Business Ethics and Environmental Fraud

Mauro Fracarolli Nunes • Camila Lee Park

Business Ethics and Environmental Fraud

Improper Competitive Advantage in the Age of Green

palgrave
macmillan

Mauro Fracarolli Nunes
OCRE-Lab
EDC Paris Business School
Courbevoie, Paris, France

Camila Lee Park
OCRE-Lab
EDC Paris Business School
Courbevoie, Paris, France

ISBN 978-3-030-73799-3 ISBN 978-3-030-73800-6 (eBook)
https://doi.org/10.1007/978-3-030-73800-6

This Palgrave Macmillan imprint is published by the registered company Springer Nature Switzerland AG.
The registered company address is: Gewerbestrasse 11, 6330 Cham, Switzerland

To our Children, the love of our lives.

Preface

The debate on the environmental impacts of corporate activities is not new. Along with the idea that companies have responsibilities toward societies, subjects such as the use of natural resources, pollution, and recycling became popular in the last decades, consolidating the view that, beyond the pursuit of profits, companies must incorporate wider goal to their strategies. The transition to Sustainable Management did not happen by chance though. Following a series of efforts by international organizations (e.g. United Nations), issues such as CO_2 emissions and the use of natural resources by companies become part of the public debate. Environmental concerns, however, have never been so in vogue. With the development of an eco-conscience among consumers, environmental goals were incorporated into corporate strategies, pushing companies to adapt the way they do business. Along with the development of new technologies and the dissemination of green practices, the call for corporate environmental responsibility raised a series of questions about the nature and the objectives of companies.

Likewise, difficulties in conciliating economic and environmental aims have put managers in challenging situations, once, although argued to be mutually supportive, the pursuit of one often demands the sacrifice of the other. When the environmental impacts of companies' operations are considered, the search for profit maximization may turn into ethical dilemmas. Still, in face of the harshening of environmental regulations and the high investment that the development of environmentally friendly technologies shall demand, the equation of these two dimensions becomes particularly difficult, with a firm's capacity to meet the environmental demands of stakeholders' becoming a powerful source of competitive advantage.

In analyzing companies' responses to these changing conditions, the book discusses a new and possibly lasting form of corporate misconduct. Based on a multidisciplinary and contextualized discussion on Business Ethics, competitive advantage, and the emergence and consolidation of the *age of green*, the concept of *environmental fraud* is developed. Through the scrutiny of some of the most pressing corporate scandals of all times (e.g. Volkswagen Dieselgate), the application of deceiving environmental strategies by companies is investigated. Beyond the description of cases, motivations, methods, and impacts of environmental fraud are discussed, in such a way that companies' financial and reputational damages may be more easily accessed. In addition, the comprehension of the impetus leading managers to cheat on environmental issues is expected to prevent, or, at least, diminish the occurrence of environmental frauds in the future.

Positioned in the intersection between Business Ethics, Management, Economics, and History, the book addresses some of the most relevant issues of the twenty-first century. Not limited to an academic audience, however, the debate proposed here must be of interest to a wide range of audiences, including executives, lawyers, students, policymakers, and all publics interested in sustainability-related issues.

Paris, France Mauro Fracarolli Nunes
Paris, France Camila Lee Park

Acknowledgments

To God.

To all the professors, educators, and colleagues that contributed to our path.

To our editor, Jessica Harrison, who believed in our project, and Charanya Manoharan, who supported us along the way.

Contents

1 **Business Ethics** 1

2 **Environmental Fraud** 47

3 **Improper Competitive Advantage** 67

4 **The Age of Green** 87

5 **The Automotive Industry Under Suspicion** 105

6 **Dieselgates: VW, FCA, Renault, and PSA** 131

7 **Not a "Privilege": Environmental Fraud Beyond the Automotive Industry** 159

8 **The Intangible Costs of Environmental Fraud: Impacts for Brands, Trust, Corporate Identity, Image, Credibility, and Reputation** 185

9 Your Fraud, Our Country: Impacts on National Brands and Reputations 207

10 Impacts on Market Value 229

11 Is Diesel Dead? 251

12 Lessons Learned, Future Research and Tendencies on Environmental Fraud 279

Index 295

Abbreviations

CAA	Clean Air Act
CAFE	Corporate Average Fuel Economy
CARB	California Air Resource Board
CEO	Chief Executive Officer
COC	Certificate of conformity
CO_{2eq}	CO_2 equivalent
EIB	European Investment Bank
EPA	U.S.' Environmental Protection Agency
FCA	Fiat Chrysler Automobiles
FTC	Federal Trade Commission
GHG	Greenhouse gas
GM	General Motors
ICCT	International Council on Clean Transportation
ISAT	Institut Supérieur de l'Automobile et des Transports (Higher Institute of Automobile and Transport)
LSP	Logistic Service Provider
OECD	Organization for Economic Co-operation and Development
OLAF	European Anti-Fraud Office (*Office Européen de Lutte Antifraude*)
PEMS	Portable Emission Measurement Systems
RBV	Resource-based view
RFID	Radio Frequency Identification Devices
SUV	Sport Utility Vehicle
TDI	Turbocharged direct injection

UNEP	United Nations Environment Programme
WCED	World Commission on Environment and Development
WHO	World Health Organization
ZEV	Zero Emission Vehicle

List of Figures

Fig. 1.1 The tripartite business ethics model. (Source: Author (s)) 26
Fig. 2.1 The fraud severity and range matrix. (Source: Author (s)) 49

List of Tables

Table 3.1 Porter's (1979, 1980) five forces 76
Table 8.1 Impact of environmental fraud on companies' intangible resources 202

1

Business Ethics

1.1 Business, People, and Ethics

Business and Ethics have always been in conflict, and will always be. Not because business is naturally hurtful, nor because businesspeople are inherently greedy or malicious (even though some are), but because businesspeople are human—and Humans and Ethics have always been in conflict, and will always be. Chief Executive Officers (CEOs), for instance, are not less human than any of us. Aside from their jobs, they have a history—maybe a family, friends, dreams, fears, ambitions. They have gone through deceptions, through moments of happiness, of pain, of desperation, of anxiety, through grace and disgrace. CEOs are not robots. They get tired. They get ashamed. They may be shy. They may be vain. They may have something to prove. They may seek glory. They may seek revenge. They may seek both in different measures, or none. The combinations are endless. The fact is that, as any human being, businesspeople are influenced by emotions and, to some extent, driven by them. They may be also driven by ambition, greed, opportunism, or simply by their natural instincts. It does not imply that businesspeople must not

M. Fracarolli Nunes, C. Lee Park, *Business Ethics and Environmental Fraud*,
https://doi.org/10.1007/978-3-030-73800-6_1

take full responsibility of their acts and omissions; it just means that one must not expect much from them. Remember: they are just humans.

Unlike the average human, however, businesspeople usually occupy positions of power, meaning that their attitudes and decisions may impact a wide range of publics. In this sense, the relevance of behavioral aspects seems sufficient to place it at the center of the business ethics debate. That includes not only the way individuals process information and stimuli, but also their reactions, beliefs, and habits. In particular, people's conception of right and wrong, and their willingness to act accordingly may be seen as the fundamental questions that permeate this discussion. Yet, in addition to the issues that are specific to the human functioning, the dynamics proper to organizations and to business environments need to be equally considered, as these are the scenarios where managers face their ethical dilemmas.

Building on the idea of ethics as the way toward a good human life (i.e. how one should live) (Weiss, 1991), we discuss business ethics as the way toward good business practices, or, how business should be done. In that direction, some inquiries emerge: how should businesspeople behave?; why do businesspeople behave the way they do?; what is a good business practice?; what is a bad one?; and why should we care? These questions have no simple answer. In fact, once they are made, more questions—instead of answers—are likely to pop up. By introducing the main concepts and ideas that support the discussion throughout the book, this chapter provides some reflection on these queries. We start by the latter.

1.2 Why Should We Care?

From a pragmatic point of view, because business is an important part of life. Business shapes the way we live, more than we usually give it credit for. By fulfilling market needs, companies generate value to customers (McNaughton et al., 2002), and by competing and pursuing profits, they create jobs, pay taxes, and innovate (Friedman, 1962, 1970). Companies produce, transform, transport, distribute, and commercialize most of the food we eat (Clapp, 2015). They develop technologies that may not only improve our comfort (e.g. smart TVs, smartphones) but also save lives (e.g. medicines, medical equipment) (Arasaratnam & Humphreys, 2013; Song et al., 2016). Companies deliver orders all over the world and make the internet work (Chiou, 2004; Jelassi & Martínez-López, 2020). They also finance new businesses (Kortum & Lerner, 2001), build roads and airports (Campos, 2017), operate sewer networks (Silva et al., 1998), and produce clothes (Remy et al., 2016). Companies make things happen and provide us with nearly all the things we need to live a safe and pleasant life.

Along with this sunny side, however, companies may also produce great harm. They are pointed, for example, as responsible for most of the greenhouse gas (GHG) emissions (Griffin, 2017), for cases of severe social damage (e.g. modern slavery, child labor) (Crane, 2013; Turker & Altuntas, 2014), having been also associated with corruption schemes (Argandoña, 2001), abuse of power (Munson et al., 1999), and illegal manipulation of markets (Austin, 2017). Among the factors supporting their relevance is the power that is peculiar to firms. The annual revenues of companies such as Amazon or Apple, for example, exceed US $230 billion (Amazon, 2019; Apple, 2018), being higher than the GDP of some Organization for Economic Co-operation and Development (OECD) countries (e.g. Iceland, Lithuania, Slovak Republic, and New Zealand) (OECD, 2020). Even if the comparison between these figures is not direct, it puts the strength of organizations—and by consequence of those who manage them—into perspective.

Yet, the prestige of top executives is not limited to the amount of money they manage. The fact that they are often inserted in networks of power may considerably add to their clout. It is not rare that executives from different companies have studied in the same schools and universities, or even belong to the same family. The CEOs of Microsoft, Adobe, and Mastercard, for instance, are all issued from the same high school in India (Hess, 2018). These relationships seem to be also common among politicians, academics, and judiciary operators (e.g. lawyers, prosecutors, judges), as well as among all these groups. As pointed out by Finkelstein (2004, p. 256), Edward McCracken—the former CEO of Silicon Graphics—regularly attended White House events in the 1990s, while Ken Lay, the founder, CEO, and chairman of Enron, "was never more than a phone call away from close friend President George W. Bush".

Examples of how companies and managers use their influence abound, with the interaction between organizations and the public power being particularly relevant on that regard. With large firms usually being critical taxpayers and assuring employment to local populations, governments may be predisposed to favor their activities, what shall demonstrate greater tolerance to transgressions. Also, cases of companies interfering in electoral processes are not rare (Levmore, 2019), with the donation of money to political campaigns often translating is several forms of corruption (Issacharoff, 2010). That includes the favoring of candidates committed to their causes, or the exchange of electoral support by future contracts with the government. In these cases, corporate involvement with the public power is seen as a sort of investment in which money given today is expected to return in the future, not only deviating valuable resources from taxpayers but also maculating democracy. Business also has an important impact on public health, with pharmaceutical and health insurance firms, deliberating, in many cases, which diseases are going to be cured, treated, or ignored. The participation of companies in the development, testing, and production of military equipment is another sphere of their influence in peoples' life, directly affecting geopolitical equilibriums and the trade balance of countries. A country's capacity to export riffles, missiles, tanks, airplanes, ships, or any other related product is also associated to its international influence, in such a way that these corporate activities end up supporting national interests, even if in indirect ways.

Within a broader perspective, companies' weight may also be detected in the consequences of their usual activities. By deciding on the financing of specific projects, bankers exert great influence in the economy, impacting, among other things, the development of new technologies. Strategic movements such as the internationalization of brands or production (i.e. strategic outsourcing) shall also have a profound effect on the development of countries. Similarly, the search for operational effectiveness favors processes of mergers and acquisitions (Porter, 1996), which may trigger a series of collateral effects. So that synergies are captured, plants are usually closed (Maksimovic et al., 2011) or relocated (Brouwer et al., 2004), concurring with the dismissal of employees (Eby & Buch, 1998; Siegel & Simons, 2010). Likewise, companies in the entertainment industry shall greatly collaborate to the building and management of countries' "soft power" (Nye 2004). By exporting fragments of culture, films, series, cartoons, books, and music, they transmit the values and visions of a given nation to others, possibly facilitating their dialog. All this means that businesses have deep roots in societies and that business practices may have strong impacts on it. In this sense, beyond a philosophical exercise, business ethics matters because the way business is done may seriously impact peoples' life. Nevertheless, while the arguments supporting that the conduct of businesspeople deserves attention are relatively straightforward (i.e. why should we care?), the discussion around the reasons why businesspeople behave the way they do tends to be more intricate.

1.3 Why Do Businesspeople Behave the Way They Do?

Far from obeying the rules of an exact science, human behavior is difficult to predict or explain. It is not by chance that assorted disciplines focus on the quest to understand the reasons, processes, and effects of people's conduct. To a greater or lesser degree, that includes Philosophy, Psychology, Sociology, Economics, History, and basically all other fields dedicated to the study of individuals and their interactions. The determination of the reasons why someone does good or bad may be particularly difficult. At the origin of ethical tensions are, perhaps, the sacrifices that the pursuit of good requires. Truth is not always pleasant, and Justice may be bitter to swallow. Temptations are great. In other words, the path of good usually seems thornier, and, at first glance, less rewarding. Businesspeople, for example, may be charmed by "shortcuts" to success, which, not rarely, translate into corporate crimes and contraventions. Likewise, pressures for financial performance may spur managers' unethical decisions, as they seek to survive in harsh competitive environments. Whether in search of undue benefits or in a sheer defense of their jobs, businesspeople are constantly faced with moral impasses (Waters et al., 1986).

Adds to that the different value that societies place on ethical and unethical behaviors. In general, this can be seen in the mechanisms of reward and recognition of social status that arise from each type of conduct. Sometimes the formation of these perceptions can be confusing to the point that, even if a certain behavior is valued at first, in practice, it can end up being understood as not rewarding in terms of its tangible results. An extract from the romance *Cannery Row* by John Steinbeck (1993) illustrates the view. The text—which also opens the first chapter of Clinard and Yeager's (2011) book *Corporate Crime*—claims that

> The things we admire in men, kindness and generosity, openness, honesty, understanding and feeling are the concomitants of failure in our system. And those traits we detest, sharpness, greed acquisitiveness, meanness, egotism and selfinterest are the traits of success. And while men admire the quality of the first they love the produce of the second. (Steinbeck, 1993, p. 89)

Even if the reasons leading managers to behave unethically must be of the most varied natures, we argue that eight main motives are manifested more frequently: greed, professional ambition, emotions, pathologies, corporate culture, opportunism, natural inclinations, and the pressures emerging from competitive markets. We briefly develop each as follows.

1.3.1 Greed

For Goodpaster (1991, p. 53), two questions would be at the center of the business ethics debate: (1) "what is ethically responsible management?", and (2) "how can a corporation, given its economic mission, be managed with appropriate attention to ethical concerns?" While the first relates to the very nature of ethics in business contexts, the second suggests the existence of a tension between the meeting of economic goals and the respect to ethical concerns, with the former being somehow an obstacle to the latter. In fact, a range of authors point out to the pursuit of financial results as the origins of unethical corporate behavior. Tang and Chiu (2003), for example, claim that the love of money is the "root of evil" for Hong Kong employees, while Singhapakdi et al. (2013) argue that it significantly impacts managers' marketing decisions. From a broader perspective, Kouchaki et al. (2013) add that the mere exposure to money has the potential to trigger people's unethical intensions and behaviors. The ideas may be translated into an immoral seek for profits, with unethical managers not refraining from breaking laws, or using any means necessary to achieve financial goals. As pointed out by Childs (2000, p. 2), however, "[g]reed is not all ostentation and spending or the lust for great wealth. It is also manifest in the hoarding compulsion that turns people into misers." In that way, it would have a "profoundly deleterious effect on everything from the quality of personal relationships to the just distribution of goods and the future of our environment".

For Mintzberg (2002, p. 67), excessive corporate greed would result in companies ignoring their social responsibilities as they focus on the creation of short-term value to shareholders. Accordingly, these dynamics would be boosted by the idea that CEOs create economic value on their own, with a "syndrome of selfishness" spreading in corporations, societies, and in individuals' minds. In that vein, Miles et al. (2004) point out that greed and self-serving behavior have become not only acceptable but also desirable in some social segments. Understood as the quest obtains superior returns, greed would then be the driving force pushing publicly held companies to innovate and pursue risky entrepreneurial activities (Cooke, 1997).

Within this view, it may be argued that an overwhelming desire for performance is not necessarily bad, possibly serving as a powerful engine for the development of economic activities. It is possible, for example, that the greed levels of successful entrepreneurs and businesspeople who end up in jail are indeed similar. What makes the fate of the two groups different, therefore, is not the destination they aspire to, but the means they are willing to use to get there. As pointed out by Gross (1978), the small proportion of individuals within organizations who strive for or end up attaining high hierarchical positions are generally characterized by ambitiousness, shrewdness, and moral flexibility. Along with other factors this may favor unethical conducts, as discussed next.

1.3.2 Professional Ambition

Corporate careers are characterized by a generally well-defined hierarchical organization. Usually, the distribution of power takes place in a pyramidal manner, so that the number of people occupying a certain level of command decreases as one moves toward the top. In addition to power itself, the rise of a professional in the hierarchical pyramids awards them with prestige and social status. From an evolutionary point of view, the achievement of positions of power is valued for guaranteeing access to scarce resources, which, in the case of organizations, translates into higher salaries, more subordinates, physical space (i.e. larger rooms), automobiles, and, depending on the company and the position in question, even private planes and helicopters. It is not uncommon for companies to dedicate some of its employees (i.e. human resources) to take care of the personal lives of senior executives, freeing them to focus on their professional activities. This may include routine tasks such as shopping or paying school fees for their children, as well as more important issues such as monitoring health treatments.

Due to the scarcity of power posts (i.e. pyramidal structure) and their attractiveness, it is normal that it leads to disputes among those who seek to occupy them. In addition to the meritocratic issues more directly linked to the candidates' professional profile and performance, filling these positions can be involved in political competition, fuelling the rivalry between groups within the organization. The excessive ambition of some candidates for professional ascension can lead them to adopt objectionable behaviors such as slander, defamation, conspiracy, and fraud of the most varied types. It must be considered that the dispute for these positions of power is not limited to organizational boundaries, with external contenders (i.e. candidates to jobs) presenting additional sources of pressure. In this sense, the search to reach or maintain positions of power within organizations stands as a potential trigger of unethical conducts on the part of managers.

1.3.3 Emotions

Just as the search for financial results or for professional status can lead managers to ignore ethical limits, it is common for deviations to occur due to impulses, or unplanned attitudes. Likewise, rooted feelings and perceptions that are built over time also seem to be important factors explaining inappropriate conducts. In this sense, emotions appear as an important factor explaining unethical behavior, with their manifestations leading managers to eventually use their power in a violent or criminal manner. When occupying the space of reason, emotions seem to give vent to everything that is most primitive in the human being, so that behaviors more adapted to a wild and uncivilized world end up emerging in situations which are, in fact, inappropriate. Power struggles within organizations, for example, can trigger the survival instinct of those who somehow feel threatened. Since instincts precede the very idea of civilization, it seems natural that those under their influence end up ignoring laws, social conventions, or customs.

Likewise, common feelings such as envy and jealousy can decisively influence the behavior of employees. The fact that organizations are structured hierarchically can act as an important catalyst for these factors, with the status achieved by a professional—and the access to resources that it guarantees—being the target of his colleagues' lust. This issue can be particularly important when an employee ascends to a hierarchically superior position. In addition to the resentment of those who eventually lost the dispute for the vacancy, the promoted employees may be the target of negative feelings on the part of colleagues who until then shared the same hierarchical level. In these cases, envy seems to be the most likely feeling, with professional ascension possibly causing important impacts on the social relations within organizations. The different types of human relationships that may emerge between co-workers can create a favorable environment for jealousy. Friendships and love affairs, for instance, can significantly increase the complexity of exchanges in these contexts, with professional aspects becoming even more confused with elements of private life. In these cases, it is possible that a passionate aspect becomes more present, keeping people involved away from a logical and objective reasoning. These personal relationships can also extend beyond the limits of the company, with the bonds developed with customers, suppliers, and financial institutions, among others, possibly hampering the pursuit of the company's best interests.

As discussed by Izard (1977), however, scholars have offered different and often contradicting views on the nature and relevance of emotions. While some claim that they are not particularly important (e.g. Duffy, 1962), others argue that they constitute the essential motivational system in human beings (e.g. Tomkins, 1963). Analogously, the duration and the impact of emotions in the human functioning are also controversial, with some academics arguing that they are either transient phenomena or a constant in people's life (e.g. Schachtel, 1959). At the same time emotions are pointed out as disruptors and disorganizers of human behavior—being the main source of human problems—(e.g. Lazarus, 1968), they are also seen as important in the organization, motivation, and support of conducts (e.g. Schachtel, 1959).

Still, emotions are also pointed out as a matter of visceral functions, meaning that they would result from the activities of organs provoked by the autonomic nervous system (e.g. Wenger, 1950). In opposition, researchers have also highlighted the importance of considering externally observable behavior such as facial expressions, as well the role of the somatic nervous system, which is generally considered to be voluntarily controlled (e.g. Tomkins, 1963). In any case, emotions are believed to have a profound effect on strategic decision-making, with the interplay between behavior, cognition, and affect being endemic to humans (Kisfalvi & Pitcher, 2003). It is thus possible that unethical conducts come to be more likely when emotions are propelling managers' decisions. In this sense, the transgression of norms, laws, and social codes, as well as all sorts of dishonest and unfair conducts may be favored.

1.3.4 Pathologies

Just as emotions can decisively influence the behavior of managers, the role that psychological and mental pathologies might play in this regard cannot be neglected. While some diseases and behavioral deviations can compromise the social life of those who suffer from them, they may come to offer a certain type of advantage in corporate environments, at least with regard to professional advancement and results. In this sense, the lack of empathy seems to be an important factor in career development, allowing those who are not able to feel compassion to extract from other people more than they would be naturally inclined to give. As pointed out by Resick et al. (2009), narcissism would be one of the most common types of dark-side personalities approached in the study of CEO leadership (e.g. Chatterjee & Hambrick, 2007; Judge et al., 2006; Kets de Vries & Miller, 1997; Lubit, 2002; Maccoby, 2003). Accordingly, beyond a "pervasive pattern of grandiosity", individuals suffering from a narcissistic personality disorder would show a constant "need for admiration and lack of empathy" (American Psychiatric Association, 2000, p. 717). The qualities of a narcissistic individual such as their tendencies to form grandiose ideas, to be boastful, aggressive, and elitist (Hogan et al., 1990; Maccoby, 2000, 2004; Rosenthal & Pittinsky, 2006) would be often helpful in getting them promoted through higher management ranks, as well as to be hired into leadership positions (Hogan & Kaiser, 2005).

It may be argued then that narcissistic leaders would be more prone to engage in immoral practices, particularly those associated with the respect of human rights. The lack of empathy that is typical of those suffering from this personality disorder would favor the crossing of ethical limits, putting the integrity and the interests of employees, customers, suppliers, and investors at risk. Despite particularly harmful, narcissism is not the only pathology capable of inducing managers to commit immoral practices. Psychopathic leaderships, for example, have also been related to bullying, staff withdraw, and higher levels of turnover, as well as to organizational declines in terms of revenues, creativity, organizational innovativeness, and employee commitment (Boddy, 2017). Accordingly, corporate psychopaths (Stevens et al., 2012) would pose serious threats to business ethics (Marshall et al., 2015).

In their seminal discussion on the organizational influence of top managers, Hambrick and Mason (1984, p. 193) argue that organizational outcomes (i.e. strategies and effectiveness) reflect "the values and cognitive bases of powerful actors in the organization". On that regard, Delgado-García and De La Fuente-Sabaté (2010) argue that CEOs' negative affective traits are associated with more typical performance, while positive ones would be linked to outcomes that deviate from the normal expectations in a given industry. Altogether, these factors indicate that, although potentially helpful in the development of individual careers, psychological and mental pathologies may harm companies' ethics and performance. In that direction, the potential of psychological and psychiatric pathologies to push unethical conducts must be recognized.

1.3.5 Corporate Culture

Along with the issues that are specific to the individual (e.g. emotions, pathologies), the environment in which they find themselves also seems to be an important factor in determining his behavior, with a company's values potentially favoring the occurrence of unethical deviations. Depending on the perception of colleagues, these unethical conducts may be more or less tolerated, thus contributing to different companies exhibiting different degrees of immoralities. In this sense, the concept of corporate culture would assume a particularly relevant role, with the understanding of the means that lead to its creation being of great importance.

As discussed by Oakes (2003), the English cliché "trajectories" would translate the idea of modernity as a "projectile launched by a piece of ancient machinery", with value spheres—among which the economy—being the domain of the Weberian "cultural being". Differently put, it seems that, for Weber, the way people exchange goods in a society shapes its values in a long-lasting way, ultimately forming the cultures in which individuals are embed. The cultural being, in turn, would be the heir of a kind of tradition of doing, and accepts that things are done in a given way that conditions their behavior. At the same time the cultural being has their acts limited by their culture, by accepting these invisible rules—even if unconsciously—they reinforce them, sending the same projectiles to future generations. Although cultures may indeed change from generation to generation, its essence shall remain relatively intact, explaining why men and women separated by centuries or even millennia sometimes behave in fascinatingly similar ways. Thus, it may be argued that the more unethical conducts are practiced within a company, the more they are incorporated to its culture. At the limit, the creation of cultures that are pervasive and tolerant to deviations shall increase the likelihood that they will take place.

1.3.6 Opportunism

If framed as a rational choice, ethical dilemmas may be discussed in terms of risk-return logics. Unethical behavior would be expected then when benefits outweigh the probability and impact of consequences. An academic author, for example, may engage in plagiarism (e.g. present the work of another author as being theirs) in case they believe that the chances of being caught are low and/or that the consequences of that are not significant. Likewise, upon the dismissal of an employee, a manager may opt not to pay the eventually due compensations. The perception that the employee is not likely to claim their rights, or that, in case they do, the costs associated with an eventual condemnation are low may lead to a higher incidence of such unethical conducts.

In that way, opportunism can be understood as one's tendency to take advantage of any moment, situation, or context to advance an objective. Although normally associated with a pejorative image, opportunism shall also count on a positive connotation. In the case of sports competitions, for example, an athlete who takes advantage of the few opportunities they may have in the course of a dispute can be highly valued. Among other modalities, football would be very illustrative of this perception. With the dynamics of matches often offering players rare opportunities to score a goal, those who are able to take advantage of them efficiently—usually attackers—are revered and, depending on the importance of their achievements, even raised to the status of heroes by supporters. On the other hand, the idea of opportunism also refers to negative, and generally illegal, conducts. In business environments this can translate into the practice of several types of corporate crimes, among them the embezzlement of resources, corruption, and fraud. Thus, the moral judgment on opportunism should not focus on the specifics of the practice, but on its ends as well as on the methods used in the pursuit of these ends.

It may be argued then that an individual's exposure to a situation of opportunism can be quite revealing of his ethical maturity. In the absence of external obstacles or punishment, moral dilemmas must be faced with an individual's moral judgment serving as his only parameter. Skepticism about the ethical rigidity of human beings, however, has contributed to the development of societies in which different means are created to prevent opportunistic conducts. Thus, a whole framework of surveillance and punishment was put in march in the most diverse fields in order to create barriers and punishments that are capable of preventing or at least discouraging such practices.

Defense strategies against opportunistic behavior would be inserted into a context in which trust between the parties is small or non-existent. The lack of confidence leads to the adoption of mechanisms that envisage the control of behavior. In business environments this translates into the formulation of contracts that aim to limit the behavior of those who agree with them. From a theoretical point of view, remedies against opportunism are treated by the literature on Transaction Cost Economics (Coase, 1937), according to which the need for safeguards would represent additional costs for the occurrence of exchanges between companies. In view of the high costs that these mechanisms can represent for economic activities, they are often ignored or at least neglected. Thus, the possibility of incurring personal gains without the proper mechanisms for surveillance and control being established can be an important motivator for the unethical conduct of managers. This discussion is summarized later in the chapter, along with the debate on the role of laws and restrictions as conditions of ethical behavior.

1.3.7 Natural Inclinations

It is also possible that people do good or bad because they are inclined to, with a possible good or bad nature determining their behaviors. But what would be the causes of such nature? Would we come into the world with a specific character, or would it be shaped as we go through life? If good and bad indoles are natural, is it possible for one to become the other during the course of a life? These questions have serious consequences. If men are considered naturally good, the responsibility for their wrongdoing cannot be attributed to them. Instead, factors surrounding the individual would be the causes of its corruption. That would support the idea that poverty precedes criminal behavior, for example. In this sense, the way toward good would not depend on a reform of man, but rather, on the reorganization of its environment.

For Treviño and Nelson (2016, p. 14), most people would not be guided by a strict internal moral compass, but, in fact, by the conditions present in their environment. Within this view, the observation of the reality in which people are embedded would serve them as a metric of morality, influencing the way they behave and even think. Phrases like "everyone is doing it" would emerge as a sort of mantra in situations of generalized unethical conducts. In that way, employees who are not naturally dishonest could have their behavior radically changed, assuming unethical conducts in case they believe that either they are expected to behave unethically (by superior or by the organization in general), or unethical behavior is the norm among the people they interact with. As put by the authors, "apples often turn bad because they're spoiled by 'bad barrels'". On the other extreme some believe that one is born good or bad and that the environment has little to no influence on the conducts on will develop in life. If it is believed that man is not naturally inclined to do good, the establishment of laws would be one of the main ways to assure ethical conducts. Intermediary views, in turn, may articulate different combinations of human nature and the influence of the environment.

The direct reasons for unethical behavior have already been briefly assessed, with managers seeing fraud and cheating as possible ways to speed up their careers or profits. The reasons leading an individual to behave in a given way, however, shall greatly vary. It is possible, for example, that an individual's behavior changes depending on their emotional state, or if they are alone or in the company of other people (e.g. family, friends, professional colleagues). Likewise, people behave differently when they are in a church, in an office, or in a stadium. As an individual seeks to be perceived in a given way, he may adapt his conducts so that a desired image is supported. Variations across groups (e.g. friends, families, and professional colleagues) and situations (e.g. church, office, and stadium) may be explained by the search to fulfill different expectations and rules. Broadly, this suggests that people's conducts are influenced both by questions related to the individual themselves and by the context in which their actions are analyzed.

1.3.8 Competitive Environments

If, on the one hand, unethical practices may be the result of individual and even circumstantial characteristics, it is likely that structural issues of economic organization will also create the conditions for them to occur. In particular, the exacerbated rivalry between competitors and the lack of opportunities for differentiation seem to form a pernicious combination that may lead some companies to opt for illegal and fraudulent mechanisms. As discussed by Porter (1979, 1980), among the factors contributing to the aggressiveness of corporate disputes are the number of players already established in a given industry, the absence or irrelevance of barriers to entry, and the growth potential of the consumer markets. The concentration of a large number of companies offering value propositions that are not significantly different from each other favors competition based on the price of products, which ends up reducing operating margins and financial performance as a whole (Porter, 1996). Just as there are several causes that can raise the level of competition in an industry, the potential for differentiation can also be influenced by a number of issues. The main one is perhaps the achievement of technological maturity so that a limit for innovation is present. Similarly, the high costs of research and development activities can prove prohibitive, which ends up interrupting cycles of creation and incorporation of new technologies.

Adds to that the increasing pressure from investors for companies to present short-term results. In reality, executives' own remuneration (i.e. bonuses) is often linked to these results, which can act as an additional incentive to unethical practices. Also, the dynamics of competitive environments may contribute to emotionally driven deviations. The high pressure for financial results in scenarios of harsh disputes with other companies may often elevate the stress levels of business leaders, as, ultimately, their jobs are constantly at risk. The combination of these factors can create an enabling environment for the factors discussed above (e.g. emotions, pathologies) to act even more strongly, increasing the likelihood of illegal and/or immoral behavior. In this context, the search for *improper competitive advantage* can be favored. In general, this seems to be the diagnosis of some of the most emblematic cases of environmental fraud. In particular, the Volkswagen Dieselgate, which is discussed in greater detail in Chap. 6. Likewise, the competitive dynamics that are characteristic of the automotive sector and which may favor disapproved practices are also addressed in Chap. 5.

1.4 How Should Businesspeople Behave?

From companies' perspective, the attention to business ethics may be also driven by issues other than moral reasoning. Ensuring that a firm respects what is deemed appropriate by its stakeholders is the most basic way of building, managing, and/or protecting its intangible resources (e.g. corporate credibility, corporate reputation). With the fast development of communication technologies and the consolidation of social networks, companies' activities have been brought to the center of public debate, with cases of unethical conducts being openly discussed. Likewise, non-governmental organizations such as Greenpeace and PETA have been organizing online campaigns linking companies to issues such as the deforestation of tropical forests, the extinction of endangered species, and the disrespect to animal welfare, which may not only trigger consumers' boycotts but also deteriorate the value of brands. The administration of what is conveyed about firms in social media nowadays seems virtually impossible. Companies' ethical conducts may be even more relevant for the building and management of positive corporate reputations, as, along with the higher scrutiny of operations by stakeholders, the creations of artificial social and environmental reputations based solely on communication efforts (Nunes & Lee Park, 2017) have become more difficult. In this set, the discussion on how managers should behave are not restricted to the ethical dimension, with the compliance of business activities with demands of society (i.e. corporate social and environmental responsibilities) representing an important factor for the survival and prosperity of organizations.

As argued by Bowie (2017, p. 7), the prescription on social conduct is often built on a reflexive manner, meaning that individuals' tolerance for the conduct of others usually serves as a metric for their own. In that way, the so-called Golden Rule—'Do unto others as you will have them do unto you'—would be common, standing as a bedrock of moral principle. The idea, however, would fail to assure good conducts, once, "so long as you are willing to let others treat you in an immoral way, it seems as if you are allowed to treat them immorally as well". Within business contexts that would possibly lead to one's tolerance to deceiving and cheating in both directions (i.e. from and toward others) because "that is how it is in business".

Differently put, the perception that the business world is ruled by savagery, compared to a jungle, would lead people to classify their own deceiving and cheating conducts as moral, as they believe that expecting similar attitudes from others would be inevitable. The Golden Rule shall be thus argued to be flawed, not because of its premises that people act in their best interest, but, in fact, because they must see their sacrifices (i.e. being ethical) as pointless. In case business environments are indeed perceived as infertile grounds for unethical exchanges, expecting the worst from others and acting accordingly may sadly be the conduct one may rationally adopt to maximize their chances for survival and success.

On that regard, the perspective that one must avoid unethical behavior not because of an intrinsic good but because immoral conducts shall validate a similar behavior from others seems to be inserted in a more pessimistic—or realistic—view of mankind. Curiously, benevolent eyes may see in such state of barbarism a primitive form of Justice, with the application of a sort of *lex talionis* being apparently embed in business contexts. As pointed out by Kollock (1993, p. 768), however, "an eye for an eye leaves everyone blind". By proposing reflections on the validity of such practices, consideration on how businesspeople should behave would end up making business viable. Just like Rajan and Zingales (2003) claim for the need to save capitalism from capitalist, business ethics could be seen as an attempt to save business from businesspeople. We may get back then to our specific question: how should businesspeople behave? As noted before, this question raises others: (1) what is an acceptable behavior?; (2) what is an ideal behavior?; (3) what is an expected behavior?; and (4) how do these notions interact? Although all related, each of these "sub-questions" fulfills a distinct role in this discussion.

An acceptable behavior, for example, refers to people's tolerance toward a given conduct, with the agreed norms, laws, and social codes representing the limits between ethical and unethical conducts. From a practical view, business ethics would refer to the observation of these limits, either through managers' inherent conscience, or through external mechanisms of control. That includes the surveillance and sanction to eventual deviations (i.e. punishment). The idea of acceptable behaviors would serve binary views of ethics, meaning that a conduct is either ethical (i.e. acceptable) or unethical (i.e. unacceptable). Ethical judgments, however, are essentially misty, as the determination of the limits is not always clear. It is possible, for instance, that the strictly legal conduct of a company is considered unacceptable, as social codes may not always be perfectly translated in laws. Even laws are often dubious in their interpretation.

Things may become even more complex when the operations of multinational companies are considered, as a given conduct may be seen as legal and morally correct in a country, but illegal and unacceptable in another. Beyond different legal systems, distinct cultures have a direct impact on the constitution of social norms. The observation of these different codes may pose significant challenges to firms operating in multiple countries, as they must carefully adapt their business models to the idiosyncrasies of different regions. Similarly, companies inserted in global value chains must ensure that the operations of all its partners respect the standards and metrics against which they are assessed, under penalty of severe reputational damage. In that way, the dissemination of socially and environmentally responsible practices across supply chains must be critical to avoid corporate scandals involving modern slavery, child labor, employees' safety, deforestation, pollution, among others.

The fact that the perception of what is acceptable shall vary among individuals reinforces the idea that the limits between ethical and unethical behaviors must be derived from collective and well-communicated views (i.e. norms, laws, and social codes). That would avoid the establishment of "personal ethics", which, depending on the distinct perceptions of each individual, may lead to damaging behaviors. While the establishment and communication of collective values must function as remedies to such personal ethics, the process through which they are created, incorporated, and communicated must be tortuous, with the development of legal systems illustrating this intricacy. Within this idea, perceptions on the ethicality of a behavior can, in fact, be separated from its contrasts with social norms, with individuals assuming the power to judge them according to their own metrics. The consequentialist view, for instance, does not start its ethical judgments with rule, but with goals (Singer, 1993). The assessment of actions would then be conditioned by their contributions to a given pre-established objective, the most popular consequentialist theory being known as utilitarianism. Still after the author, a classical utilitarian would thus judge an action as right in case it grants all parts involved with equal or higher level of happiness than any alternative action, and wrong, if it does not. Under these lenses, a lie would be considered ethically wrong or right not because of its intrinsic value, but, rather, for its consequences. These extreme views can give rise to behaviors that are harmful to societies, with acts of violence being justified on account of the results they produce. The fact that law and order can be disregarded denotes the anarchic nature of these views, meaning that caution is necessary upon the interpretation of their conclusions.

Beyond the differentiation between acceptable and unacceptable conducts, ethical assessments may be done in a more nuanced way, meaning that a sort of order among behaviors must be established. Deontologists, for example, would resolve their ethical conflicts by finding positions of no-conflict between rules, or, in case of inevitable conflicts, by organizing these rules in a hierarchical form, opting for the highest in ranking (Singer, 1993). Along with proposing a more detailed understanding of the issue, the graduation of ethical and unethical behaviors allows for the overcoming of the Boolean logics (Boole, 1847, 1854) that surrounds the binary distinction of a conduct. While all acceptable behaviors are ethical, it is possible that some come to be more ethical than others. On that regard, the closer a conduct is to the limits of norms, laws, and social codes, the less ethical it is—although still ethical. On the other hand, the more distant an acceptable behavior is from these limits, the more ethical it would be.

Yet, at the same time there are lower limits, there would be no upper ones. In fact, these limits are imposed by the practicality of the conducts, meaning that a more ethical conduct can only be considered to the point that it is possible. From the intersection between the progression of conducts to an ever higher ethical level, and the restrictions imposed by reality, the concept of an ideal conduct emerges. An ideal behavior refers then to those conducts that are not only acceptable but also preferred among all other. In the opposite direction, the same reasoning would be possible when it comes to unacceptable (i.e. unethical) conducts, with the proximity to norms making them less unethical, and the distance to it making them more unethical. The feasibility of an unethical conduct would set the maximum point of these conducts, being then diametrically opposed to an ideal one. This unacceptable extreme is here defined as an anti-ideal behavior.

An expected behavior, in turn, refers to the set of conducts that are typical from an individual. Differently from the other types of conducts, it does not demand abstract exercises. Rather, the observation of the typical human behavior would be sufficient. This does not make its practical determination simpler, as, although some patterns may even be observable, they are not free of surprises and deviations. In this sense, the idea of expected behavior borrows a basic concept of statistics (i.e. expected value), which, within probability theory is represented by the sum of the multiplications of a series of outcomes by the probabilities of them occurring (Kenton, 2020). The expected behavior of an individual would be thus a function of the average behavior of all individuals, possibly assuming any of the forms proposed here (i.e. unacceptable, acceptable, ideal).

In a certain sense, the discussion on managers' ideal behavior of is heir to a long philosophical tradition, which has among its main concerns the discussion on human behavior. As discussed by the Brazilian philosopher Luiz Felipe Pondé (2018), the so-called moral philosophers represent a group of thinkers—predominantly from the twelfth century in France—dedicated to the study of human nature and behavior, mainly around its obscure aspects. In this sense, philosopher Michel de Montaigne (1533–1592) would be one of the initiators of this philosophical current even in the fourteenth century, although still strongly influenced by his characteristic skepticism. Still according to the author, thinkers such as Blaise Pascal (1623–1662), François de La Rochefoucauld (1613–1680), and Jean de la Bruyère (1645–1696) would be some of the most important members of this tradition that, at least from a chronological point of view, predates the Enlightenment.

1.5 The Role of the Law

Considered the difficulties or even the impossibility of changing the essence of human nature, the way toward real business ethics shall be more effective in the shaping of institutions which may function under the rule of law. Within this set, severe punishment of deviations from ethical conducts may be necessary as a way to discourage such behavior. By raising the costs of being caught, the imposition of the law may unbalance the risk-return equilibrium that sometimes seem to convince those engaging in reprehensible acts that their misconducts are worth it. The reasoning appears to be linked to the views of Irish Philosopher Edmund Burke (1729–1797), who is considered by many the predecessor of conservative thinking. The aphorism traditionally credited to him claims that "[t]he only thing necessary for the triumph of evil is for good men to do nothing". In adapting the saying to "our technologically specialised realities", Bandura (2002, p. 113) proposes a rephrasing, according to which "[t]he triumph of evil requires a lot of good people, doing a bit of it, in a morally disengaged way, with indifference to the human suffering they collectively cause".

In this sense, keeping businessmen and women under strict vigilance is, perhaps, our best chance to see business being done as it should. That includes harsh inspection and punishment as possibly the most efficient manners to minimize the negative outcomes of unethical behavior. Diligence would be necessary to prevent, for example, the unfair treatment of those occupying lower hierarchical positions within organizations, as well as to avoid injustices toward other classes of stakeholders such as customers, investors, suppliers, governments, and society as a whole. The close watch and punishment of businesspeople may restrict some of the most pressing issues within the modern business ethics debate, among which poor working conditions offered to employees, modern slavery, child labor, moral harassment, environmental damage, corruption, fraud, piracy, promiscuous relations with politicians, and the formation of cartels, to name a few.

In his introduction to Max Weber's *Economy and Society* ([1922] 1978, p. 35), German-American sociologist Guenther Roth stresses that the book "clearly states that men act as they do because of belief in authority, enforcement by staffs, a calculus of self-interest, and a good dose of habit". The reasoning is coherent with Wilson and Kelling's (1982) broken window theory. Building on an experiment conducted by Philip Zimbardo and Scott Fazer on vandalism against abandoned cars (Zimbardo, 1969), the authors defend that negligence to deviations ends up favoring the occurrence of new deviations. A metaphor to the dynamics and incentives of criminal behavior is proposed, arguing that if a window of a given building is broken and left unrepaired, other windows of that building will soon be broken. Accordingly, the lack of response to the first episode (i.e. the non-repairment of the first window broken) signs that no one is particularly worried about it, meaning that, from the point of view of a vandal, the cost of breaking another window is close to zero.

In applying this rational to business contexts, it must be argued that coercive measures against unethical conducts is, in fact, essential to avoid the proliferation of such practices. In these cases, a causal relation between the enforcement of the law and ethical behavior would be evident, with the non-materialization of unacceptable or undesirable conducts being conditioned to an expectation of punishment if they take place. Differently put, the way toward the "right conducts" would not be dependent on one's own conscience, but on the vigilance and action of an external and more powerful entity that oversees, judges, and corrects eventual deviations. People would embrace ethical conducts not because of their inner morality but because a higher power is enforcing it.

That seems to be part of the rationale supporting the creation of social structures that, through the imposition of the order, seek to organize the existence of its members. Following conscious or unconscious accords in which individuals recognize the authority of another entity (e.g. another individual, group of individuals, institutions), power is concentrated, and the conducts that are agreed to be the right ones can be imposed to the conjunct of persons living under that authority. Broadly, we may think of these mechanisms as the origins of what is known as "the rule of law", which, by setting what is considered to be right and wrong in a society (i.e. the law), opposes personal discretions to do justice (Scalia, 1989). The Hammurabi code, for example, shows that concerns with the regulation of human behavior through sanctions have been applied since the earliest stages of civilization, being itself, perhaps, a fundamental step in the organization of social order. In that direction, the adoption of some extracts of the code—among which the famous and previously addresses *lex talionis*—would oppose the normalization of unacceptable practices, with retaliation and revenge being used as mechanisms of immediate Justice.

As highlighted by Aristotle in his *Politics*,

> Rightly constituted laws should be the final sovereign; and personal rule, whether it be exercised by a single person or a body of persons, should be sovereign only in those matters on which law is unable, owing to the difficulty of framing general rules for all contingencies, to make an exact pronouncement. (Scalia, 1989, p. 1176)

Once more, the enforcement of the good and fairness would not be dependent on personal values, but from the establishment and formalization of a general rule. Personal judgments such as the ones conducted by notable monarchs throughout history (e.g. King Solomon; Louis IX of France, Saint Louis) would be substituted by peoples' general will (Scalia, 1989). From a broader perspective, religions would be also anchored in the need to create structures of power and punishment to control general misbehavior. On that regard, Arnold (1867) argues that conduct and obedience would be particularly influent notions within Hebraism, forging what he called a strictness of conscience. As discussed by Fried (2001), the author positioned Hebraism and Hellenism as metaphors for a response to authority and experience, with both being part of human nature and having perfection and salvation as their goals. Coherently, Tang and Liu (2012) argue that, along with higher levels of

Machiavellianism and low self-esteem, one's propensity to engage in unethical behavior is correlated with low intrinsic religiosity. Indeed, religions have traditionally worked as a sort of moral rule, meaning they have the power to differentiate right from wrong. The weakening of religions throughout history seems to have contributed to the valorization of the debate on ethics as a guide for human conduct. The process is curious as, in many cases, the philosophical debate precedes the appearance of religions themselves. Within business contexts, the development of business ethics as a discipline seems to be an attempt to fulfill the vacuum.

1.6 Business Ethics Versus Ethics

Beyond the discussion on the uses and misuses of Business Ethics, authors have also challenged its legitimacy as a separate field of study. On that regard, Drucker (1981, p. 18) questions its necessity and even its sheer existence, as Ethics itself has accommodated philosophers' struggles with human behavior for centuries. Accordingly, despite being taught in departments of philosophy, business schools, and even in theological seminaries, the idea of Business Ethics would be highly controversial, with question like "where does 'business ethics' fit in—or does it fit in anywhere at all?" deserving full consideration. Embedded in the criticism of the author is the idea that Business Ethics would unfairly single out businesses for special ethical treatment, subordinating ethical to political concerns (Hoffman & Moore, 1982). Accordingly, Drucker's (1981) arguments would not grant Business Ethics with its due status, claiming that, instead of real ethics, it would be a form of "ethical chic", or, as put by Ciulla (1991), no more than a fad. Based on these and on other passages of Peter Drucker's work, it seems that the author not only questioned the need for Business Ethics but actually showed a certain contempt for it. For Hoffman and Moore (1982) these positions, however, would be fruit of a great ignorance.

It is possible that, as argued by Drucker (1981), the idea of Ethics is sufficient. Yet, the combinations of factors such as the abstract nature of the concept, the role of business in contemporary life, the flawed human condition, and the great power of those owing or occupying high positions in large companies shall justify the existence of a sub-filed dedicated to human behavior in business contexts. Since issues such as slavery and deforestation seem to be inserted in a sort of historical continuity, Business Ethics should not be seen as a sheer fad located in a specific point in time, as Drucker (1981) proposes. Instead, it would be better understood as a member of a much larger family of scholars who, through the centuries, have systematically discussed moral problems of doing business (Ciulla, 1991). Still, as approached earlier, businesspeople are subject to moral dilemmas, just like any other human being. What differentiates them, however, is the strength and reach of their attitudes, decisions, and omissions. These, in turn, are conditioned by the particular dynamics of power in which they are inserted, as well as by the very nature of business environments. Broadly, it means that businesspeople are presented to situations which are not only specific, but that shall have a considerable impact in the numerous lives, as well as in the environment. These ideas gave rise to the here proposed *tripartite business ethics model* (Fig. 1.1), as discussed later in the chapter.

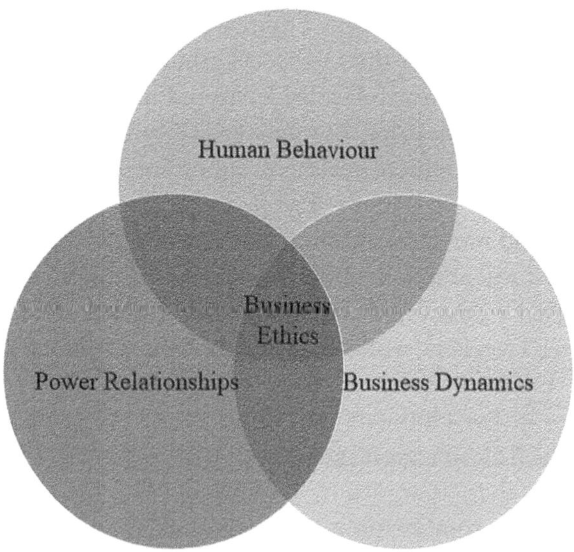

Fig. 1.1 The tripartite business ethics model. (Source: Author (s))

In that way, the recognition of Business Ethics as a distinct field of study does not imply its differentiation with Ethics, but, in fact, the acceptance that a critical and focused assessment of business issues may be necessary. Reflecting these peculiarities, we position Business Ethics as a sub-field of Ethics, as, at the same time, the study of the moral behavior of businesspeople shares the essence of generic moral assessments; it also has particularities when compared to other situations. The delimitation of Business Ethics would not target then the segregation or the hierarchization of ethical issues, nor grant ethical questions in business a privileged treatment. Instead, it would stand as an excerpt from a more general discussion on Ethics, in such a way that the specificities, idiosyncrasies, and complexities of morality in business contexts shall be properly addressed.

The reasoning developed for the justification of Business Ethics also supports the existence of other sub-fields. On that regard, Robinson (2008) points out to the increasing interest and assessment of public office ethics in the Western world, with particular focus on military activities (i.e. Military Ethics). Accordingly, among the reasons for this increased concern is the fact that military missions are being justified as humanitarian actions, with terms such as "humanitarian intervention" and "the responsibility to protect" being common. The British Armed Forces, for example, claim to be a "force for good". As pointed out by the author, in case such claims indeed express their purpose, military personnel must necessarily uphold the highest ethical standards, meaning that military institutions must be increasingly concerned with providing the appropriate ethical educations to their members. With companies positioning themselves in similar ways, the same argument may be used in the defense of Business Ethics. It is not rare, for example, that firms of the most diverse industries—including oil, mining, and tobacco—claim to care for the environment and for people.

Just as in companies, ethical impasses in military operations, however, go well beyond their role in humanitarian matters, with their destructive power being, perhaps, the source of most of these issues. The decision to fire a missile, for example, involves the consideration of a range of distinct questions that find no parallel outside the military field. That includes the life and safety of troops, those of enemies and of civilian populations eventually at risk. Adds to that the fact that such decisions are typically taken in contexts of great tension and uncertainty, contributing to the complexity of decision-making processes. Once more, an analogy with Business Ethics shall be traced. Considered the great power and reach of businesspeoples' decisions and the high-pressure contexts in which these decisions are made, ethical impasses in business contexts would also deserve the highest consideration. The decision of a pharmaceutical company between developing a drug that could save millions of lives in 30 years and be (hopefully) profitable only in the long run, and investing in the advertising of its current products to ensure the financial results of the next quarter have both great potential impact and ethical challenges which deserve to be addressed in a focused manner. It does not mean that every distinct area demands the development of a specific typology of Ethics, but in face of the intricacies of some—among which business—the approach shall be useful.

The delimitation of specific fields in related disciplines also corroborates the delimitation of Business Ethics within Ethics. On that regard, Driskell and Olmstead (1989, p. 43) discuss military psychology as a sub-field of Psychology. Accordingly, it would not be defined by a set of techniques, nor by a shared set of problems, but, instead, by an area of context of application (i.e. the military). As summarized by the authors, "military psychology is the application of psychology to military needs". Still accordingly, "[i]n many cases, military needs reflect concerns similar to those of other large civilian institutions, only magnified". When translated to the discussion proposed here, that means that the delimitation of Business Ethics has a lot to do with the context in which it may be more valuable, being business its natural *locus.* Likewise, it implies in the closer consideration of the issues that are specific, without, however, ignoring what is common. Metaphorically speaking, that dynamics could be understood as an observation under a microscope, as if, on the lenses of Ethics, a zoom was applied in business issues, revealing its details and specificities.

Donaldson and Dunfee (1994), however, display Business Ethics as a field suffering from a lack of direction, and intrinsically absorbed by its own logics, with research on the area being informed either by empirical ideas or by normative concepts. While the former comprehends the description and the explanation of factual states of affairs (e.g. managerial motivation, organizational accountability structures, relationships between ethical conduct, and financial performance), the latter would be centered on ideas which, despite possibly not grounded in actual business practices and structures, serve as guides to what one should do (i.e. prescriptions). Still after the authors, business school researchers would be at the origin of the empirical vein, as they adapted techniques typically used in Management disciplines (e.g. Marketing, Finance) to investigate relevant matters in corporate and organizational ethics. Often, this empirical stream produces frameworks propounding relationships among key behavior variables, as well as connections with the normative view. These frameworks, in turn, would be used in the prediction or understanding of ethical behavior, generally incorporating broad statements from ethical theory (e.g. utilitarianism, rights and justice, Ferrell & Gresham, 1985), or from moral psychology (Jones, 1991; Treviño, 1986).

Following similar developments in the areas of legal and medical ethics, researchers counting on philosophical training introduced these purely normative approaches to the business ethics debate, which, along with the use of nonempirical methods, have forged the contribution of the philosophical tradition of ethical theory to the field. Regardless of the efforts to reconcile the "is" and the "ought" perspectives (empirical and normative approaches, respectively), these two views would remain distant from each other, being the methods used by each the main cause of such gap (Treviño & Weaver, 1994). It is, in fact, possible that part of the resistance to Business Ethics is due to its philosophical origins, which can be linked to the sophists and casuists, "considered the quacks and horsethieves of moral philosophy" (Ciulla, 1991, p. 167). Accordingly, such is the resistance to these streams that the terms sophistry and casuistry assume a negative connotation, often describing hair-splitting argumentations. Still after the author, while false advertising and dangerous practices have traditionally been attributed to sophists, casuists have been accused of defending a case approach to ethics, recklessly disregarding moral principles, and serving the interests of the rich and powerful.

1.7 A Model for Business Ethics

This gray area between (1) human behavior, (2) the dynamics of power in business, and (3) business dynamics itself is proposed here as the delimitation of the Business Ethics debate. Inspired on Elkington's (1997) approach to sustainable management (i.e. the triple bottom line in business), we introduce then the *tripartite business ethics model* (Fig. 1.1), that serves as a guide to more structured analysis and discussions on the theme. The cases and concepts approached throughout the book are positioned in relation to its different dimensions, being the intersections between them of particular interest.

Although beyond the scope of the book, the framing of military ethics in a tripartite model may be useful for the sedimentation of the approach proposed here. Within the human behavior dimension, militaries—as well as managers or any other class we may analyze—present both what is common to the average person and what is specific in the behavior of those performing in a certain group. It is likely, for example, that over the course of a military career, certain psychological characteristics will be selected, shaping the profile of a typical individual that occupies command positions. On the specificities of military, Driskell and Olmstead (1989) stress their mission orientation (e.g. defend the country, fight, and win a war), being anything that does not contribute to the meeting of objectives secondary in their views. The dynamics of power in the military are particular as, most likely, in no other context hierarchy is so valued. Among other things, this means that obedience to higher orders must mitigate internal power struggles, creating an environment of greater stability in this regard. It does not express, however, that ethical dilemmas are only presented to generals. From the moment one enters a military career, specific moral and ethical questionings will be presented. It is possible, however, that these questions are at least partially suppressed in the name of respect for hierarchy. Thus, a low-ranking military officer would stand only as an executor of the decisions made by his superiors, meaning that, while this transfer of responsibility toward the top may make military operations viable, they increase the responsibilities of those in charge. This concentration of responsibilities and, thus, of the ethical burden on commanders is, perhaps, an important characteristic of the relationships in military environments. When it comes to the third dimension (i.e. the military dynamics), Driskell and Olmstead (1989) point out to the military context as a source of differentiation between military and civilian institutions. Accordingly, the military environment is, in a way, more serious than the civilian one, since those operating in the former must be ready to defend their country, and eventually die if necessary. The conjunction of these three dimensions would compose then the delimitation of the debate on military ethics.

Similar paths could be developed for other fields such as medical ethics, judicial ethics, sports ethics, academic ethics, and so on. That shows the versatility of tripartite models, such as the one developed here. Models, however, represent simplifications of reality, so that in face of the complexity of real life, many facets are necessarily ignored upon their construction. One must not expect the *tripartite business ethics model* to explain or predict the ethical conduct of businesspeople in its entirety, but rather to serve as a bridge between the main theoretical current and practical matters. One of its main limitations comes from the fact that contexts are not easily isolated and intersect with one another. Business and military ethics, for instance, are linked as most of the equipment employed in the pursuit of military goals (e.g. weapons, missiles, bombs, planes, warships, submarines, and radars) are developed and produced by companies. It must be argued then that the responsibility of military commanders is partially shared with the businesspeople behind the production of this material. Thus, just like a decision of dropping a bomb on the enemy is extremely serious, the decision to develop, produce, and commercialize such a bomb is not free of ethical considerations.

1.8 Historical Development

Even though the debate on Business Ethics has accelerated in the last years, it has occupied the minds of philosophers for centuries, even for millennia. As pointed out by Ciulla (1991), Cicero already approached unscrupulous business practices back in 44 B.C., having dedicated part of his classic *De Officiis* to the issue. Likewise, Medieval Church would also have the morality of business among its concerns, with themes such as wage labor, usery, and the determination of fair prices being addressed on some of its treatises. Still, debates held by European social thinkers in the seventeenth and eighteenth centuries would also compose this forming discussion, particularly those focused on the interaction between self-interest and the greatest good (Hirschman, 1977; Vogel, 1991).

Intellectual efforts, however, have not always been against what is now perceived as serious ethical faults. In his theory of natural slavery, Aristotle, for example, justifies the practice, arguing that "the majority of human beings may be enslaved without injustice, because they are slaves by nature" (Heath, 2008, p. 243). While the reasoning may have been accepted by the time, by today's standards it would be not only immoral but also criminal. Radical mutations in moral judgments such as this illustrate the dynamic nature of the business ethics debate. This evolution in the way of thinking, however, is not fully reflected in practice, as slavery is still well disseminated, particularly in low labor cost zones. While the morality of business has been a common subject throughout history, Business Ethics did not consolidate as an independent field of study before the last decades of the twentieth century. From an apparent marginal issue to its current status as one of the main themes of modern Management, the Business Ethics debate experienced a fast growth in what Donaldson and Dunfee (1994, p. 252) classify as a "meteoric rise" from the mid-1970s. Although arguably inappropriate—as meteors actually fall—the meaning commonly attributed to the expression denotes the rapid rise of Business Ethics as a field.

On that regard, Ciulla (1991) features some of the initial landmarks in the debate. Accordingly, the "Conference on Company Philosophy and Codes of Business Ethics" held in London in 1986 is possibly a starting point in that direction. Following the initiative, a mixed group of managers and academics created the European Business Ethics Network one year later. In 1988, in turn, the journal *Ethica Degli Affari* was published in Milan, Italy, being considered the first European publication on the issue. Also in 1988, the Hitachi Institute received funding from the Japanese government destined to the implementation of a large cross-cultural investigation on corporate responsibility, while the Dominican Catholic University Madre y Maestra inaugurated its ethics programs.

Likewise, the Instituto de Estudios Superiores de Administracion in Caracas, Venezuela, received a donation for the creation of a chair in business ethics from a wealthy businessman of the country. Still after Ciulla (1991), the Business Ethics debate faced resistance, particularly on its earliest stages. Among the criticisms was the idea that the notion of Business Ethics was a sort of American form of self-righteousness, meaning that beyond keeping the world safe for democracy, the United States would be engaged in a mission to preserve it from business practices considered to be unscrupulous.

1.9 Business Ethics in Practice

The discussions proposed throughout the chapter have, in general, a more conceptual and abstract nature. If, on the one hand, this seems to be characteristic of debates around more philosophical themes, the consideration of practical issues can be useful not only to verify the applicability of these concepts, but also to a better understanding of their relevance. Unlike other topics related to the discussion on Ethics and Morality, issues centered around Business Ethics find numerous practical applications. Among them, we highlight modern slavery and child labor. Although situated in the social dimension of sustainability, the discussion of the enormous offenses that these practices represent is useful in the understanding of the broader impacts of environmental fraud, particularly on what relates to its potential negative effects to public health. Despite not exhausting the debate on Business Ethics, these themes have shown increasing relevance for different groups of stakeholders, being briefly addressed below.

1.9.1 Modern Slavery

Although it is difficult to rank the severity of unethical business practices slavery or "slave modes of production" (Campbell, 2011) represents, perhaps, the most critical issue on that regard. Sadly, History is full of examples of such practices. Among the most notorious is the massive use of slave labor in the economic models adopted for the commercial exploitation of European colonies in America. On that regard, Singleton (2001) discusses some of the acts employed by coffee producers in colonial Cuba, where more than one million African slaves were taken to between the beginning of the Spanish domination from 1511 until the abolition of slavery in 1886. Among those is what Moreno Fraginals (1977) classified as a jail-like structure. That comprehended the housing of enslaved people in prison-like quarters that were often locked at night and were kept under great surveillance by guards. Similarly, extremely poor working conditions were offered to slaves in Brazil until the last decades of the nineteenth century, which included intense vigilance, punishment, escape prevention, and recapture of fugitives (Versiani, 1994). Analogous practices took place in other parts of the American continent, but also in practically all other regions where human presence has been established.

Yet, the moral and ethical issues associated with slave labor go beyond the idea that one human being can possess another. Within this relationship of domination, there are also issues related to the means employed to establish this relationship, as well as to the techniques used to guarantee that the slave fulfills the wishes of the one who owns him. This includes the different practices of capture and imprisonment, destruction or modification of the original cultures, and the various forms of punishment used when deviations are observed. These issues are not limited to the last centuries, being possible to trace them back to much earlier times. Slavery has been a common business practice for millennia, with the morality of the practice being the subject of important philosophical debates throughout history. As discussed by Yavetz (1988), following a shortage of manpower—and the economic problems that come with it—great quantities of slaves were absorbed in Ancient Rome, with the practice being common both in agricultural and in industrial activities.

Regardless of all the noble efforts to eradicate slavery through history, the practice persists. Despite belonging to specific historical moments, the examples discussed still serve as references for the working conditions observed today. In September 2012, for example, a riot broke out in one of Foxconn's factories, arguably due to the harsh working conditions offered to employees. According to messages posted online, the revolt was due to the mistreatment and physical punishment imposed on workers by company guards (Duncan & Jim, 2012), while the company has among its customers some of the most important players in the electronics industry, being Foxconn itself the world's largest contract maker of electronic goods by the time. Still accordingly, the riot involved nearly 2000 employees dedicated to the assembly of Apple's iPhones. Qiu (2019) compares the working conditions at Foxconn to those typical of the transatlantic triangular trade and discusses the emergence of the term "iSlave" among labor activists to address the issue. Subsequently, that would encompass two distinct forms of slavery: (1) manufacturing iSlave (i.e. production mode iSlavery); and (2) manufactured iSlave, (i.e. consumption mode iSlavery). While the first type refers to the poor working conditions associated with the iPhone production lines (such as the ones in Foxconn), the second would relate to the use of the device, encompassing what the author refers to as Facebook free labor and the addiction of people by electronic gadgets.

The differentiation seems pertinent, even if both types fit as cases of unethical conducts. If, on the one hand, the association of poor working conditions with business abuses is arguably more direct, the "voluntary work" for social networks and the addiction related to the use of electronic devices also stand as potential risks to the physical and emotional health of the individuals involved. On the other hand, although the damages resulting from each situation are different and shall have very distinct degrees of severity, both represent negative social impacts that may arise from one same economic activity. The fact that the first type is usually more visible may be associated to a greater identification of employees with companies, while the delimitation of consumer groups may be significantly more difficult, regardless of firms' efforts to know their publics. Even if techniques and practices of market segmentation have dramatically evolved, the client, as an individual, is, in general, diluted in a group, particularly when it comes to mass consumption products. That means that the perception of the damage caused by the second type of "slavery" is hardly noticed, except for those who are dedicated to the study of these topics in greater detail. This illustrates the importance of multi-stakeholder analysis in practice, so that the Business Ethics debate is not restricted to its philosophical and theoretical foundations. Despite critical, they do not seem to be sufficient to advance moral and ethical practices in businesses.

1.9.2 Child Labor

Like slavery, child labor seems to have been part of economic activities practically since its inception. It is not uncommon that images dating from the industrial revolution portray minors performing jobs of high physical demand, especially in coal mines. Correspondingly, representations of children working in the most diverse activities are common in the literature and painting from the most diverse eras such as the Middle Age and the Renaissance periods. The conception that children are special beings who deserve a distinguished treatment seems to be relatively recent, with the very notion of childhood being a concept that does not appear very often in historical records. For centuries, children were considered only as small adults, in such a way that responsibilities and duties similar to the ones assigned to older people were usually appointed to them. In addition to the obligations associated with work, children were also commonly exposed to situations that today are generally reserved for grown-ups. This includes participating in wars and even early marriages. Unfortunately, in many parts of the world these practices remain trivial and present.

Issues relating to the preservation of childhood are of general interest and pose a greater challenge than those presented in discussions on Business Ethics. The disrespect of childhood can have lasting consequences in societies, with its effects extending for generations. In this sense, it is important to highlight aspects related to children's access to both public health and education policies. If, on one side, the lack of appropriate medical care can have permanent consequences for the child (e.g. infantile paralysis due to failures in the distribution of vaccines), it should also generate high costs for the whole social body. In addition to the values necessarily dispensed in medicines, exams, and treatments of various kinds, the impairment of an individual's physical health carries with it an immense opportunity cost, since in adulthood this child will possibly not be able to integrate the workforce or it will do so only partially. With regard to deprivation of access to education, the costs are similar. A child who does not have access to quality basic education will find it difficult to enter the labor market and, even if they succeed, they will probably occupy lower-paid positions. When taking a child's time, child labor prevents them from studying properly, condemning them to a more economically modest life. It is necessary to take into account, therefore, that, in addition to its more immediate effects, child labor ends up acting as an important factor of social inequality. In this way, issues related to the employment of children acquire a fundamental importance within the Business Ethics debate.

Despite all its harms, child labor still appears as a fundamental part for the survival of millions of families around the world. In particular, rural activities have been a breeding ground for the employment of children as a workforce. It is common, for instance, to small landowners to employ their own children in activities related to planting, harvesting, and transporting food. Once again, the dynamics of the industry can serve as an important factor explaining unethical behavior. While it holds a large number of producers, food manufacturing offers very low opportunities for differentiation. The production and marketing of agricultural commodities (e.g. corn, soybeans, and rice) are configured in many cases as examples of activities that approach the dynamics of perfectly competitive markets. In addition to the irrelevance of individual producers and consumers (i.e. atomization of production and consumption), the fact that the products are practically identical reinforces the mechanism for determining prices through the quantities demanded and offered.

Currently, child labor has been also highlighted in areas that theoretically represent advances in terms of environmental management. As discussed in more detail in Chap. 11, the transition to electric car technology caused a rush for inputs. Among them, lithium is among the main components of its batteries. If the fact that lithium should be mined—which can hardly be defended from an environmental standpoint—was not enough, working conditions in the exploration areas have been pointed out as being particularly bad. Along with issues related to the safety of workers and the use of violence against them, child labor appears as one of the main problems of this business model. This appears to be particularly common in lithium mines in underdeveloped countries in Africa and Latin America. For these and other reasons, the ethical issues related to the transition of the automobile industry to electrical technology can be understood as being particularly challenging.

As discussed throughout the chapter, businesspeople face moral dilemmas in virtually every activity they perform. Similarly, issues of Business Ethics extend to basically all industries. The examples discussed here are evidently far from considering all topics on this subject. A more comprehensive discussion should consider a number of other industries and activities that appear to be rich in moral and ethical challenges. Among these are the industries related to tobacco, gambling, pornography, and others. Although these themes are not covered in more detail in this book, readers are invited to apply the concepts developed here in their analysis of these issues. In general, discussions about the motivations of unethical behavior, the ways in which it develops, and possible ways of discouraging them can be useful in this direction.

References

Amazon. (2019). 2018 Annual Report. https://s2.q4cdn.com/299287126/files/doc_financials/annual/2018-Annual-Report.pdf

American Psychiatric Association. (2000). *Diagnostic and Statistical Manual of Mental Disorders* (4th ed.). American Psychiatric Association.

Apple. (2018, September 29). Annual Report Pursuant to Section 13 or 15(d) of the Securities Exchange act of 1934 for the Fiscal Year Ended. https://s2.q4cdn.com/470004039/files/doc_financials/2018/q4/10-K-2018-(As-Filed).pdf

Arasaratnam, A., & Humphreys, G. (2013). Emerging Economies Drive Frugal Innovation. World Health Organization. *Bulletin of the World Health Organization, 91*(1), 6–7.

Argandoña, A. (2001). Corruption: The Corporate Perspective. *Business Ethics: A European Review, 10*(2), 163–175.

Arnold, M. (1867). Hebraism and Hellenism. In M. Arnold (Ed.), *(1913), Selections from the Prose of Matthew Arnold*. Houghton Mifflin.

Austin, J. (2017). *Insider Trading and Market Manipulation: Investigating and Prosecuting Across Borders*. Edward Elgar Publishing.

Bandura, A. (2002). Selective Moral Disengagement in the Exercise of Moral Agency. *Journal of Moral Education, 31*(2), 101–119.
Boddy, C. R. (2017). Psychopathic Leadership a Case Study of a Corporate Psychopath CEO. *Journal of Business Ethics, 145*(1), 141–156.
Boole, G. (1847). *The Mathematical Analysis of Logic*. Philosophical Library.
Boole, G. (1854). *An Investigation of the Laws of Thought: On Which Are Founded the Mathematical Theories of Logic and Probabilities* (Vol. 2). Walton and Maberly.
Bowie, N. E. (2017). *Business Ethics: A Kantian Perspective* (2nd ed.). Cambridge University Press.
Brouwer, A. E., Mariotti, I., & Van Ommeren, J. N. (2004). The Firm Relocation Decision: An Empirical Investigation. *The Annals of Regional Science, 38*(2), 335–347.
Campbell, G. (2011). Slavery in the Indian Ocean World. In G. Heuman & T. Burnard (Eds.), *The Routledge History of Slavery*. Routledge.
Campos, P. H. P. (2017, August 28–30). A trajetória das mendes júnior: um caso emblemático de uma das empreiteiras da ditadura. *XII Congresso Brasileiro de História Econômica*. Niterói.
Chatterjee, A., & Hambrick, D. C. (2007). It's All About Me: Narcissistic CEOs and Their Effects on Company Strategy and Performance. *Administrative Science Quarterly, 52*, 351–386.
Childs, J. M. (2000). *Greed: Economics and Ethics in Conflict*. Fortress Press.
Chiou, J. S. (2004). The Antecedents of Consumers' Loyalty Toward Internet Service Providers. *Information & Management, 41*(6), 685–695.
Ciulla, J. B. (1991). Why Is Business Talking About Ethics? Reflections on Foreign Conversations. *California Management Review, 34*(1), 67–86.
Clapp, J. (2015). ABCD and Beyond: From Grain Merchants to Agricultural Value Chain Managers. *Canadian Food Studies / La Revue Canadienne des Études sur l'Alimentation, 2*(2), 126–135.
Clinard, M. B., & Yeager, P. C. (2011). *Corporate Crime*. Transaction Publishers New Brunswick. Originally Published in 1980 by Free Press.
Coase, R. H. (1937). The Nature of the Firm. *Economica, 4*(16), 386–405.
Cooke, E. F. (1997). Greed Leads to Better Marketing, Healthier Competition, Economy. *Marketing News, 31*(23), 4.
Crane, A. (2013). Modern Slavery as a Management Practice: Exploring the Conditions and Capabilities for Human Exploitation. *Academy of Management Review, 38*(1), 49–69.

Delgado-García, J. B., & De La Fuente-Sabaté, J. M. (2010). How Do CEO Emotions Matter? Impact of CEO Affective Traits on Strategic and Performance Conformity in the Spanish Banking Industry. *Strategic Management Journal, 31*(5), 562–574.

Donaldson, T., & Dunfee, T. W. (1994). Toward a Unified Conception of Business Ethics: Integrative Social Contracts Theory. *Academy of Management Review, 19*(2), 252–284.

Driskell, J. E., & Olmstead, B. (1989). Psychology and the Military: Research Applications and Trends. *American Psychologist, 44*(1), 43–54.

Drucker, P. (1981). What Is Business Ethics. *The Public Interest, 63*, 18–36.

Duffy, E. (1962). *Activation and Behavior*. Wiley.

Duncan, M., & Jim, C. (2012). Foxconn China Plant Closed After 2,000 Riot. *Reuters*. https://www.reuters.com/article/us-hon-hai/foxconn-china-plant-closed-after-2000-riot-idUSBRE88N00L20120924

Eby, L. T., & Buch, K. (1998). The Impact of Adopting an Ethical Approach to Employee Dismissal During Corporate Restructuring. *Journal of Business Ethics, 17*(12), 1253–1264.

Elkington, J. (1997). *Cannibals with Forks: The Triple Bottom Line of 21st Century Business*. Capstone.

Ferrell, O. C., & Gresham, L. G. (1985). A Contingency Framework for Understanding Ethical Decision Making in Marketing. *Journal of Marketing, 49*(3), 87–96.

Finkelstein, S. (2004). *Why Smart Executives Fail: And What You Can Learn from Their Mistakes*. Penguin Group.

Fried, L. (2001). Creating Hebraism, Confronting Hellenism: The Menorah Journal and Its Struggle for the Jewish Imagination. *American Jewish Archives Journal, 53*(1/2), 147–174.

Friedman, M. (1962). *Capitalism and Freedom*. University of Chicago Press.

Friedman, M. (1970, September 13). The Social Responsibility of Business Is to Increase Its Profits. *The New York Times Magazine*. https://www.nytimes.com/1970/09/13/archives/article-15-no-title.html

Goodpaster, K. E. (1991). Business Ethics and Stakeholder Analysis. *Business Ethics Quarterly, 1*(1), 53–73.

Griffin, P. (2017). *The Carbon Majors Database*. CPD Carbon Majors Report.

Gross, E. (1978). Organizational Crime: A Theoretical Perspective. In N. K. Denzin (Ed.), *Studies in Symbolic Interaction* (Vol. 1, pp. 55–85). JAI Press.

Hambrick, D. C., & Mason, P. A. (1984). Upper Echelons: The Organization as a reflection of Its Top Managers. *Academy of Management Review, 9*(2), 193–206.

Heath, M. (2008). Aristotle on Natural Slavery. *Phronesis: A Journal for Ancient Philosophy, 53*(3), 243–270.

Hess, A. (2018). How on High School Produced the CEOs of Microsoft, Adobe and Mastercard. *CNBC.* https://www.cnbc.com/2018/04/05/one-high-school-produced-the-ceos-of-microsoft-adobe-and-mastercard.html

Hirschman, A. O. (1977). *The Passions and the Interests.* Princeton University Press.

Hoffman, W. M., & Moore, J. M. (1982). What Is Business Ethics? A Reply to Peter Drucker. *Journal of Business Ethics, 1*(4), 293–300.

Hogan, R., & Kaiser, R. B. (2005). What We Know About Leadership. *Review of General Psychology, 9*(2), 169–180.

Hogan, R., Raskin, R., & Fazzini, D. (1990). The Dark Side of Charisma. In K. E. Clark & M. B. Clark (Eds.), *Measures of Leadership* (pp. 343–354). Leadership Library of America, Inc.

Issacharoff, S. (2010). On Political Corruption. *Harvard Law Review, 124*(118), 118–142.

Izard, C. E. (1977). *Human Emotions.* Springer Science and Business Media New York.

Jelassi, T., & Martínez-López, F. J. (2020). The Strategic Approach of the World's Biggest e-Tailing Companies: Amazon and Alibaba. In *Strategies for e-Business* (pp. 467–500). Springer.

Jones, T. M. (1991). Ethical Decision Making by Individuals in Organizations: An Issue-Contingent Model. *Academy of Management Review, 16*(2), 366–395.

Judge, T. A., LePine, J. A., & Rich, B. L. (2006). Loving Yourself Abundantly: Relationship of the Narcissistic Personality to Self and Other Perceptions of Workplace Deviance, Leadership, and Task and Contextual Performance. *Journal of Applied Psychology, 91*, 762–776.

Kenton, W. (2020). Expected Value (EV). *Investopedia.* https://www.investopedia.com/terms/e/expected-value.asp#:~:text=The%20expected%20value%20(EV)%20is,summing%20all%20of%20those%20values

Kets de Vries, M. F. R., & Miller, D. (1997). Narcissism and Leadership: An Object Relations Perspective. In R. P. Vecchio (Ed.), *Leadership: Understanding the Dynamics of Power and Influence in Organizations.* University of Notre Dame Press.

Kisfalvi, V., & Pitcher, P. (2003). Doing What Feels Right. The Influence of CEO Character and Emotions on Top Management Team Dynamics. *Journal of Management Inquiry, 12*(1), 42–66.
Kollock, P. (1993). "An Eye for an Eye Leaves Everyone Blind": Cooperation and Accounting System. *American Sociological Review, 58*(6), 768–786.
Kortum, S., & Lerner, J. (2001). *Does Venture Capital Spur Innovation?* Emerald Group Publishing Limited.
Kouchaki, M., Smith-Crowe, K., Brief, A. P., & Sousa, C. (2013). Seeing Green: Mere Exposure to Money Triggers a Business Decision Frame and Unethical Outcomes. *Organizational Behavior and Human Decision Processes, 121*(1), 53–61.
Lazarus, R. S. (1968). Emotions and Adaptation: Conceptual and Empirical Relations. In W. J. Arnold (Ed.), *Nebraska Symposium on Motivation* (pp. 175–266). Nebraska University Press.
Levmore, S. (2019). *Outside Influence on Democratic Elections*. University of Chicago, Public Law Working Paper.
Lubit, R. (2002). The Long-Term Organizational Impact of Destructively Narcissistic Managers. *Academy of Management Executive, 16*, 127–138.
Maccoby, M. (2000). Narcissistic Leaders. *Harvard Business Review, 78*, 68–78.
Maccoby, M. (2003). *The Productive Narcissist: The Promise and Peril of Visionary Leadership*. Broadway.
Maccoby, M. (2004). Narcissistic Leaders: The Incredible Pros. *the inevitable cons. Harvard Business Review, 82*, 92–101.
Maksimovic, V., Phillips, G., & Prabhala, N. R. (2011). Post-Merger Restructuring and the Boundaries of the Firm. *Journal of Financial Economics, 102*(2), 317–343.
Marshall, A. J., Ashleigh, M. J., Baden, D., Ojiako, U., & Guidi, M. G. (2015). Corporate Psychopathy: Can "Search and Destroy" and "Hearts and Minds" Military Metaphors Inspire HRM Solutions? *Journal of Business Ethics, 128*, 495–504.
McNaughton, R. B., Osborne, P., & Imrie, B. C. (2002). Market Oriented Value Creation in Service Firms. *European Journal of Marketing, 36*(9/10), 990–1002.
Miles, M. P., Munilla, L. S., & Covin, J. G. (2004). Innovation, Ethics, and Entrepreneurship. *Journal of Business Ethics, 54*(1), 97–101.
Mintzberg, H., Simons, R., & Basu, K. (2002). Beyond Selfishness. *MIT Sloan Management Review, 44*(1), 67–74.

Moreno Fraginals, M. (1977). Africa in Cuba: A Quantitative Analysis of the African Population in the Island of Cuba. In V. Rubin, & A. Tuden (Eds.), *Comparative Perspectives on Slavery in New World Plantation Societies. Annals New York Academy of Sciences* (Vol. 292, pp. 187–201).

Munson, C. L., Rosenblatt, M. J., & Rosenblatt, Z. (1999). The Use and Abuse of Power in Supply Chains. *Business Horizons, 42*(1), 55–56.

Nunes, M. F., & Lee Park, C. (2017). Self-Claimed Sustainability: Building Social and Environmental Reputations with Words. *Sustainable Production and Consumption, 11*, 46–57.

Nye, J. E. (2004). *Soft Power: The Means to Success in World Politics*. Public Affairs.

Oakes, G. (2003). Max Weber on Value Rationality and Value Spheres: Critical Remarks. *Journal of Classical Sociology, 3*(1), 27–45.

OECD. (2020). *National Accounts of OECD Countries*. OECD Publishing, Issue 1, Paris. https://doi.org/10.1787/629805bc-en. https://read.oecd-ilibrary.org/economics/national-accounts-of-oecd-countries/volume-2020/issue-1_629805bc-en#page14

Pondé, L. F. C. S. (2018). O que é moralismo em filosofia?. https://www.youtube.com/watch?v=HsBR_5gbIIU

Porter, M. E. (1979, March–April). How Competitive Forces Shape Strategy. *Harvard Business Review*, pp. 137–145.

Porter, M. E. (1980). *Competitive Strategy: Techniques for Analyzing Industries and Competitors*. Free Press.

Porter, M. E. (1996). What Is Strategy? *Harvard Business Review, 74*(6), 61–78.

Qiu, J. L. (2019). Goodbye iSlave: Making Alternative Subjects Through Digital Objects. In D. Chandler & C. Fuchs (Eds.), *Digital Objects, Digital Subjects: Interdisciplinary Perspective on Capitalism, Labour and Politics in the Age of Big Data*. University of Westminster Press.

Rajan, R., & Zingales, L. (2003). *Saving Capitalism from the Capitalists: How Open Financial Markets Challenge the Establishment and Spread Prosperity to Rich and Poor Alike*. Crown Business.

Remy, N., Speelman, E., & Swartz, S. (2016). Style That's Sustainable: A New Fast-Fashion Formula. *McKinsey & Company*. https://www.mckinsey.com/business-functions/sustainability/our-insights/style-thats-sustainable-a-new-fast-fashion-formula#

Resick, C. J., Whitman, D. S., Weingarden, S. M., & Hiller, N. J. (2009). The Bright-Side and the Dark-Side of CEO Personality: Examining Core Self-Evaluations, Narcissism, Transformational Leadership, and Strategic Influence. *Journal of Applied Psychology, 94*, 1365–1381.

Robinson, P. (2008). Introduction. In P. Robinson, N. de Lee, & D. Carrick (Eds.), *Ethics Education in the Military*. Ashgate Publishing Company.
Rosenthal, S. A., & Pittinsky, T. L. (2006). Narcissistic Leadership. *The Leadership Quarterly, 17*, 617–633.
Scalia, A. (1989). The Rule of Law as a Law of Rules. *The University of Chicago Law Review, 56*(4), 1175–1188.
Schachtel, E. (1959). *Metamorphosis*. Basic Books.
Siegel, D. S., & Simons, K. L. (2010). Assessing the Effects of Mergers and Acquisitions on Firm Performance, Plant Productivity, and Workers: New Evidence from Matched Employer-Employee Data. *Strategic Management Journal, 31*(8), 903–916.
Silva, G., Tynan, N., & Yilmaz, Y. (1998, August). Private Participation in the Water and Sewerage Sector: Recent Trends. *The World Bank Group*. Note No. 147, pp. 1–8.
Singer, P. (1993). *Practical Ethics* (2nd ed.). Cambridge University Press.
Singhapakdi, A., Vitell, S. J., Lee, D. J., Nisius, A. M., & Grace, B. Y. (2013). The Influence of Love of Money and Religiosity on Ethical Decision-Making in Marketing. *Journal of Business Ethics, 114*(1), 183–191.
Singleton, T. A. (2001). Slavery and Spatial Dialectics on Cuban Coffee Plantations. *World Archaeology, 33*(1), 98–114.
Song, J., Lee, K., & Khanna, T. (2016). Dynamic Capabilities at Samsung: Optimizing Internal Co-Opetition. *California Management Review, 58*(4), 118–140.
Steinbeck, J. (1993). *Cannery Row*. Penguin Books.
Stevens, G., Deuling, J., & Armenakis, A. (2012). Successful Psychopaths: Are They Unethical Decision-Makers and Why? *Journal of Business Ethics, 105*, 139–149.
Tang, T. L. P., & Chiu, R. K. (2003). Income, Money Ethic, Pay Satisfaction, Commitment, and Unethical Behavior: Is the Love of Money the Root of Evil for Hong Kong Employees? *Journal of Business Ethics, 46*(1), 13–30.
Tang, T. L. P., & Liu, H. (2012). Love of Money and Unethical Behavior Intention: Does an Authentic Supervisor's Personal Integrity and Character (ASPIRE) Make a Difference? *Journal of Business Ethics, 107*(3), 295–312.
Tomkins, S. S. (1963). *Affect, Imagery, and Consciousness: The Negative Affects* (Vol. 2). Springer and Company.
Treviño, L. K. (1986). Ethical Decision Making in Organizations: A Person-Situation Interactionist Model. *Academy of Management Review, 11*(3), 601–617.

Treviño, L. K., & Nelson, K. A. (2016). *Managing Business Ethics—Straight Talk About How to Do It Right* (5th ed.). John Wiley & Sons.
Treviño, L. K., & Weaver, G. R. (1994). Business Ethics/Business Ethics: One Field or Two? *Business Ethics Quarterly, 4*(2), 113–128.
Turker, D., & Altuntas, C. (2014). Sustainable Supply Chain Management in the Fast Fashion Industry: An Analysis of Corporate Reports. *European Management Journal, 32*(5), 837–849.
Versiani, F. R. (1994). Escravidão no Brasil: uma Análise Econômica. *Revista Brasileira de Economia, 48*(4), 463–478.
Vogel, D. (1991). The Ethical Roots of Business Ethics. *Business Ethics Quarterly, 1*(1), 101–120.
Waters, J. A., Bird, F., & Chant, P. D. (1986). Everyday Moral Issues Experienced by Managers. *Journal of Business Ethics, 5*(5), 373–384.
Weber, M. ([1922] 1978). *Economy and Society* (G. Roth & C. Wittich, Eds.). University of California Press.
Weiss, R. L. (1991). *Maimonides' Ethics: The Encounter of Philosophic and Religious Morality*. The University of Chicago Press.
Wenger, M. A. (1950). Emotion as Visceral Action: An Extension of Lange's Theory. In L. Reymert (Ed.), *The Second International Symposium on Feelings and Emotions* (pp. 3–10). McGraw-Hill.
Wilson, J. Q., & Kelling, G. L. (1982, March). Broken Windows. *Atlantic Monthly*, pp. 29–38.
Yavetz, Z. (1988). *Slaves and Slavery in Ancient Rome*. Transaction Publishers.
Zimbardo, P. G. (1969). The Human Choice: Individuation, Reason, and Order Versus Deindividuation, Impulse, and Chaos. *Nebraska Symposium on Motivation, 17*, 237–307.

2

Environmental Fraud

2.1 Fraud, Criminology, and Corporate Crimes

Fraud can be defined as any initiative that aims to deceive an interlocutor, making them believe that what is presented is something that is not. Such forgeries can have the most diverse objectives, being applied, for example, to documents, products, and services, among others. Likewise, fraudsters can use a practically infinite range of means to achieve their goals, with the practice often being an illustration of the misuse of human creativity. As for the motivations of fraudulent conducts, they can be as diverse as the means of applying them. It is possible, for instance, that individuals engage in such practices to avoid punishment. This would be the case of a driver who simulates a parking ticket so that he is not fined, or a child who tries to hide the pieces of a broken vase to avoid parental sanctions. There also seem to be situations in which one person seeks to deceive the other for the simple pleasure of doing so. In these cases, it is possible that the practice of fraud gives the person who engages on it a sense of intellectual superiority, with this sensation resting their only gain. Despite the

M. Fracarolli Nunes, C. Lee Park, *Business Ethics and Environmental Fraud*,
https://doi.org/10.1007/978-3-030-73800-6_2

myriad of reasons that may possibly lead to fraudulent practices, the prospect of financial gains appears to be among the most important ones.

Regarding the consequences of fraudulent practices, they can be analyzed in terms of both their seriousness and scope. While some can be banal and have a relatively small impact, others shall be at the origin of important and lasting damages. In the first group are what might be called day-to-day frauds. In addition to the examples discussed above, small lies and falsehoods may be common within basic social interaction (e.g. an employee who lies to justify his delay by pointing to a flat tire, a friend who lies saying to have gotten a flu to skip attending a pre-scheduled appointment). In general, these common little deviations do not have prior planning, being adopted in the management of situations that were not initially foreseen. Although they cause harm to people who are cheated on, the consequences of these actions can be considered mild. Likewise, their effects are limited to a small number of people, being usually restricted to the direct victims.

At the other extreme, widespread fraud can have a profound and far-reaching impact, harming not just a few specific individuals but entire communities. This is the case of fraud involving medicines, vaccines, medical devices, or anything that relates to health care. In the case of vaccines, for example, the ineffectiveness of an adulterated product can lead to the proliferation of epidemics and/or condemn individuals to live with chronic diseases. The continuity of the damage to public health is also manifested in the large expenditures these issues represent as the valuable and scarce resources of the public budget need to be reallocated to address them. The various cases of environmental fraud in the automobile industry fall into this category. As discussed in Chap. 6, the implementation and use of cheating devices to defraud emission tests in the United States allowed Volkswagen to market vehicles that emitted pollutants—in particular NO_x—well above legal limits. This extra load of pollutants can have a direct effect not only on the quality of life of the populations exposed to it but also on people's life expectancy. With these substances being associated with the development of serious illnesses that can manifest themselves for decades (e.g. cancer), the fraud perpetrated by Volkswagen appears to have both acute and long-term impacts.

Between the extremes of day-to-day fraud (i.e. low and restricted impact) and widespread fraud (i.e. high and collective impact), it is possible to distinguish types of fraud that alternate two other combinations of these variables. A fraud that has a high impact but is restricted in terms of the number of people affected is here defined as a punctual fraud. In this category are frauds to creditors, to investors, to the assets of third parties, among others, as, depending on the values involved in these deviations, their impact can be quite relevant for the victims (typically formed by individuals or small groups). Likewise, frauds that have a relatively small impact but have their effects distributed for a large number of people are here defined as diluted fraud. This category includes cases of corruption and embezzlement of public money involving small amounts. Although the effects of these minor offenses often go unnoticed, their effects can be extended to the whole of society. The perception of these four types of fraud allows for their differentiation, possibly contributing to a greater understanding of their nature. Figure 2.1 below summarizes these four fraud classifications in what is here named *the fraud severity and*

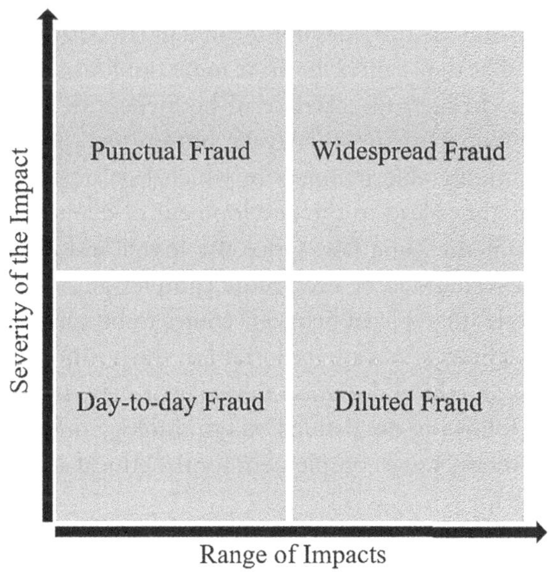

Fig. 2.1 The fraud severity and range matrix. (Source: Author (s))

range matrix, separating them in terms of the relevance and the scope of their impacts. The distinction of these categories is relevant to our debate as it allows a clearer understanding of relevance of environmental fraud. As discussed ahead in the chapter, this specific type of deviation usually classifies as widespread fraud.

Despite covering different types of conducts, fraudulent practices can, in some cases, be treated as crimes. In this sense, the literatures on both General and Corporate Criminology may offer useful insights in the comprehension of this sort of behavior. In addition to offering the theoretical basis for the understanding of fraud as a manifestation of human interactions, this debate allows for a greater comprehension of the different natures of fraudulent conducts, paving the way for more specific discussions on environmental fraud. This analysis complements the considerations made in Chap. 1 on the reasons why businesspeople eventually behave unethically.

It must be noted, however, that the classification of a conduct as a crime is not always aligned with its ethical and moral assessments. While the first depends on what is allowed or prohibited under the law, the second demands an understanding of values which are not always well defined or determined. This does not mean that laws do not require interpretation, and that they cannot be as or more dubious than the so-called informal values. In fact, the exercise of hermeneutics accompanies the career of all law operators (e.g. lawyers, prosecutors, judges), in such a way that the innumerable manners in which legal texts can be understood may sometimes lead to the development of diametrically opposed interpretations of the same law. Once the moral and ethical issues are considered, the results can be even more complex and diverse. It is possible, for example, that a legal behavior comes to be considered immoral and vice-versa. These points are important in the positioning of environmental fraud as an ethical deviation that may or may not be criminal. In this sense, the following discussions on criminology must be seen not as a substitute, but rather as a complement for the ethical and moral debates proposed in Chap. 1.

2.1.1 Environmental Fraud and Crime

In discussing fraudulent behavior, Albrecht (2014) points out to the work of earlier criminology researchers Edwin Sutherland and Donald Cressey as the first references in that direction. Accordingly, Sutherland would be responsible for the Differentiation Association Theory, which, among other things, focuses on the reasons why people commit crimes. On that regard, Tittle et al. (1986, p. 405) position Sutherland's (1939) reasoning "as the prime factor in the genesis of crime", with the exposition of individuals to favorable or unfavorable cultural patterns configuring a major driver of crime. In this set, criminal behavior would be learned mostly through interpersonal interaction, with the frequency, the extent, the intimacy, and the intensity of associations with favorable criminal cultures pushing the process (Sutherland, 1942; Sutherland & Cressey, 1978). Coherently, Gaylord and Galliher (1988) add that, unlike the European schools of criminology—which would typically associate deviant behaviors with economic influences—the consideration of proximate and observable causes should be favored under Sutherland's perspective. Thus, the association and interaction of groups of people would be the main source of criminous conducts. Sutherland's Differential Association Theory views crime as a way of life, which is basically conditioned to one's attachment to groups that value it as a measure of success.

Concerning the practice of environmental fraud, Sutherland's arguments would be relevant for two main reasons. First, the emphasis on the environment's role corroborates the assumption of organizational cultures as possible triggers of unethical behavior. As discussed in Chap. 1, in case employees realize that deviations are tolerated or even valued by their surroundings, they should feel encouraged to commit them. This can translate into a series of frauds that may have a major impact on the environment, including the use of technologies aimed at circumventing emissions inspections, the falsification of classifications (e.g. conventional products being sold as organic), and the incorrect minimization of environmental impacts of alternative sources of energy (e.g. wind, solar). These and other forms of environmental fraud are discussed in greater detail in Chap. 7. Second, the discussion of environmental factors also reinforces the idea that industry practices can justify, encourage, or validate the practices of a particular company. Thus, if any company in the industry incurs environmental fraud, the others may feel entitled to do the same, especially if the fraud in question allows the offending company to develop a competitive advantage. This seems to be the case for some companies in the automotive industry that, as discussed in Chap. 6, have adopted practices very similar to those attributed to Volkswagen, even if they have not gained the same prominence.

The meaning of Differentiation Association Theory, however, has been uncertain, mainly due to Sutherland's argued lack of precision in defining its concepts (Tittle et al., 1986). The connotation of regular terms and ideas (e.g. association, excess, (un)favorableness to law violation, direction of attitudes and rationalizations) would be often relegated to those applying or testing it. Along with leading to diverse interpretations, it would also make the comparison and application of research results difficult. Beyond that, the way conceptual variables affect each other would not be sufficiently clear, making the case for a range of variations of the underlying causal structure of the theory. Competing theorists such as Sheldon Glueck (1960, p. 293) also harshly criticized Sutherland's views, claiming that Differential Association Theory "is a very thin and distant abstraction without capacity to guide practical research". Despite the objections, Sutherland is claimed to have "established the sociological model of crime as the dominant paradigm in criminology", standing as "the most influential criminologist of the [twentieth] century" (Laub & Sampson, 1991, p. 1402). Likewise, Gaylord and Galliher (1988) position Sutherland as the founder of criminology as a separate research area within sociology.

Sutherland's theory required him to demolish individual level or non-sociological perspectives on criminal conduct, with the work of Sheldon and Eleanor Glueck appearing as a counterpoint on that regard (Laub & Sampson, 1991). Based on a multiple-factor theory of crime, the investigation conducted by the Glueck couple is seen as a competing research paradigm, in which the development of criminal careers and the power of correctional measures to reduce criminal behavior were privileged. Still accordingly, the Gluecks' conclusions would be more strongly rooted in empiricism, with results suggesting, for example, that delinquent boys tend to be more often characterized as having greater levels of self-assertion and social-assertion, as well as presenting defiant and narcissistic characteristics (Baumeister et al., 1996).

The study *Unraveiling Juvenile Delinquency* (Glueck & Glueck, 1950), perhaps their most influential work, received great attention from a range of publics, including researchers, psychiatrists, anthropologists, students of criminology, and juvenile court judges, among others. Indeed, the Supreme Court of Japan was particularly interested, having ordered its translation right after its publication and distributed it to assorted classes of law operators in the country (e.g. judges, prosecutors, probation officers) (Glueck, 1960), what denotes the popularity of the Gluecks' contribution among practitioners. In that way, despite often ignored or sharply criticized—mainly by sociologists—their work represents a fundamental part of research in criminology, particularly on the causes of crime (Laub & Sampson, 1991). For Sutherland, however, the Gluecks' work was far from convincing, with the author classifying it as "a threat to the intellectual status of sociological criminology" (Laub & Sampson, 1991, p. 1404).

Regardless of these criticisms, it seems that the views proposed by the Gluecks favor individual factors as sources of criminal conducts, corroborating some of the elements pointed as possible motives for unethical behavior in Chap. 1, such as greed and emotions. When it comes to the practice of environmental fraud, this implies in the consideration factors at the individual level which may or may not be aligned with the corporate or industry cultures managers are inserted in. For the purposes of the book, Sutherland's and the Gluecks' views must be seen then as complementary. To some extent, these contrast perspectives are inserted in a more profound debate around individual responsibilities on the one side and the relevance of the environment in conditioning one's conduct on the other. Chapter 4 approaches these issues in more details, discussing the work of prominent thinkers in that direction, exemplified by Jean-Jacques Rousseau and Denis Diderot.

As highlighted by Sutherland (1945, p. 132) himself, legal scholars often defend that the definition of crime requires the combination of two abstract ideas, being them a "legal description of an act as socially injurious" and a "legal provision of a penalty for the act". In that way, when crimes are committed within business contexts, injured persons shall be divided into two groups: the first refers to a relatively small number of individuals who engage either in the same or in related activities as the offender. The second, in turn, concerns the general public, who may happen to be affected as consumers or simply as members of the social institutions damaged by the violations of the laws. As discussed by the author, while antitrust laws, for instance, would be designed to protect competitors, they would be also intended to protect the institution of free competition, which regulates the economic system. Not only consumers would be protected against the practice of arbitrary prices, but, in a larger sense, the institution of democracy would be shielded against the concentration of wealth around monopolies. Likewise, the protection offered by laws against false advertising is twofold, with competitors being preserved from unfair competition, and consumers from fraud. Other examples offered by the author relate to the National Labour Relation Law, which protect employees against coercion by employers, but also the general public from turbulence due to strikes and lockouts, and the laws against infringements, conceived to defend the owners of patents, copyrights, and trademarks from deprivation of their property and from unfair competition, as well as to preserve institution of patents and copyrights, established to "promote the progress of science and the useful arts" (Sutherland, 1945, p. 133). As violations to each of these laws are legally defined as injuries and provide a penal sanction, both the first and the second criteria to define a crime are met. This views dialogs with the fraud severity and range matrix proposed earlier, with both the severity and the range of effects being considered.

If, on the one hand, a more general discussion around the different theoretical currents of criminology is of great relevance for the delimitation of environmental fraud, then the fact that companies are, in general, on the other hand the stage where these deviations occur demands a more objective discussion about corporate crimes. In the search to fulfill this gap, a discussion on corporate criminology is proposed, as follows.

2.1.2 Environmental Fraud and Corporate Criminology

In comparing individuals and organizations, Gross (1978) stresses that, while psychiatrists tend to consider wide personality splits as symptoms of some disorder, division of labor and departmental specialization are not indicative of any sort of schizophrenia, but the basis of organizational structure. Organizations would have what the scholar calls a "criminogenic nature". Indeed, companies have been the scenario to basically all sorts of crimes, illegalities, and misbehaviors. On this view, Clinard and Yeager (2011) argue that serious unethical conducts and law violations have characterized large corporations since their chartering, with deviations being the object of analysis of journalists, writers, and sociologists. Accordingly, attention to unscrupulous business operators was already a reality in the beginning of the twentieth century, with authors such as Ross (1907) generically calling these groups "criminaloids". In fact, the most compelling offenses against the environment—whether intentional or not—originate in companies. This includes oil spills (e.g. 2010 BP Oil Spill in the Gulf of Mexico; EPA, 2010), tailings dam failure (e.g. as happened in the Brazilian cities of Mariana, Philips & Brasileiro, 2018, and Brumadinho, Philips, 2019, in 2015 and 2019, respectively), waste disposal in drinking water (Tingting, 2017), the use of pesticides (Carrington, 2020), deforestation (Harvey, 2013), and overfishing (Österblom, 2015), among a series of other infractions. In this sense, the understanding of the different levels of responsibility attributed to the diverse hierarchical levels in organizations can also be a determining factor for the nature of crimes that involve damage to natural systems.

For Clinard and Yeager (2011), three main categories of crime would co-exist: conventional, occupational, and organizational. While occupational crimes encompass acts of physical violence (e.g. assault, murder) and against properties (e.g. theft, burglary, robbery), occupational ones relate to violations of the law within the practice of a legitimate occupation, typically those made by lawyers, doctors, pharmacists, and politicians, among others. Due to the different social status of individuals often linked to such practices, they are commonly known as blue- and white-collar crimes, respectively. Braithwaite (1989) highlights the Bonger and Sutherland traditions as two important attempts to integrate the crimes often linked to the "powerless" (i.e. blue-collars) and to the "powerful" (i.e. white-collars). Accordingly, in the Marxist Prisma of Willem Bonger (1916), capitalism would be to blame by crimes of both natures, as the transformation of work it promotes (i.e. from value for use to value of exchange) would favor the development of egoism at the expense of altruism. The misery afflicted on individuals of the working class would be the trigger of their criminality. For the members of the bourgeoisie, criminal behavior would arise from the avarice fostered by the capitalist mode of production. In line with Bonger's views, Coleman (1987) points out to the "culture of competition" fed by capitalism as the main motivation of white-collar crime. As with Sutherland's views discussed earlier, these perspectives point to a greater influence of the environment in determining criminal behavior, ignoring the role of individual choices.

Organizational crimes, in turn, refer to the use of illegal methods by firms, corporations, industries, labor unions, as well as by other types of organizations in the pursuit of their objectives. On that regard, Gross (1978. p. 55) argue that companies shall be predicted to engage in criminal behavior if (1) their success is measured by performance or the attainment of goals, (2) there is uncertainty around a firm's capacity to attain its goals, and (3) criminal behavior is seen as a necessary condition for goals to be attained. That would represent the commonly accepted generalization that when individuals are placed in a position where performance is emphasized, pressure to violate norms will exist. Usually demanding complex coordination systems that comprehend several hierarchical levels, the author classifies practices of the most diverse nature within the organizational crime category, including accounting malpractices (e.g. false statements of corporate assets and profits), the offering of poor working conditions to employees, unfair labor practices, the production and commercialization of hazardous products, misleading packaging, false advertising, abuses of competition that restrains trade (e.g. antitrust and cartels), environmental violations (e.g. air and water pollution, illegal dumping of hazardous materials), illegal political practices, and bribery.

This view of corporate crime appears to be particularly useful for both understanding and predicting environmental fraud. As discussed in Chap. 6, Volkswagen's success in the American market appeared as a fundamental point of its long-term strategy, as the company sought to become the largest car manufacturer in the world. Due to the great rivalry of that market and the regulatory issues encountered (i.e. the strict American environmental protection laws), the company found itself in difficulties to achieve its objectives. It then opted for the use of illegal mechanisms to achieve its ambitions, as, apparently, that would be the only way to do so. In this sense, it must be argued that the dynamics of the environmental fraud perpetrated by the German company fulfill all the three conditions proposed by Gross (1978).

From a theoretical point of view, Braithwaite (1989) argues that, although relevant, general crime theories (e.g. the "Sutherland project") would be capable to explain only a modest part of the variance of particular sorts of crimes, with tailor-made theories being necessary for these cases. For the study of organizational crimes, more specifically, pertinent approaches are likely to emerge from organization theory, as shown by a number of scholars (e.g. Clinard & Yeager, 2011; Geis, 1984). The author claims, however, that organizational crime should not be assumed to be significantly different from individual crime to the point of requiring a different paradigm to treat it.

2.2 Fraud and Environmental Fraud

Although all types of fraud have some common characteristics, one must highlight their specific features. Understood as any initiative, activity, or measure intended to hide or disguise environmental impacts of any kind, environmental fraud, for example, may be discussed through its similarities and differences in relation to other types of fraud. This includes questions regarding the reasons leading someone to engage on it (i.e. motivations), the ways it may be applied, and its expected consequences. Regarding the former, it seems that the reasons pushing the practice may not be significantly different from those favoring other types of misconducts. In this sense, the possible greed of administrators, coupled with the lack of solid moral values, seems to create a favorable environment for deviations to occur. In addition, pressure for financial results may also appear as an important factor, increasing the likelihood of environmental fraud. As managers are pressured to perform, they may be more prone to consider illegal alternatives to reach their goals. Pressures arising from competition between companies can also represent an important element in that regard.

In relation to the means by which environmental fraud can be applied, it should be noted that, just like any other type of fraud, they can be of the most diverse nature, with human creativity being the determining driving force in this direction. What can differentiate environmental fraud in this sense is precisely its primary objective, which, as discussed above, is to hide or disguise environmental impacts. In this sense, the most diverse practices can be considered, ranging from the most banal to the application of sophisticated schemes. It is possible, for instance, that environmental fraud refers to a simple manipulation of information in a company's sustainability report. In other situations, the search for misleading stakeholders may require the application of complex technologies, such as those used in the Volkswagen Dieselgate.

The main difference between environmental fraud and other types of fraud is, perhaps, the extent and the gravity of the damage they can cause. In this sense, the fraud severity and range matrix previously developed can be useful in positioning this type of crime. In this sense, basically all types of environmental fraud can be understood as a widespread fraud. Given the seriousness of the various negative consequences that can result from these practices (e.g. extinction of animal and plant species, depletion of natural resources, changes in landscape), as well as their irreversibility, the practice of environmental fraud can in some cases be considered not just a serious offense against humanity, but also a crime against all nature. The effects of environmental crimes—including environmental fraud—can span generations, affecting people who, in addition to not being responsible for the damage, will have to live with its effects.

In this context, the work of the Brundtland Commission in 1987 seems to be of great relevance. The idea of sustainability as being associated with the preservation of resources for future generations (Brundtland Commission Report, 1987) translates this understanding. From a philosophical point of view, the preservation of natural resources for human beings who have not yet been born seems to approach the ideas of Edmund Burke (1790), for whom the concept of society is a contract between those who have lived, those who live, and those who will live in the future. As pointed out by the author himself,

> [Society] is a partnership in all science; a partnership in all art; a partnership in every virtue and in all perfection. As the ends of such a partnership cannot be obtained in many generations, it becomes a partnership not only between those who are living, but between those who are living, those who are dead, and those who are to be born. (Burke, 1790, p. 80)

Important impacts of environmental fraud are discussed in greater detail later in the chapter.

2.3 Differences Between Environmental Fraud and Greenwashing

In some respects, environmental fraud resembles so-called greenwashing practices, especially with regard to companies' search to create a "green façade", with both concepts representing forms of corporate hypocrisy. The most significant differences between the two seem to be in (1) the level of sophistication of the techniques applied, (2) in the degree of the infractions committed, and (3) in their scope. While greenwashing can be seen as a set of more gross moral infractions (e.g. packaging products in green packaging), environmental fraud may rely on complex arrangements that aim to circumvent technical and/or bureaucratic inspections. These two dimensions sometimes mix, resulting in situations that include falsification of products and documents, falsehoods about the raw materials used, and the improper alteration of the functioning of equipment so that they are approved in environmental tests, among others.

With regard to the degree of the infractions committed, the very nature of the techniques used suggests the potential of each type of transgression to cause damage. While greenwashing techniques often exploit loopholes in legislation, environmental fraud is more related to disregard for laws, so that in addition to the ethical component, they also have a legal one. It is not uncommon, for example, for cases of environmental fraud to be treated as a criminal case, usually being resolved in courts. Not rarely this leads to lengthy legal disputes that may take years to be settled, sometimes decades. In terms of scope, on the one hand, environmental fraud seems to have a greater potential to affect a larger number of people. Within a stakeholder view, greenwashing appears to have its immediate effects more restricted to consumers who end up being deceived. As discussed, environmental fraud, on the other hand, seems to have a greater potential for damage.

2.4 Impacts of Environmental Fraud

In the same way that environmental fraud may have the most different motivations and shall be applied in diverse ways, its results can also widely vary. Complementing the previous discussions in this regard, some of the possible results of environmental fraud are discussed in more detail. Building once more on the Volkswagen Dieselgate, the impacts of the fraud perpetrated by the German company on the environment and on public health are addressed. As discussed in Chap. 6, among the main negative outcomes of the scandal is the excessive emission of NO_x (i.e. Nitrogen oxides). Therefore, our analysis remains centered on the harmful effects that this pollutant can cause. In addition, a brief discussion on the impacts to the company itself is proposed.

2.4.1 Consequences to the Environment

As pointed out by the United States Environmental Protection Agency (EPA, 1999), NO_x represents a family of seven compounds: N_2O—nitrous oxide, NO—nitric oxide, N_2O_2—dinitrogen dioxide, N_2O_3—dinitrogen trioxide, NO_2—nitrogen dioxide, N_2O_4—dinitrogen tetroxide, and N_2O_5—dinitrogen pentoxide. Accordingly, among these seven possibilities, nitrogen dioxide (NO_2) would be the most prevalent anthropogenically generated form of NO_x (i.e. resulting from human activities), being not only an important air pollutant all alone, but also reacting in the atmosphere to form tropospheric ozone (O_3) (i.e. ozone in the ambient air that one can breathe) and acid rain. While stratospheric ozone (i.e. ozone present in the upper atmosphere that one cannot breathe) prevents excessive solar radiation, tropospheric ozone is a primary constituent of smog, being a significant vector of air pollution. Still after the EPA (1999), about half of the anthropogenic NO_x that is emitted comes from automobiles and other mobile sources. Electric power plants would account for 20% of emissions and other sources such as "industrial boilers, incinerators, gas turbines, reciprocating spark ignition and Diesel engines in stationary sources, iron and steel mills, cement manufacture, glass manufacture, petroleum refineries, and nitric acid manufacture" (EPA, 1999, p. 4) represent 30% of NO_x emissions, and other problems related to damages in marine habitats would also be related to them.

In collaboration with a range of stakeholders including auto and oil companies, states, and organizations related to public health and environmental protection, the EPA launched the "Tier 2 Vehicle & Gasoline Sulfur Program", defined as a landmark scheme "that affects every new passenger vehicle and every gallon of gasoline sold in the U.S." (EPA, 2019). Basically, it stood that large passenger vehicles of all natures (e.g. SUVs, pickups, vans) would be subject to the same national emission standards applied to cars. Also, the new emission standards would apply to passenger vehicles independently of the fuel they are run on (i.e. gasoline, diesel, or alternative fuels). The EPA has progressively introduced more rigorous emission standards for light-duty vehicles since the 1970s, when the Clean Air Act (CAA) established its authority to regulate pollution from motor vehicles (EPA, 2016). EPA's Tier 2 standards, which began phasing in with the 2004 model year, replaced EPA's Tier 1, which was in force since mid-1990s. The most recent emission standards are set by EPA's Tier 3 regulations, valid since model year 2017.

By choosing to defraud the emission tests, Volkswagen ignored the harmful effects of NO_x. Given the large volume of irregular vehicles that have been marketed, and the relatively long time required to detect the irregularities, it is possible to assume that the environmental damage caused by these excess emissions is considerable. However, since NO_x can come from several sources, determining the real effect of the fraud is controversial. Adds to that the matter that the impacts are neither immediate nor concentrated in a particular region. What stands out the most is the fact that the company apparently had no plans to interrupt the scheme, having only adjusted its conduct when its practices were discovered. The case evidences the value of the work performed by the control agencies, which, in this specific case, prevented an even greater damage.

2.4.2 Impacts on Public Health

In addressing the issue of air pollution, some sectors of the mainstream media outlets are often quite blunt about the harm it causes to people's health. The opinion session of the British newspaper *The Guardian*, for instance, points out to a series of studies linking the poor conditions of the air to health issues such as loss of intelligence (Zhang et al., 2018) and dementia (Chen et al., 2017), as well as to more traditional conditions affecting the heart and lungs of people exposed to contaminated air. Likewise, French newspaper *Le Monde* also discusses scientific studies in that direction, such as the one that estimates that air pollution is the cause of around 800,000 premature deaths (i.e. before the age of life expectancy) a year in Europe (Lelieveld et al., 2019).

The position of some international bodies seems to be aligned with these pessimistic views. The World Health Organization, for example, estimates that between one-quarter to one-third of deaths from a series of disorders (e.g. heart attack, stroke, lung cancer, and chronic respiratory disease) shall be attributed to air pollution (Ghebreyesus, 2018). Among the threats pointed out by the organization is the potential damage that contaminated air may cause in the development of babies when the mother is exposed to pollution during pregnancy. That includes disturbances in vital organs (e.g. the brain, heart, and lungs), as well as a series of conditions such as asthma, heart disease, and different types of cancer. The risks would not be limited to unborn babies, with brain development issues being also observable during childhood. Accordingly, that would lower the chances of affected children to succeed in school, as well as their employment possibilities as they grow old. In view of all these matters, it may be argued that the damage caused by Volkswagen to public health is invaluable. Once again, however, the exact determination of the extent of these harmful effects is practically impossible. In any case, by choosing to defraud the emission tests, Volkswagen demonstrated that it did not care about the health of its stakeholders, in a clear demonstration of contempt for the most basic pillars of corporate social responsibility.

2.4.3 Consequences to the Company

From the perspective of its consequences for the company, environmental fraud can result in the compromise of its intangible resources, especially those related to the trust of stakeholders. In this sense, the concept of corporate credibility takes on special importance, with its two dimensions (trustworthiness and expertise, Newell & Goldsmith, 2001) being potentially impacted. With regard to the first, the perception that the company has adopted dishonest behavior may result in consumers' disbelief in the messages that are sent to the environment. This includes advertisements, advertisements, and all the effort directed toward building the brand. Likewise, investors may be suspicious of both accounting figures and projections of future results, which, in any case, should result in a disinterest in the company's stocks, and a consequent drop in their market value. Concerning employees, they may stop believing in agreements that regulate important aspects of their relationship with the company, such as salary level, working hours, and security, among others. This could lead to a deterioration in the quality of these relationships, which, depending on the severity of the issue, could even result in strikes, and, in the medium term, in the company's operational unfeasibility.

Likewise, the impacts of environmental fraud on the aspect of expertise can be even more critical, especially for companies linked to innovation and technology. Simplistically understood as the perception of the company's technical capacity to perform a certain task, project, or activity (Newell & Goldsmith, 2001), corporate credibility—expertise can indeed prove to be a determining factor between the success and failure of companies in industries such as pharmaceuticals, healthcare, food, air, and automobile. The particular relevance of expertise in these activities is due to the fact that potential operational failures could have catastrophic results for the health of users, or even for their lives. The issues related to the possible impacts of environmental fraud on corporate credibility will be discussed in more detail in Chap. 8, as well as the effects of this practice on other intangible assets (brand, corporate image, corporate identity, and corporate reputation). Likewise, Chap. 10 discusses in more detail the effects of fraud in terms of market value destruction.

References

Albrecht, W. S. (2014, July/August). Iconic Fraud Triangle Endures. *Fraud Magazine*. https://www.fraud-magazine.com/article.aspx?id=4294983342

Baumeister, R. F., Boden, J. M., & Smart, L. (1996). Relation of Threatened Egotism to Violence and Aggression: The Dark Side of High Self-Esteem. *Psychological Review, 103*(1), 5–33.

Bonger, W. A. (1916). *Criminality and Economic Conditions*. Little Brown.

Braithwaite, J. (1989). Criminological Theory and Organizational Crime. *Justice Quarterly, 6*(3), 333–358.

Brundtland Commission Report. (1987). Report of the World Commission on Environment and Development: Our Common Future. *United Nations*. https://sustainabledevelopment.un.org/content/documents/5987our-common-future.pdf

Burke, E. (1790). Reflection on the Revolution in France and on the Proceedings in Certain Societies in London Relative to That Event. https://socialsciences.mcmaster.ca/econ/ugcm/3ll3/burke/revfrance.pdf

Carrington, D. (2020, February 20). Firms Making Billions from 'Highly Hazardous' Pesticides, Analysis Finds. *The Guardian*. https://www.theguardian.com/environment/2020/feb/20/firms-making-billions-from-highly-hazardous-pesticides-analysis-finds

Chen, H., Kwong, J. C., Copes, R., Tu, K., Villeneuve, P. J., van Donkelaar, A., Hystad, P., Martin, R. V., Murray, B., Jessiman, B., Wilton, A. S., Kopp, A., & Burnett, R. T. (2017). Living Near Major Roads and the Incidence of Dementia, Parkinson's Disease, and Multiple Sclerosis: A Population-Based Cohort Study. *The Lancet, 389*(10070), 718–726.

Clinard, M. B., & Yeager, P. C. (2011). *Corporate Crime*. New Jersey: Transaction Publishers New Brunswick. Originally published in 1980 by Free Press, New York.

Coleman, J. W. (1987). Toward an Integrated Theory of White-Collar Crime. *American Journal of Sociology, 93*(2), 406–439.

EPA. (1999). *Nitrogen Oxides (NO_x), Why and How They Are Controlled*. https://www3.epa.gov/ttncatc1/dir1/fnoxdoc.pdf

EPA. (2010). *Deepwater Horizon—BP Gulf of Mexico Oil Spill*. https://www.epa.gov/enforcement/deepwater-horizon-bp-gulf-mexico-oil-spill

EPA. (2016). *Laws and Regulations Related to Volkswagen Violations*. https://www.epa.gov/vw/laws-and-regulations-related-volkswagen-violations

EPA. (2019). *What Is the Tier 2 Vehicle & Gasoline Sulfur Program?* https://www.epa.gov/fuels-registration-reporting-and-compliance-help/what-tier-2-vehicle-gasoline-sulfur-program

Gaylord, M. S., & Galliher, J. F. (1988). *The Criminology of Edwin Sutherland*. Transaction Publishers.

Geis, G. (1984). White-Collar and Corporate Crime. In R. F. Meir (Ed.), *Major Forms of Crime* (pp. 137–166). Sage.

Ghebreyesus, T. A. (2018, October 27). Air Pollution Is the New Tobacco. Time to Tackle This Epidemic. *The Guardian*. https://www.theguardian.com/commentisfree/2018/oct/27/air-pollution-is-the-new-tobacco-time-to-tackle-this-epidemic

Glueck, S. (1960). Ten Years of Unraveling Juvenile Delinquency. *The Journal of Criminal Law, Criminology and Police Science, 51*(3), 283–308.

Glueck, S., & Glueck, E. T. (1950). *Unraveling Juvenile Delinquency*. Harvard University Press.

Gross, E. (1978). Organizational Crime: A Theoretical Perspective. In N. K. Denzin (Ed.), *Studies in Symbolic Interaction* (Vol. 1, pp. 55–85). JAI Press.

Harvey, F. (2013, February 5). Leading Paper Firm Pledges to Halt Indonesian Deforestation. *The Guardian*. https://www.theguardian.com/environment/2013/feb/05/paper-firm-indonesian-deforestation

Laub, J. H., & Sampson, R. J. (1991). The Sutherland-Glueck Debate: On the Sociology of Criminological Knowledge. *The American Journal of Sociology, 96*(6), 1402–1440.

Lelieveld, J., Klingmüller, K., Pozzer, A., Pöschl, U., Fnais, M., Daiber, A., & Münzel, T. (2019). Cardiovascular Disease Burden from Ambient Air Pollution in Europe Reassessed Using Novel Hazard Ratio Functions. *European Heart Journal, 40*(20), 1590–1596.

Newell, S. J., & Goldsmith, R. E. (2001). The Development of a Scale to Measure Perceived Corporate Credibility. *Journal of Business Research, 52*, 235–247.

Österblom, H. (2015, May 28). A Handful of Corporations Could Hold the Answer to Crisis in the Seafood Industry. *The Guardian*. https://www.theguardian.com/sustainable-business/2015/may/28/seafood-industry-overfishing-corporations-control-potential-solution

Philips, D. (2019, January 28). Brazil Dam Collapse: Bodies Pulled from Toxic Mud as Hope Fades for Survivors. *The Guardian*. https://www.theguardian.com/world/2019/jan/28/brazil-dam-collapse-mining-disaster-victim-search-latest-news

Philips, D., & Brasileiro, D. (2018, March 1). Brazil Dam Disaster: Firm Knew of Potential Impact Months in Advance. *The Guardian*. https://www.theguardian.com/world/2018/feb/28/brazil-dam-collapse-samarco-fundao-mining

Ross, E. A. (1907). *Sin and Society: An Analysis of Latter-Day Iniquity*. Houghton Mifflin.

Sutherland, E. H. (1939). *Principles of Criminology* (3rd ed.). Lippincott.

Sutherland, E. H. (1942). Development of the Theory. In A. K. Cohen, A. Lindesmith, & K. F. Schuessler (Eds.), *The Sutherland Papers*. Indiana University Press.

Sutherland, E. H. (1945). Is "White-Collar Crime" Crime? *American Sociological Review, 10*(2), 132–139.

Sutherland, E. H., & Cressey, D. R. (1978). *Criminology* (10th ed.). Lippincott.

Tingting, D. (2017, June 2). In China, the Water You Drink Is as Dangerous as the Air You Breathe. *The Guardian*. https://www.theguardian.com/global-development-professionals-network/2017/jun/02/china-water-dangerous-pollution-greenpeace

Tittle, C. R., Burke, M. J., & Jackson, E. F. (1986). Modeling Sutherland's Theory of Differentiation Association: Toward an Empirical Clarification. *Social Forces, 65*(2), 405–432.

Zhang, X., Chen, X., & Zhang, X. (2018). The Impact of Exposure to Air Pollution on Cognitive Performance. *Proceedings of the National Academy of Sciences of the United States of America, 115*(37), 9193–9197.

3

Improper Competitive Advantage

3.1 Competition and Environmental Fraud

Among the many factors concurring with the practice of environmental fraud, competition is probably one of the most critical. In this sense, both the characteristics of firms and those of the industries they are inserted in seem to directly influence the adoption of dishonest conducts. Apparently, the fiercer the competition, the greater the chances that unethical managers will pursue shortcuts to either match or overcome competitors. There is, however, no well-defined rule that allows us to predict or explain cases of environmental fraud solely on the basis of corporate rivalry. As discussed in Chap. 1, a range of other factors must be taken into account on that regard. That includes executives' emotional and psychological conditions, the robustness of institutional environments, the mechanisms of control and punishment, and, to a certain degree, corporate and national cultures, among others. Although logical, the combination of these factors is not trivial. When brought together, they create a complex dynamic that can make it difficult to identify the contribution of each to the final result. Yet, competition appears to be the stage where all other variables

M. Fracarolli Nunes, C. Lee Park, *Business Ethics and Environmental Fraud*,
https://doi.org/10.1007/978-3-030-73800-6_3

interact. Unlike an arena, however, it is in constant metamorphosis, usually getting tougher.

The allegedly unethical conducts of companies facing harsh competition illustrate the issue. As further discussed in Chap. 7, firms such as Apple and Samsung have been accused of pushing the obsolescence of smartphones even further by installing programs that artificially slowed the functions of their devices when they went through software updates (Gibbs, 2018). Not by chance, competition in the smartphone industry is among the most ferocious. Likewise, the production of agricultural commodities (e.g. cotton, soybeans) also suffers from similar problems, with the premium prices paid for organic products serving as an important incentive in that direction. In search to capture some of the value of these goods, farmers have been falsely labeling their crops as organic, even if pesticides, fertilizers, and other polluting chemicals were used in their cultivation. Once more, the high competition of these industries—which is among the causes for the low price of conventional products—appears as a factor possibly pushing fraudulent practices. The automotive industry is no exception to that, having been a particularly favorable atmosphere for cases of environmental fraud. As discussed in Chap. 5, it evolved to become particularly competitive, gathering a considerable number of players and offering limited sources of differentiation. Still, from a social point of view, companies' search to produce faster and cheaper often translates into degrading working conditions, both in terms of security and respect for fundamental human rights. Once more, problems of this nature have been common in firms operating in extremely competitive environments. Along with companies of the electronics industry, that has also been the case with fast fashion, and food and beverage enterprises. These questions are also further developed in Chap. 7.

Several factors contributed to the intensification of competition in the most diverse sectors, with the consolidation of mass consumption societies being particularly important. As pointed out by Matsuyama (2000, p. 3), a mass consumption society stands as one "where not a few individuals, nor a thin upper class, but the majority of families enjoys the benefits of increased productivity and constantly expands their range of consumer goods". As pointed out by the author, the phenomenon would be relatively recent in human history, with virtually all industrialized countries reaching the status of mass consumption societies only after WWII. On that regard, Katona (1964) stresses that poverty has been the rule throughout times, with people—even in the rich countries of the past—struggling for mere subsistence. By contrast, minimum standards of nutrition, housing, and clothing were assured to the majority in the United States of that time. Still after the author, the triumph of mass consumption markets would be responsible to turn former luxuries such as homeownership, durable goods, travel, recreation, and entertainment accessible to the average citizen.

In that way, it may be argued that despite favoring the accumulation of wealth (Bonefeld, 2011) and deepening economic inequality (Muller, 2013), the capitalist mode of production—in which competition is embedded—was responsible for a marked improvement in the living condition of the poorest. From a material point of view, people considered underprivileged today have a better standard of living than those upper classes from a not-so-remote past used to have, even if the inequality between them has, in some cases, worsened. Yet, while the development of mass consumption societies democratizes access to material goods, it intensifies the use of natural resources, as well as problems related to waste management and pollution. These contradictions between the economic aspects on the one hand and the environmental/social ones on the other are at the heart of the debate on the viability of sustainable development. Among the main characteristics of these arrangements is the constant shortening of products' life cycle (Mason et al., 2002), with many consumption goods being designed to last for relatively brief periods (e.g. electronics, clothes).

From a strategic point of view, the emergence of mass consumption societies had a major impact in competition, as well as in the way companies organized to answer to these new challenges. Due to the increase in the consumption base (i.e. more people having access to companies' offers), criteria that used to be commonly associated with the success of products and services (e.g. quality) progressively gave way to other operational priorities. In this set, cost and time-based competition became the dominant business paradigm in the last decades (Christopher, 2016). In this sense, the race to serve customers faster and cheaper seems to have boosted corporate rivalry, particularly for offers counting on little or no differentiation. In this progressively customer-centered business environment (Gill et al., 2019), companies' survival and success depend then on their ability to adapt to constant social and economic transformations (Zhao et al., 2014), as well as on their capacity to anticipate (Finger et al., 2014) and respond to competitors' moves (Homburg et al., 2007). As firms seek to fulfill the needs and expectations of increasingly demanding customers, they had to radically reorganize production and distribution processes (Gattorna & Ellis, 2019). Among the main consequences of these dynamics was the unfolding of processes of massive strategic outsourcing (Quinn & Hilmer, 1994), as companies partially or totally transferred their production to low labor-cost zones (e.g. Asia, Eastern Europe, Latin America). These changes are anchored in new consumption habits, which not only filled the development of market economies, but are also at the origin of many of the sustainability issues we face today.

In his seminal article "What is Strategy?", Porter (1996) discusses how cost-based competition can negatively affect companies in the long-term. With the price of offers being the main benchmark for customers' decisions, margins tend to be compressed, pushing firms to constantly look for ways to increase their operational effectiveness. In this way, cost-based competition would put firms in self-destructive dynamics. Cost reductions in exchange of quality, for example, would be common on that regard. Likewise, the search for gains of scale would be a main reason supporting mergers and acquisitions among competitors. As pointed out by the author, these would be frequent movements in industries such as the automotive. At this point, a distinction between operational effectiveness and strategy is proposed. While the former relates to the efficient management of operations, the latter would be the essence of strategy, with the construction of unique positions (i.e. different from those of competitors) standing as the basis of competitive advantage.

The discussion is relevant as it supports our propositions about the likelihood of environmental fraud due to the level of differentiation of companies. In this sense, we hypothesize that, because of the limited opportunities for differentiation, companies engaged in cost-based competition may be more tempted to incur in environmental fraud as they seek to escape the self-destructive dynamics approached. By offering an alleged solution for the trade-off between economic and environmental performance—even if through illegal or immoral mechanisms—companies that opt to make use of environmental fraud do so in an attempt to differentiate themselves from their competitors. The search to overperform competition through the use of such subterfuge paves the way to what is here called *improper competitive advantage*. Defined as the reach and maintenance of superior performance through the use of illegal or immoral mechanisms, *improper competitive advantage* represents a deviation of ethical business conducts, and stands as one of the main challenges faced by companies, legal authorities, consumers, and the society in general. In this sense, a discussion about the concept of competitive advantage itself is necessary.

3.2 Competitive Advantage: Wide Usage and Main Theoretical Currents)

Broadly, competitive advantage refers to whatever allows a company to grant an abnormal performance (i.e. above what could be expected initially). As put by Naveh and Marcus (2005, p. 16) "(T)he abnormal performance of a firm in a given year is defined as realized performance less expected performance". A company that has significantly higher profit margins than its competitors, for instance, may be argued to have competitive advantage(s). If, on the one hand, the abstraction of these concepts is relatively simple, then, on the other hand, their application is often complex. The estimation of expected performance, for example, requires a thorough analysis of companies' macro environments, as well as their resources and capabilities. In this set, the study of the reasons why companies that compete in the same industry have different levels of return—in particular, above-normal returns—would be on the basis of disciplines such as strategy.

Despite often misused, competitive advantage is among the most employed terms in business contexts. Along with other popular concepts (e.g. 4Ps—Culliton, 1948; Borden, 1965; McCarthy, 1964; Kotler, 1984, and Maslow's (1954) hierarchy of needs), it composes the basic

Management vocabulary, supporting the arguments of both scholars and practitioners in the field. In fact, it is used in the analysis of the most distinct situations, ranging from day-to-day activities to companies' strategic decisions. The application of the term by some of the largest companies of the world illustrates its versatility. Nike, for example, links its competitive advantage to innovation (Nike, 2019), while Nestlé associates it with research and development (Nestlé, 2010). Bain & Company, in turn, argues that competitive advantage may result from positive organizational cultures (Meehan et al., 2006), and General Electric highlights the role of intellect and technology transfer in that direction (Lurie, 2015). Likewise, Cargill claims that competitive advantage may be sourced in the formulation of low sugar products (Cargill, 2019).

When the nature of modern business is considered, however, the complexity of the debate may significantly increase, particularly in the context of globalization and the consequent boom in strategic outsourcing (Quinn & Hilmer, 1994) in the last decades. Within this view, competitive advantage is also argued to be sourced outside the limits of organizational borders, with the arrangement of companies in the form of supply chains becoming particularly relevant (Liao et al., 2017). On that regard, Boeing points out to its suppliers' capacity to exceed cost performance goals as a critical element of its success (Boeing, 2019), and Inditex (2018)—Zara's parent company—credits part of its competitive advantage to the stability, agility, flexibility, and high level of specialization of suppliers.

Despite often valid, the broad employment of the concept may lead to confusion about its meaning, with the practical difficulties in measuring it (Bromiley & Rau, 2016) possibly adding to the problem. As stated by Stigler (1957, p.1), "No concept in economics—or elsewhere—is ever defined fully, in the sense that its meaning under every conceivable circumstance is clear"—in fact, encompassing the work of classic authors such as Schumpeter (1934), Coase (1937), Mason (1939), Bain (1956, 1968), Simon (1961), Stigler (1961), Williamson (1975), Spence (1979), Rumelt, 1984, and Hoskisson et al., 1999, among others. Since a more grounded discussion on competitive advantage is beyond the scope of the book, we concentrate on the main theoretical developments and currents of thought orbiting the debate, in such a way that the use of the concept throughout the book becomes clearer. Questions such as "what are the antecedents of sustained abnormal performance?" or "what makes a company constantly more profitable than its competitors?" shall be useful starting points.

3.2.1 SWOT Analysis

As discussed by Barney (1995, p. 49), the quest for sustained competitive advantage has traditionally concentrated on the environmental opportunities and threats faced by firms, as well as on their internal strengths and weaknesses. Accordingly, the reasoning would be summarized in the work of Learned et al. (1969), on what came to be known as the SWOT (i.e. Strengths, Weaknesses, Opportunities, and Threats) analysis. Still after the author, its "logic suggests that firms that use their internal strengths in exploiting environmental opportunities and neutralizing environmental threats, while avoiding internal weaknesses, are more likely to gain competitive advantages than other kinds of firms". Within this view, the SWOT analysis would be seen as a powerful analytical tool in the categorization of relevant factors that rest both inside and outside organizations, being praised for its simplicity and practicality (Pickton & Wright, 1998). It would also stand as a building block of the strategic management process, complementing the definition of companies' vision (i.e. the desired future position of the organization), mission (i.e. what an organization aims to be and avoid in the long run), and objectives (i.e. concrete organizational goals) (Gürel & Tat, 2017).

By scrutinizing its environment (i.e. external analysis), a company would not only identify potential threats and opportunities, but also examine the probable evolution of competition. In the internal analysis, firms shall recognize resources and capabilities which may and may not be sources of competitive advantage, in such a way that they can choose appropriate strategies to navigate competitive environments. For Hoskisson et al. (1999), the interchangeable focus of strategic management theory and research would be similar to the swings of a pendulum, with attention moving from the environment to internal resources and vice-versa. The integration of these two focuses would represent then one of the main merits of the SWOT analysis.

The application of the SWOT analysis has been wide, being an important technique in any field that requires strategic planning (Gürel & Tat, 2017). If used simplistically, however, it shall be considered naïve and lead to strategic errors (Pickton & Wright, 1998). The history of strategic management research could be seen as an effort to fill in the blanks of the SWOT analysis, in such a way that models and frameworks may be used in the investigation of competitive advantage (Barney, 1995). Yet, as discussed by Galbreath and Galvin (2008), this expedition has created a bifurcated view: on the one hand, the set of ideas known as industry structure—mainly represented by Michael Porter's (1980) five-forces model—focuses on the structural characteristics of industries as determinants of performance. On the other, proponents of the resource-based view (e.g. Penrose, 1959; Rumelt, 1984; Wernerfelt, 1984; Conner, 1991; Barney, 1991) claim that firms' specific resources are at the origins of competitive advantage. Sometimes isolated, and sometimes combined (Barney, 1991), these perspectives have dominated strategic management debate in the last decades (Galbreath & Galvin, 2008). We briefly discuss each, as follows:

3.2.2 Industry Structure

Theoretically based on the work of Mason (1939) and Bain (1956, 1968), the so-called industry structure privileges strategic analysis that is based on the conditions of competitive environments (i.e. exterior to companies), as well as on the positions firms occupy (Hoskisson et al., 1999). Accordingly, the reasoning implies the gathering of companies in strategic categories in face of their similarities and differences across groups. In this sense, the specific characteristics of an industry would determine both its potential return and the risks associated with it, ultimately establishing its attractiveness. The reasoning would be also greatly supported by literature on industrial organization economics around game theory (see Camerer & Weigelt, 1988 and Grimm & Smith, 1997, for further information) and oligopolistic competition (Edwards, 1955).

Despite the numerous contributions that concurred to the sedimentation of the Industry Structure, the vision proposed by Michael Porter seems to be the most widespread among academics and practitioners. Accordingly, it would be based on the idea that both the nature and the degree of competition in a given industry fundamentally depends on five distinct forces: (1) the industry jockeying for position among current competitors; (2) threat of new entrants; (3) threat of substitute products or services; (4) bargaining power of suppliers; and (5) bargaining power of customers (Porter, 1979, 1980). The stronger the forces collectively, the lower the potential for superior performance. The weaker they jointly are, however, the greater the opportunities for above-normal returns. As highlighted by the author, a company must understand the dynamics of these forces in its industry and how they may affect it, so that it may establish a strategic agenda and grow despite them.

Competition in a given industry would be a function of its underlying economics, in such a way that the intensity of competitive forces shall vary from one context to another. As stated by the author, "intense competition in an industry, is neither coincidence nor bad luck" (Porter, 1979, p. 137). Competition would then range from intense in industries where no company earns particularly high returns on investments (e.g. tires, metal cans, and steel) to mild in industries allowing for higher returns (e.g. oil field services and equipment). Perfectly competitive industries, for instance, would offer the worst prospect of profits, as, in face of low barriers to entry, disputes for positions tend to be intense. Regardless of the market structure a company operates in, its strategy must be driven to find a position where it can either best defend itself from market forces or influence them in its favor (Porter, 1979). Table 3.1 resumes Porter's (1979, 1980) five forces that would shape strategy.

Porter (1980) adds that competitive advantage would be gained in terms of either cost or differentiation. Accordingly, the value created by a company is measured by the amount that buyers are willing to pay for its products or services, meaning that a company will only be profitable if it is able to produce value in excess of the cost of obtaining it. Competitive advantage would be gained thus as a company gets either to produce value at a lower cost than its competitors (i.e. cost advantage) or to perform value activities in such a way that premium prices may be charged

Table 3.1 Porter's (1979, 1980) five forces

Force	Influencing factors	
The industry jockeying for position among current competitors	Summary	Relates to the rivalry among the players already established in a given industry. Typically, disputes comprehend price competition, the introduction of new products, and advertising war.
	Example	Harsh competition in hotels and airline industry.
	Influencing factors	• Number of players • Similarity of players in terms of power and size • Growth level of the industry, with slower growth pushing competition for existing market share • Products or services levels of differentiation or switching costs Low differentiation and pushing price-based competition • High fixed costs or perishable products, offering incentives to constant price cuts • Capacity is typically augmented in large increments, creating periods of excessive offer • High exit barriers, pushing companies to keep competing, even when returns are low or negative • Heterogeneous competitors' profiles, favoring chaotic competition

(*continued*)

Table 3.1 (continued)

Force	Influencing factors	
Threat of new entrants	Summary	Refers to the possibility and likelihood of companies outside the industry to enter it, and thus, become new competitors. In the fight for market share, companies entering new markets tend to leverage their resources, increasing the pressure on the other players. Often, entrance movements take place in the form of acquisitions.
	Example	Tobacco company Philip Morris entering the beer market through the acquisition of Miller back in the 1970s.
	Influencing factors	• Barriers to entry in six major sources: economies of scale, product differentiation, capital requirements, cost disadvantages independent of size, access to distribution channels, government policy • Reaction from existing competitors, conditioned by incumbents' possession or access to resources (e.g. cash, unused borrowing power), likely to cut prices to preserve market share, as well as by the growth rate of the industry
Threat of substitute products or services	Summary	This force focuses on the potential of products or services from other industries to offer equal or similar attributes, in a way that customers may have a realistic alternative. The condition may push prices down and damage industry growth, in case the threatened companies are not capable to upgrade the quality or differentiate its products.
	Example	High-fructose corn syrup substituting sugar.
	Influencing factors	• Products which are subject to trends that improve price-performance trade-offs of an industry. • The profitability level of the company offering substitute products.

(continued)

Table 3.1 (continued)

Force	Influencing factors	
Bargaining power of suppliers	Summary	Indicate the potential of suppliers to raise prices and reduce the quality of their products or services in face of their power. Powerful suppliers may thus significantly pressure the profitability of companies that cannot fully transfer cost increases to their own customers.
	Example	By raising prices, producers of soft drink concentrate may erode the profitability of bottling companies, as, in face of intense competition from other beverages, bottlers have limited freedom to increment their prices.
	Influencing factors	• The concentration level of a supplier group • The uniqueness or differentiation of goods supplied • Switching costs • Alternative products • Possibility of forward integration • Relevance of customer industry to supplier group
Bargaining power of customers	Summary	Accounts for the possibility or likelihood of powerful buyers to pressure the profitability of suppliers, through the demand of price cuts or better quality of products or services.
	Example	Walmart constantly demanding suppliers to reduce their prices. In this case, the dependency of suppliers on Walmart's distribution power and the high volumes bought by the company pressure suppliers to agree on price cuts.

(continued)

Table 3.1 (continued)

Force	Influencing factors	
	Influencing factors	• The concentration level of a buyer group • Purchasing volume • The level of differentiation of purchased products • Representativeness of purchasing value in the cost of products • Profitability of buyers' industry, and importance of supplies to buyers' products or services, both impacting buyers' price sensitivity • Purchased products do not save buyers' funds • Possibility of backward integration

Source: Adapted from Porter (1979, 1980)

(i.e. differentiation). In this sense, "the myriad activities that go into creating, producing, selling, and delivering a product or service are the basic units of competitive advantage" (Porter, 1996, p. 61). By representing the set of interdependent technological and economic activities a company performs to do business, the concept of value chain (Porter, 1985, p. 26) would be particularly relevant for this debate. As pointed out by the author, it would stand as "the basic tool for diagnosing competitive advantage and finding ways to enhance it". Within this perspective, the reaching of competitive advantage would depend on the configuration of a company's value chain, reflecting the contribution of all its individual activities (Porter & Kramer, 2011). In that way, one could not understand competitive advantage by looking at a firm as a whole (Porter, 1985). Instead, attention to each of these elements would be necessary, as potential sources of cost advantage and differentiation may be found in any part of the arrangement (Porter & Millar, 1985).

3.2.3 Resource-Based View

In contrast with the industry structure, the resource-based view (RBV) concentrates on the relationship between firms' internal characteristics and performance (Barney, 1991). The major question posed by the RBV is: "Why do firms in the same industry vary systematically in performance over time?" (Hoopes et al., 2003, p. 889), with scholars focusing on "explaining the differences between the relatively few firms with sustained competitive advantage and all other" (Bromiley & Rau, 2016, p. 95). On that regard, Barney (1991) proposes three concepts as being central to the debate: firm resources, competitive strategy, and sustained competitive advantage. Accordingly, firm resources relate to instruments controlled by the firm and that allow it to conceive and implement strategies, particularly those driven to advance its efficiency and effectiveness (Daft, 1983) (e.g. all assets, capabilities, organizational processes, firm attributes, information, and knowledge). Likewise, competitive strategy refers to the implementation of a value-creating strategy which must not be implemented simultaneously by another company. In turn, sustained competitive advantage requires competitors to be unable to reproduce the benefits of such strategy. As argued by the author, only resources that are valuable, rare, imperfectly imitable, and not substitutable would grant firms with sustained competitive advantage. In that way, while sustained competitive advantage is the dependent variable in the RBV (i.e. what one seeks to explain or predict), these resources would stand as the explanatory ones (Bromiley & Rau, 2016; Barney, 1991).

The ideas seem to have been well absorbed by practitioners, with companies constantly pointing out to such issues when discussing their sources of abnormal performance. In assessing its ability to compete, Fiat Chrysler Automobiles (FCA) states that—

> Much of our value is derived from our confidential business information, including vehicle design, proprietary technology and trade secrets, and to the extent the confidentiality of such information is compromised, we may lose our competitive advantage and our vehicle shipments may suffer. (FCA, 2018, p. 88)

Likewise, Apple (2019, p. 5) claims that "if the Company is unable to continue to develop and sell innovative new products with attractive margins or if competitors infringe on the Company's intellectual property, the Company's ability to maintain a competitive advantage could be adversely affected".

Despite its success, RBV is not free from critics. Bromiley and Rau (2016), for example, argue that the reasoning would not be useful to treat Operations Management issues, as the focus on sustained competitive advantage and the comparison between firms that follow (i.e. contrast between firms that have it and those that do not) would lead researchers to ignore performance variations within most companies. Also, the fact that RBV considers competitive advantage to rest either at the business or at firm levels would extrapolate the typical scope of Operations Management research. Still after the authors, under the premises of RBV, prescription would be troublesome, as one may not specify what firms could readily implement. If that is the case, they would probably be easily imitable. Another common critic to RBV relates its argued tautology. Building on Popper's (1959) view that a tautology cannot be falsified, Priem and Butler (2001, p. 58) argue that "the RBV statement 'if a resource is valuable and rare, then it can be a source of competitive advantage' is necessarily true by logic (i.e. a tautology) if 'valuable' and 'competitive advantage' are defined in the same terms". Bromiley and Rau (2016, p. 100), in turn, argue that "(i)f we define resources as having a positive impact on performance, then we have ruled by definition that resources cannot negatively influence performance, creating the tautology".

As discussed throughout the chapter, the search for competitive advantages is among managers' greatest concerns, with differentiation being seen as a path to prosperity. In this sense, the offer of value propositions that come to be superior to those of competitors appears as a powerful instrument that allows companies to escape the dynamics of cost-based competition. In addition to favoring higher returns, the search for differentiation would increase the chances of survival in increasingly harsh competitive environments. If, on the one hand, this logic seems to have accompanied the evolution of market economics throughout history, the structural changes in industrial organization in recent decades have highlighted the importance of competitive advantages. The introduction of new production technologies and the consolidation of business models based on strategic outsourcing, for example, have significantly increased the levels of operational efficiency, making the sources of superior performance even more valuable. In this context, the combination of increasing pressures for financial returns and the scarcity of sources of value creation in an environment hostile to profits result, in many cases, in an incentive to the practice of unethical activities. In general, this translates into companies engaging in several illegal activities that can include counterfeiting, breach of contract, abuse of economic power, and corruption, among many others.

Thus, the search for *improper competitive advantages* must be understood as a strategic choice that can have a negative impact that goes far beyond those that are more easily identifiable. In addition to harming consumers, illegal activities corrupt the logic of the market, and can decisively affect the incentive mechanism that leads entrepreneurs and investors to move forward with their projects. If the competition is perceived as dishonest, or, in some way, biased, it is possible that players who have some value to offer prefer not to do so for fear of not having their efforts justly rewarded. By unbalancing the relationship between risk and return on economic activities, *improper competitive advantages* can hinder the development of a series of economic initiatives, especially regarding investments in research and development of companies and their innovation policies. The use of subterfuges in the search for abnormal returns may have effects that go far beyond the organizational boundaries of the source company (i.e. the one directly engaged in such attitudes). It is possible, for example, that illicit activities end up tarnishing the reputation of entire industries, even when irregularities are committed by a single firm. In these cases, illegal activities would contribute to the stigmatization of certain activities, which represents an additional burden for competitors who compete honestly. This spillover can also be extended to other players in the supply chain, illustrating the large scope of the harmful effects of illicit practices.

References

Apple. (2019). Annual Report Pursuant to Section 13 or 15(d) of the Securities Exchange Act of 1934 for the Fiscal Year Ended September 28, 2019. https://s2.q4cdn.com/470004039/files/doc_financials/2019/ar/_10-K-2019-(As-Filed).pdf

Bain, J. S. (1956). *Barriers to New Competition*. Harvard University Press.

Bain, J. S. (1968). *Industrial Organization* (2nd ed.). Wiley.
Barney, J. (1991). Firm Resources and Sustained Competitive Advantage. *Journal of Management, 17*(1), 99–120.
Barney, J. B. (1995). Looking Inside for Competitive Advantage. *Academy of Management Perspectives, 9*(4), 49–61.
Boeing. (2019). Supplier Recognition. http://www.boeingsuppliers.com/awards.html
Bonefeld, W. (2011). Primitive Accumulation and Capitalist Accumulation: Notes on Social Constitution and Expropriation. *Science & Society, 75*(3), 379–399.
Borden, N. H. (1965). The Concept of the Marketing Mix. In G. Schwartz (Ed.), *Science in Marketing* (pp. 386–397). John Wiley & Sons.
Bromiley, P., & Rau, D. (2016). Operations Management and the Resource Based View: Another View. *Journal of Operations Management, 41*, 95–106.
Camerer, C. F., & Weigelt, K. (1988). Experimental Tests of a Sequential Equilibrium Reputation Model. *Econometrica, 56*, 1–36.
Cargill. (2019). Sweet Solutions: Formulating Low Sugar Products for Competitive Advantage. https://www.cargill.com/doc/1432136521904/formulating-low-sugar-products.pdf
Christopher, M. (2016). *Logistics & Supply Chain Management*. Pearson UK.
Coase, R. H. (1937). The Nature of the Firm. *Economica, 4*(16), 386–405.
Conner, K. (1991). An Historical Comparison of Resource-based Logic and Five Schools of Thought Within Industrial Organization Economics: Do We Have a New Theory of the Firm Here? *Journal of Management, 17*, 121–154.
Culliton, J. W. (1948). *The Management of Marketing Costs*. Division of Research, Graduate School of Business Administration, Harvard University.
Daft, R. (1983). *Organization Theory and Design*. West.
Edwards, C. D. (1955). Conglomerate Bigness as a Source of Power. In University-National Bureau (Ed.), *Business Concentration and Price Policy* (pp. 331–352). Princeton University Press.
FCA. (2018). Annual Report. https://www.fcagroup.com/en-US/investors/financial_regulatory/financial_reports/files/FCA_NV_2018_Annual_Report.pdf
Finger, A. B., Flynn, B. B., & Paiva, E. L. (2014). Anticipation of New Technologies: Supply Chain Antecedents and Competitive Performance. *International Journal of Operations & Production Management, 34*(6), 807–828.
Galbreath, J., & Galvin, P. (2008). Firm Factors, Industry Structure and Performance Variation: New Empirical Evidence to a Classic Debate. *Journal of Business Research, 61*(2), 109–117.

Gattorna, J., & Ellis, D. (2019). *Transforming Supply Chains: Realign Your Business to Better Serve Customers in a Disruptive World*. Pearson UK.

Gibbs, S. (2018). Apple and Samsung Fined for Deliberately Slowing Down Phones. *The Guardian*, October 24. https://www.theguardian.com/technology/2018/oct/24/apple-samsung-fined-for-slowing-down-phones

Gill, L., McCarthy, V., & Grimmett, D. (2019). Voice of the Customer: Creating Client Centered Cultures in Accounting Firms For Retaining Clients and Increasing Profitability. *Journal of Accounting, Business and Management, 26*(2), 46–58.

Grimm, C. M., & Smith, K. G. (1997). *Strategy as Action: Industry Rivalry and Coordination*. South-Western College Publishing.

Gürel, E., & Tat, M. (2017). SWOT Analysis: A Theoretical Review. *Journal of International Social Research, 10*(51), 994–1006.

Homburg, C., Grozdanovic, M., & Klarmann, M. (2007). Responsiveness to Customers and Competitors: The Role of Affective and Cognitive Organizational Systems. *Journal of Marketing, 71*(3), 18–38.

Hoopes, D. G., Madsen, T. L., & Walker, G. (2003). Guest Editors' Introduction to the Special Issue: Why is there a Resource-based View? Toward a Theory of Competitive Heterogeneity. *Strategic Management Journal, 24*(10), 889–902.

Hoskisson, R. E., Wan, W. P., Yiu, D., & Hitt, M. A. (1999). Theory and Research in Strategic Management: Swings of a Pendulum. *Journal of Management, 25*(3), 417–456.

Inditex. (2018). Annual Report. https://www.inditex.com/documents/10279/619384/Inditex+Annual+Report+2018.pdf/25145dd4-74db-2355-03f3-a3b86bc980a7

Katona, G. (1964). *The Mass Consumption Society*. McGraw-Hill.

Kotler, P. (1984). *Marketing Management: Analysis, Planning and Control* (5th ed.). Prentice-Hall.

Learned, E. P., Christensen, C. P., Andrews, K. P., & Guth, W. (1969). *Business Policy*. Homewood.

Liao, S. H., Hu, D. C., & Ding, L. W. (2017). Assessing the Influence of Supply Chain Collaboration Value Innovation, Supply Chain Capability and Competitive Advantage in Taiwan's Networking Communication Industry. *International Journal of Production Economics, 191*, 143–153.

Lurie, D. (2015). GE: A Simpler, More Valuable Digital Industrial Company. https://www.ge.com/reports/ge-simpler-valuable-digital-industrial-company/

Maslow, A. H. (1954). *Motivation and Personality*. Harpers.

Mason, E. S. (1939). Price and Production Policies of Large Scale Enterprises. *American Economic Review, 29*, 61–74.
Mason, S. J., Cole, M. H., Ulrey, B. T., & Yan, L. (2002). Improving Electronics Manufacturing Supply Chain Agility through Outsourcing. *International Journal of Physical Distribution and Logistics Management*.
Matsuyama, K. (2000). The Rise of Mass Consumption Societies. In *London School of Economics and Political Sciences*. http://eprints.lse.ac.uk/6656/1/The_Rise_of_Mass_Consumption_Societies.pdf
McCarthy, E. J. (1964). *Basic Marketing*. Richard D. Irwin.
Meehan, P., Gadiesh, O., & Hori, S. (2006). Culture as a Competitive Advantage. *Bain & Company*, January 1. https://www.bain.com/insights/culture-as-competitive-advantage/
Muller, J. Z. (2013). Capitalism and Inequality: What the Right and the Left Get Wrong. *Foreign Affairs, 92*, 30–51.
Naveh, E., & Marcus, A. (2005). Achieving Competitive Advantage Through Implementing a Replicable Management Standard: Installing and Using ISO 9000. *Journal of Operations Management, 24*(1), 1–26.
Nestlé. (2010). Nestlé to Invest in R&D Centre in India. https://www.nestle.com/media/pressreleases/allpressreleases/nestle-to-invest-in-rd-centre-in-india
Nike. (2019). Shareholders' Letter. July 23. https://s1.q4cdn.com/806093406/files/doc_financials/2019/annual/nike-shareholders-letter-2019.pdf
Penrose, E. T. (1959). *The Theory of the Growth of the Firm*. John Wiley.
Pickton, D. W., & Wright, S. (1998). What's SWOT in Strategic Analysis? *Strategic Change, 7*(2), 101–109.
Popper, K. R. (1959). *The Logic of Scientific Discovery*. Hutchinson.
Porter, M. E. (1979). How Competitive Forces Shape Strategy. *Harvard Business Review, 57*, 137–145.
Porter, M. E. (1980). *Competitive Strategy: Techniques for Analyzing Industries and Competitors*. Free Press.
Porter, M. E. (1985). *Competitive Advantage*. Free Press.
Porter, M. E. (1996). What is Strategy? *Harvard Business Review, 74*(6), 61–78.
Porter, M. E., & Kramer, M. R. (2011). Creating Shared Value. *Harvard Business Review, 89*, 62–77.
Porter, M. E., & Millar, V. E. (1985). How Information Gives You Competitive Advantage. *Harvard Business Review, 63*(4), 149–160.
Priem, R. L., & Butler, J. E. (2001). Tautology in the Resource-based View and the Implications of Externally Determined Resource Value: Further Comments. *The Academy of Management Review, 26*(1), 57–66.

Quinn, J. B., & Hilmer, F. G. (1994). Strategic Outsourcing. *MIT Sloan Management Review, 35*(4), 43–55.
Rumelt, R. P. (1984). Towards a Strategic Theory of the Firm. In R. Lamb (Ed.), *Competitive Strategic Management* (pp. 556–570). Prentice-Hall.
Schumpeter, J. A. (1934). *The Theory of Economic Development*. Harvard University Press (Original Publication 1911).
Simon, H. A. (1961). *Administrative Behavior* (2nd ed.). Macmillan.
Spence, A. M. (1979). Investment, Strategy and Growth in a New Market. *Bell Journal of Economics, 10*, 1–19.
Stigler, G. J. (1957). Perfect Competition, Historically Contemplated. *Journal of Political Economy, 65*(1), 1–17.
Stigler, G. J. (1961). The Economics of Information. *Journal of Political Economy, 69*(3), 213–225.
Wernerfelt, B. (1984). A Resource-based View of the Firm. *Strategic Management Journal, 5*(2), 171–180.
Williamson, O. E. (1975). *Markets and Hierarchies: Analysis and Antitrust Implications*. Free Press.
Zhao, M., Park, S., & Zhou, N. (2014). MNC Strategy and Social Adaptation in Emerging Markets. *Journal of International Business Studies, 45*, 842–861.

4

The Age of Green

4.1 Definition

Although not a novelty, the sustainability debate has developed enormously in recent decades, evolving from a series of diffuse and heterodox views to become a mainstream subject (Jebe, 2019). In that path, a range of ideas were incorporated, with the relationship humans keep with their surroundings being central. As the debate took shape, it also gained complexity, as issues such as the preservation of endangered species, the use of natural resources, pollution, renewable sources of energy, public policies, and corporate environmental responsibility being all brought together. With the environmentalist cause occupying the most diverse spaces in modern society, a sort of shared mindset emerged, according to which environmental concerns assume a prominent space in consumption, investment decisions, political choices, and lifestyle in general. The *age of green* is here defined then as a *zeitgeist* (i.e. spirit of the time) in which issues related to sustainability acquire a high status in society. In this sense, it stands as a collective conscience formed by values and expectations, in such a way that the worth attributed to individuals, governments, and organizations is, to some extent, related to their adherence to it.

M. Fracarolli Nunes, C. Lee Park, *Business Ethics and Environmental Fraud*,
https://doi.org/10.1007/978-3-030-73800-6_4

4.2 Philosophical Roots

The *age of green* results from a long tradition of thinkers, who have dedicated to discussing not only the role of mankind in the environment, but also the very essence of the relationships between one and the other. As is common in the development of currents of thought—particularly on their earlier stages—the ideas appear diffused in a multitude of works, whose authors are not always aware that they are contributing to the construction of a certain theoretical or conceptual body. Often, by the time ideas start to connect, the currents of thought are not well defined, what makes it difficult to identify their origins and clearly trace their philosophical development. That seems to be the case of the sustainability debate. Although the stream of thought sponsored by the United Nations may be considered the starting point of an organized and global discussion on sustainable development, concerns on the relationship between mankind and environment could be traced back to earlier works. As pointed out by Harlow et al. (2013, p. 270), that includes "[eighteenth] and [nineteenth] century political-economic thought, Rousseauian ideals, the modernism founded on Bacon and Descartes, early Christian utopianism, and classical utopias such as Republic and New Atlantis, which expressed themes of social justice, environmental stewardship and economic growth".

As discussed by Lumley and Armstrong (2004), the nineteenth century saw a proliferation of ideas associating political economy and nature. In this sense, authors such as Richard Cantillon (1680–1734), François Quesnay (1694–1774), Nicolas de Condorcet (1743–1794), Ferdinando Galiani (1728–1787), Karl Marx (1818–1883), and Henry George (1839–1897) would be particularly relevant in the conciliation between the improvement of human condition and mankind's dependence upon nature. In particular, British Victorian thinkers such as Charles Darwin (1809–1882), Thomas Malthus (1766–1834), Harriet Martineau (1802–1876), and John Stuart Mill (1806–1873) developed the idea that "conserving nature while trying to improve the distribution of wealth was not a paradox, but a moral duty" (Lumley & Armstrong, 2004, p. 367). Within this notion, Adam Smith's pursuit of self-interest could only be put in march in case it did not interfere with "the rules of justice". The way these authors conceptualized their theories would stand then as "the nineteenth century origins of sustainability concepts".

In his famous "*Discours sur l'origine et les fondements de l'inegalité parmi les hommes*" (Discourse upon the origin and foundation of the inequality among mankind, Rousseau [1754] 2011), Jean-Jacques Rousseau develops the concepts of state of nature, perfectibility, sociability, and culture, with the notions generally opposing each other (Guichet, 2002). Accordingly, the pure state of nature would be an inert one, in which resides human perfectibility. The awakening from such a state would be both the effect and cause of society, and, by consequence, of all culture and history. In the state of nature, man would be free from pain, with little to no need for medicines or doctors (Rousseau [1754] 2011). Still, just like domesticated animals lose their qualities when taken away from nature, when man is civilized (i.e. taken away from its savagery), it would become less virtuous. For Rousseau, the corruption of man would not be due to its intrinsic nature, but, in fact, to society.

This reasoning seems to have directly influenced not only philosophes in the following centuries, but also the environmentalist movements we have been watching in the last decades. Beyond setting the bases for more optimistic views on the essence of human nature, the idea that *l'homme sauvage* (the sauvage man) is virtuous seems to blame civilization for nearly all bad. Within this view, the return to *l'état de nature* (the state of nature) would condition the elimination,—or, at least, the reduction—of this same bad. In doing so, inequalities that emerge from political and social interactions would be eliminated, along with the pretense system of domination that they allow. In fact, inequalities would be restricted to those which are natural, because God wanted them to be present since the creation.

In discussing Rousseau's influence, LaFreniere (1990) highlights the impact of his ideas in the thinking of authors such as Ralph Waldo Emerson (1803–1882), Henry David Thoreau (1817–1862), and John Muir (1838–1814), as well as in the attitude of many Americans toward nature. The publication of works such as *La Nouvelle Héloïse* (The New Heloise, Rousseau [1761] 1849), *Emile ou de l'education* (Emilie, or On Education, Rousseau [1762] 1856), and *Lettres sur la Botanique* (Letters on the Elements of Botany, Rousseau [1771–1773] 2020) would be pivotal on the regard. In that way, the modern American tradition of environmentalism—dating from the 1960s—would not be solely rooted in the conservationist and preservationist movements of the late nineteenth century. It neither would be fully indigenous nor based on Thomas Jefferson's agrarian republicanism, as often argued. Instead, European ideas would have been key in the construction of this "transatlantic culture of the [eighteenth] and [nineteenth] centuries" (LaFreniere, 1990, p. 41). Beyond Jean-Jacques Rousseau himself, a range of authors associated with the development of "social science and literature toward a modern philosophy and aesthetics of nature" would have had a great influence on the consolidation of American environmentalism. That include well-known names such as Denis Diderot (1713–1784), Johann Wolfgang con Goethe (1749–1832), and William Wordsworth (1770–1850). Likewise, authors issued from the natural sciences who were precursors of ecology as a discipline would have also largely contributed to this direction. Along with previously mentioned Darwin and Malthus, intellectuals like Carolus Linnaeus (1707–1778) would be equally relevant in this construction.

A more detailed examination of the recent history of the sustainability debate, however, may greatly contribute to the understanding of its current meaning and use. In particular, the chain of developments sponsored or supported by the United Nations in the last decades offers valuable insights on the construction of the *age of green*.

4.3 Recent History

Since 1990, 12 major conferences have been convened by the international community, all seeking to commit Governments to address—as contended by the United Nations—pressing problems of the world (United Nations, 2020a). Within a historical perspective, however, the evolution of the sustainability debate seems to be marked by two inflection points before that: (1) the UN Conference on the Human Environment, held in 1972 in Stockholm, Sweden, and (2) the World Commission on Environment and Development (WCED), also known as the Brundtland Commission, in 1987. Both produced important discussions and documents defining some of the objectives, concepts, and terminologies that have influenced the dynamics of the sustainability discussion, as well as the political and economic agendas of the following decades.

4.3.1 *Blueprint for Survival* (1972)

In organizing the evolution of this debate, Basiago (1995) proposes a timeline for the development of sustainability as a concept, with the notion appearing for the first time in an issue called "A Blue Print for Survival" (Goldsmith et al., 1972). Published by the *Ecologist* magazine just before the Stockholm Conference in 1972, this "radical and influential issue" was a "catalyst for political change", having sold more than 500,000 copies and being published in book format later (Hubbard, 2012). Accordingly, concerns with the increase of both human populations and *per capita* consumption permeated the issue, with the call for radical changes being pointed out as necessary and inevitable. In February 1972 an extraction of the document was published in the American newspaper *The New York Times*, which argued that the aim of its authors was to "herald the dawn of a new age", where "Man will learn to live with the rest of Nature, rather than against it" (The New York Times, 1972).

Critics to the supposed expansive nature of "the industrial way of life" (The New York Times, 1972) are also made in the extract, with its sustainability being harshly questioned. The end of this mode of production is then foreseen to take place in a short period of time, unless its existence is extended to the profit of an "entrenched minority at the cost of imposing great suffering on the rest of mankind". In fact, authors claim that there are only two possible ends to this industrial way of life. Either through a "succession of famines, epidemics, social crises and wars" or through the creation of "a society which will not impose hardship and cruelty upon our children—in a succession of thoughtful, humane and measured changes".

4.3.2 *Stockholm Conference* (1972)

As argued by Basiago (1995), the 1972 conference of the United Nations (UN), held in Stockholm in June of that year, would have been directly inspired by this quest to make modern civilization sustainable. For the first time, scientists and world leaders were brought together to debate growing international environmental concerns (Seyfang, 2003). Officially entitled "United Nations Conference on the Human Environment in Stockholm", it is argued to be the first organized debate on the human impact on the environment, representing a primary attempt to forge a basic common understanding on how to preserve and enhance it (Handl, 2020). The conference, however, was not unanimous among all countries. As recalled by Maurice Strong—a Canadian diplomat that chaired the Stockholm Conference—developing countries considered to boycott the summit, as some believed that concerns about the environment should distract them from relieving poverty and promote economic development. Only 113 nations were present in the conference and among the main absences were the Soviet Union and its allies (Black, 2012).

The debate around the preservation of natural environment was mixed with assorted themes, mainly those including the geopolitical tensions of the time. The US action in Vietnam, for example, was brought to the spotlight of the conference, being classified as an ecocide by the then-Swedish Prime Minister Olof Palm. In his words, "The indiscriminate bombing, the large-scale use of bulldozers, the use of herbicides, is an outrage" (Black, 2012). The United States attempted to deflect the negative press received on the issue by focusing on other topics. As the country had stopped the commercial hunting of whales—as well as its allies UK, Germany, and the Netherlands—it insisted on pointing out that the practice was only carried on by the USSR and Japan, precisely its main political and economic rivals. In that way, despite whale hunting had not received great attention in the documents prepared leading up to the conference, a moratorium on commercial whaling was called by an approved resolution, outcome that was possibly the most present in the headlines following the conference. In that way, still after Black (2012), the further protection of the life of whales "may have been ecologically justified—but there is little doubt that the main motivation was political, at least on the governmental level".

Among the other outcomes of the Stockholm Conference was the establishment of a United Nations Environment Programme (UNEP) (Black, 2012), self-described as "the leading global environmental authority that sets the global environmental agenda, promotes the coherent implementation of the environmental dimension of sustainable development within the United Nation systems, and serves as an authoritative advocate for the global environment" (UNEP, 2020). Headquartered in Nairobi, Kenya, it is dedicated to the broad areas of climate change, disasters and conflicts, ecosystem management, environmental governance, chemicals and waste, resource efficiency, and environment under review. In analyzing the political impact of the summit, UN collaborator Jan-Gustav Strandenaes recalls that, before the Stockholm Conference, no country in the world counted on a ministry of the environment, having Norway been the first to establish one in the aftermath of the discussions. Sweden would have followed, creating its own a few weeks later (Black, 2012).

In 1973, the Declaration of the United Nations Conference on the Human Environment (United Nations, 1973) was released, with the body proclaiming that both aspects of man's environment (i.e. the natural and the man-made) are essential to his well-being and to the respect of his human rights, including the right to life itself. Yet, the document asserts that, at the same time man's capacity to transform its surroundings allows people to enjoy the benefits of development and enhance the quality of their lives, it shall also be sharply detrimental, potentially causing great harm to human beings and the environment. Also, a distinction is made between the causes of environmental problems in developed and developing countries. While industrialization and technological development would be to blame in the first case, underdevelopment would be the main explanation in the second. Likewise, populational growth is highlighted as a major source of environmental problems, with the adoption of policies and measures to face it being necessary. The document stresses the importance of citizens, communities, enterprises, and institutions at every level accepting their responsibility toward the environment, with all equitably sharing a common effort.

Local and national governments, however, would be more in charge of large-scale environmental policy and actions to be implemented within their jurisdictions, with international cooperations being necessary to raise resources, so that developing countries may properly attack their environmental problems. Finally, actions by international organizations would be critical, as environmental problems may be global and affect the common international realm. Along with these declarations, 26 principles and 109 recommendations are stated in what seems an attempt to equilibrate human activity and the preservation of natural environments. In this sense, a range of issues are treated, from man's right to freedom, equality, and adequate conditions of life, to his responsibility to safeguard and wisely manage the heritage of wildlife and its habitat. The expected role of national States is also approached, including their duty to ensure the capacity of international organizations to promote the protection and improvement of environmental conditions, as well as the non-utilization of environmental concerns as a way to reduce the access of other nations to markets or to implement discriminatory trade policies. In face of its pioneering spirit, however, the Stockholm declaration would not be centered on detailed normative positions. Instead, the approach to environmental policies and goals would be located in a more macro level, treating these issues from a broader perspective. Despite that, a dramatic increase on the global awareness of environmental issues would have followed the Stockholm Conference (Handl, 2020).

At the request of the chair of the 1972 conference, British economist Barbara Ward and French biologist—and Nobel Laureate—René Dubos wrote "*Only One Earth: The Care and Maintenance of a Small Planet*" (Ward & Dubos, 1972). Considered to be the first book on sustainable development, it stressed the necessity to combine the meeting of human needs with the recognition of the finite limits of the planet on what relates to resources and pollution. The idea that measures should be taken to guarantee that the planet would rest a suitable place for human life not only at that moment, but also for future generations would be the basis for the definition of sustainable development by the Brundtland Commission 15 years later (Satterthwaite, 2006).

4.3.3 *World Commission on Environment and Development (WCED)* (1987)

The World Commission on Environment and Development (WCED) was sponsored by the UN and led by Gro Harlem Brundtland (Sneddon et al., 2006), a Norwegian politician that served three terms as prime minister of Norway (1981, 1986–1989, 1990–1996) and as the director-general of the World Health Organization (WHO) between 1998 and 2003 (Britannica, 2020). For Sneddon et al. (2006), the publication of WCED report "Our Common Future" in 1987 represented watershed in the way we think about the environment, development, and governance. As discussed by the authors, it issued an audacious call for the recalibration of institutional mechanisms at global, national, and local level, so that economic development could be equated with "the security, well-being and very survival of the planet" (WCED, 1987, p. 27). In that way, the report is positioned as a "global agenda for change" (WCED, 1987, p. 5) that would answer an urgent call by the General Assembly of the United Nations. That included the proposition of long-term environmental strategies allowing for the achievement of sustainable development by the year 2000 and beyond, the recommendation of ways to increase the collaboration between countries, the consideration of the role of the international community in the treatment of environmental issues, and the definition of shared perceptions of the necessary measures to be taken.

As pointed out by Basiago (1995), the relationship between sustainability and "futurity" would follow the works of the Brundtland Commission, as it defined sustainable development as the one that ensures the meeting of present needs "without compromising the ability of future generations to meet their own needs" (WCED, 1987, p. 16). From a social viewpoint, the report also argues that sustainable development would be an important step in the eradication of widespread poverty. Accordingly, "sustainable development requires meeting the basic needs of all and extending to all the opportunity to fulfil their aspirations for a better life" (WCED, 1987, p. 16). A direct link to the environmental nature of the commission rests in the argument that a "world in which poverty is endemic will always be prone to ecological and other catastrophes".

4.3.4 *Bergen Declaration on Sustainable Development* (1990)

In turn, the precaution principle would have been affirmed in the Bergen Declaration on Sustainable Development in 1990 (Basiago, 1995), produced by the United Nations European Commission for Europe. As discussed by Stevens (2002, p. 13), it essentially advocates for the use of precaution in cases where scientific uncertainty is present, anticipating, or avoiding potential environmental damage. The preventive measures would then lower mitigation costs, being, however, the implementation of the principle problematic, once it places more responsibility on the potential sources of environmental risk than in the past. Still after the author, "[i]ts most important—and debatable—feature is that it shifts the burden of scientific proof from those who would like to prohibit or slow down a potentially dangerous activity to those who conduct the activity".

4.3.5 *The United Nations Conference on Environment and Development* (1992)

Between June 3 and 14, 1992, the United Nations Conference on Environment and Development took place in Rio de Janeiro, Brazil (United Nations, 2020a). Also known as the Earth Summit, it established that sustainable development should be regarded as the most important policy of the twenty-first century (Basiago, 1995). Among the main outcomes of the conference are the Rio Declaration on Environment and Development, the Statement of Principles for the Sustainable Management of Forests and the Agenda 21, with the latter representing a "comprehensive plan of action to be taken globally, nationally and locally by the organizations of the United Nations System, Governments, and Major Groups in every area in which human impacts on the environment" (United Nations, 2020b).

Once more, issues such as the need for "international cooperation to accelerate sustainable development in developing countries" (United

Nations, 1992, p. 1) and the combat to poverty were discussed throughout the document, being organized around the definitions of clear objectives and activities. As highlighted by Basiago (1995), by focusing on the debate of sustainability, the Earth Summit would have heralded a new paradigm in the relation between society, economics, and the environment. The harmonization of these three distinct but interrelated concepts came to be further developed by Elkington (1997) in his famous book "*Cannibals with Forks: The Triple Bottom Line of 21st Century in Business*". Accordingly, sustainability in business would depend on the simultaneous meeting of social, environmental, and economic goals, summing up the ideas of the triple bottom line.

Several other related events followed, including the Earth Summit 2002 in Johannesburg, South Africa—often nicknamed Rio + 10 –, the Earth Summit 2012—or Rio + 20 –, once again in Rio de Janeiro, Brazil (National Geographic, 2020), and the 2015 United Nations Climate Chance Conference (COP 21), in Paris, France. For Jordan and O'Riordan (2004), however, global summits such as these ones promoted by the UN would have become "circuses with a serious cause", once, along with people committed to relevant discussions, they would end up attracting groups more interested in self-promotion. The focus on agendas beyond initial goals would delay diplomatic agreements, with the final outcome typically being a new version of commitments previously made, possibly in a downgraded form.

Nevertheless, as a result of these events, the concept of sustainability has become widely employed in the most different areas of knowledge, including biology, economics, sociology, urban planning, and ethics, being "regarded as tantamount to a new philosophy, in which principles of futurity, equity, global environmentalism and biodiversity must guide decision-making" (Basiago, 1995, p. 109). Allied with its wide applications in marketing (Fracarolli Nunes & Lee Park, 2017) and the high levels of social and environmental conscience of consumers and citizens in general, the incorporation of sustainability as a main value of contemporary societies forms the basis of what is here defined as the *age of green*.

4.4 Sustainable Consumption

Beyond more abstract debates, the emergence and consolidation of the *age of green* seems to have caused profound changes in consumption habits, with consumers' emotions playing an important role in that direction. The development of negative sentiments toward unsustainable products, for example, would be a major incentive for the manufacturing of green goods, with guilt being particularly common. In fact, the association of consumption with the use of natural resources and pollution may have a thorough impact in those more sensitive to environmental issues. As they seek to balance concerns with nature and their basic needs (e.g. nutrition, clothing, and transportation), these groups shall develop contradictory and often negative sensations. The proliferation of the use of plastic is one of the main triggers of such feelings, with the material suffering from a double conviction. At the same time it is derived from oil—a finite natural resource—it is associated with ocean pollution, and a slow absorption by nature. As the material is largely employed in packages, clothes, home appliances, cars, and nearly all sorts of consumption goods, it serves as a constant reminder that environmentalists are themselves responsible for the degradation of the planet. Likewise, the great dependence of fossil fuels for transportation does not allow them to escape their dose of environmental damage. The search for relief from negative feelings would work then as an important driver for the consumption of green products.

On that regard, Lindenberg and Steg (2007) add that environmental behavior would be framed by hedonic, gain, and normative goals. While a hedonic goal refers to the feeling of positive sensations in the present, gain ones relate to the preservation or improvement of resources. Normative goals, in turn, are associated with the idea of acting appropriately, or in conformity with something. Pro-environmental consumption behavior would be also motivated by these same factors (Rezvani et al., 2018). For Lim (2017), sustainable consumption encompasses three distinct but interrelated dimensions: responsible consumption, mindful consumption, and anti-consumption. While the former refers to decisions that include social, environmental, and ethical concerns, the idea of mindful consumption would be associated with consumption derived from a mindset of awareness and attention, with care for the self, the community, and the nature. Anti-consumption, in turn, relates to rejection based on ones' personal interests and/or social-environmental worries.

From a practical point of view, the dissemination of responsible and mindful consumption is probably the direct reason for the success of products, companies, and technologies perceived as environmentally responsible. The main difference among them, however, seems to be their respective selfish and altruistic essences. Based on the notions of social value, emotional value, and functional value proposed by Sheth et al. (1991), it appears that both responsible and mindful consumptions grant individuals with all three forms, as, at the same time they may believe their attitudes indeed have a positive impact (i.e. functional value), they also make them feel better about themselves (i.e. emotional value), and, depending on the eyes of observers, improve their social status (i.e. social value).

Similarly, anti-consumption may offer customers the same benefits. One of the most recent examples of this nature is the movement known as flight shame. Among other things, it basically preaches that the use of air services should be avoided due to its high consumption of fossil fuels. In this sense it is also used to expose alleged hypocritical behaviors. Upon the 2019 Alphabet Inc.'s climate change summit held in Sicily, Italy, for example, a great number of private jets were used in the transportation of activists, politicians, businesspeople, and other public figures who were ironically gathering to discuss current environmental challenges. Among the most notable participants was the British royal Prince Harry, who was nicknamed the "Carbon Footprince" (Bryant, 2019). Accordingly, criticism was motivated mainly because traveling in private jets results in carbon dioxide emissions that are several times higher than doing so in an economy seat on a commercial flight. The "do as I say, not what I do" attitude would be particularly triggering to those disapproving the flights. Still after the author, beyond exposing the environmentally unfriendly behavior of some of the most prominent green campaigners, flight shaming would be a problem to the jet industry, with the potential to negatively affect its sales.

The same may be extended to the whole commercial flight industry, as more and more people involved in the sustainability public debate seek to avoid flying whenever possible. That is the case of Swedish activist Greta Thunberg, who crossed the Atlantic in a boat to attend a UN summit on zero emissions in New York (Milman, 2019). It seems, however, that the entire crew had to travel by plane to the United States to return the boat back to Europe (ABC News, 2019). Thus, despite having managed to avoid flight shaming, the environmental impact of the alternative displacement would have been greater than if she had opted for a conventional flight, exposing what might be interpreted as hypocritical behavior.

4.5 Points of Attention

Based on the discussion above, the *age of green* may thus be understood as a set of values and beliefs that conditions social behavior. By influencing peoples' views and opinions, the sustainability debate ends up shaping companies' activities as they search to fulfill the demands of the markets in that regard. Yet, at the same time, the search to minimize environmental impacts has a range of positive externalities; the overestimation of sustainability issues makes room for unethical conducts, particularly when managers believe that looking green is more important than actually being green. In this sense, unethical schemes may be used to sustain the gap between false corporate environmental reputations and companies' operational realities (Fracarolli Nunes & Lee Park, 2017).

Beyond its consequences, the process through which the sustainability debate consolidated as a major societal concern also merits attention. As addressed throughout the chapter, discussions in that direction did not emerge from popular segments. Instead, it seems to be the result of the work of intellectuals, including some of the most prominent philosophers of all time. Despite the theoretical robustness of this debate, it remained limited to small circles for centuries. The popularization of this discussion results—to a large extent—from the intensive efforts promoted by the United Nations since the second half of the twentieth century. Through a series of conferences and events, the entity played a major role in the consolidation of a solid global eco-conscience.

The rise of the *age of green* suggests then that society may indeed be shaped, validating the views of social engineering (Friedman, 2005). Yet, the fact that the sustainability agenda was "imposed" on society raises important concerns. It must not be assumed, for example, that intellectual and economic elites are ethical by definition. Among other things, this means that vigilance over their movements is necessary, including the pointing of eventual moral deviations, particularly when they are disguised as good intentions.

References

ABC News. (2019). Sailing Team to Fly 2 Crew to US to bring Thunberg Boat Back. August 16. https://abcnews.go.com/Technology/wireStory/sailing-team-fly-crew-us-bring-thunberg-boat-65021301

Basiago, A. D. (1995). Methods of Defining 'Sustainability'. *Sustainable Development, 3*(3), 109–119.

Black, R. (2012). Stockholm: Birth of the Green Generation. *BBC*, June 4. https://www.bbc.com/news/science-environment-18315205

Britannica. (2020). Gro Harlem Brundtland—Prime Minister of Norway. https://www.britannica.com/biography/Gro-Harlem-Brundtland

Bryant, C. (2019). Prince Harry's Shaming is Bad News for Private Jets. *Bloomberg*, August 23. https://www.bloomberg.com/opinion/articles/2019-08-23/climate-change-prince-harry-shaming-is-bad-news-for-private-jets

Elkington, J. (1997). *Cannibals with Forks: The Triple Bottom Line of 21st Century Business*. Capstone.

Fracarolli Nunes, M., & Lee Park, C. (2017). Self-claimed Sustainability: Building Social and Environmental Reputations with Words. *Sustainable Production and Consumption, 11*, 46–57.

Friedman, J. (2005). Popper, Weber, and Hayek: The Epistemology and Politics of Ignorance. *Critical Review, 17*(1–2), 1–58.

Goldsmith, E., Allen, R., Allaby, M., Davull, J., & Lawrence, S. (1972). A Blueprint for Survival. *The Ecologist, 2*(1).

Guichet, J. L. (2002). L'homme et la nature chez Rousseau: L'homme de la nature, un homme absolument isolé ou détenteur déjà d'une certaine culture? *Revue des Sciences Philosophiques et Théologiques, 86*(1), 69–84.

Handl, G. (2020). Declaration of the United Nations Conference on the Human Environment / Rio Declaration on Environment and Development. *United Nations Audiovisual Library of International Law*. https://legal.un.org/avl/ha/dunche/dunche.html

Harlow, J., Golub, A., & Allenby, B. (2013). A Review of Utopian Themes in Sustainable Development Discourse. *Sustainable Development, 21*(4), 270–280.

Hubbard, B. (2012). The Ecologist January 1972: A Blueprint for Survival. *The Ecologist,* January 27. https://theecologist.org/2012/jan/27/ecologist-january-1972-blueprint-survival

Jebe, R. (2019). The Convergence of Financial and ESG Materiality: Taking Sustainability Mainstream. *American Business Law Journal, 56*(3), 645–702.

Jordan, A., & O'Riordan, T. (2004). Institutions for Global Environmental Change. *Global Environmental Change, 14*(4), 367.

LaFreniere, G. F. (1990). Rousseau and the European Roots of Environmentalism. *Environmental History Review, 14*(4), 41–72.

Lim, W. M. (2017). Inside the Sustainable Consumption Theoretical Toolbox: Critical Concepts for Sustainability, Consumption, and Marketing. *Journal of Business Research, 78*, 69–80.

Lindenberg, S., & Steg, L. (2007). Normative, Gain and Hedonic Goal Frames Guiding Environmental Behavior. *Journal of Social Issues, 63*(1), 117–137.

Lumley, S., & Armstrong, P. (2004). Some of the Nineteenth Century Origins of the Sustainability Concept. *Environment, Development and Sustainability, 6*(3), 367–378.

Milman, O. (2019). 'Let's do it now': Greta Thunberg Crosses Atlantic and Calls for Urgent Climate Action. *The Guardian*, August 29. https://www.theguardian.com/environment/2019/aug/28/greta-thunberg-arrival-in-new-york-delayed-by-rough-seas

National Geographic. (2020). Earth Summit 2002—Rio+10. August 26. https://www.nationalgeographic.org/thisday/aug26/earth-summit-2002rio10/

Rezvani, Z., Jansson, J., & Bengtsson, M. (2018). Consumer Motivations for Sustainable Consumption: The Interaction of Gain, Normative and Hedonic Motivations on Electric Vehicle Adoption. *Business Strategy and the Environment, 27*(8), 1272–1283.

Rousseau, J. J. ([1761] 1849). *La Nouvelle Héloïse*. Gustave Havard.

Rousseau, J. J. ([1762] 1856). *Emile ou de l'Education*. J. Bry Ainé, Libraire-Éditeur.

Rousseau, J. J. ([1754] 2011). *Discours sur l'origine et les fondements de l'inegalité parmi les hommes*. Les Échos du Maquis (Édition électronique). 1st edition 1754. https://philosophie.cegeptr.qc.ca/wp-content/documents/Discours-sur-lin%C3%A9galit%C3%A9-1754.pdf

Rousseau, J. J. ([1771–1773] 2020). *Lettres sur la Botanique*. Burlapapey—Bibliothèque Numérique Romande.

Satterthwaite, D. (2006). *Barbara Ward and the Origins of Sustainable Development*. International Institute for Environment and Development (IIED).

Seyfang, G. (2003). Environmental Mega-Conferences – From Stockholm to Johannesburg and beyond. *Global Environmental Change, 13*, 223–228.

Sheth, J. N., Newman, B. I., & Gross, B. L. (1991). Why We Buy What We Buy: A Theory of Consumption Values. *Journal of Business Research, 22*(2), 159–170.

Sneddon, C., Howarth, R. B., & Norgaard, R. B. (2006). Sustainable Development in a Post-Brundtland World. *Ecological Economics, 57*(2), 253–268.

Stevens, M. (2002). The Precautionary Principle in the International Arena. *Sustainable Development Law & Policy, 2*(2), 13–15.

The New York Times. (1972). A Blueprint for Survival. 5 February. https://www.nytimes.com/1972/02/05/archives/a-blueprint-for-survival.html

UNEP. (2020). Why does UN Environment Matter? https://www.unenvironment.org/about-un-environment/why-does-un-environment-matter

United Nations. (1973). Report of the United Nations Conference on the Human Environment—Stockholm, 5–16 June 1972. https://digitallibrary.un.org/record/523249?ln=en#record-files-collapse-header

United Nations. (1992). Agenda 21. https://sustainabledevelopment.un.org/content/documents/Agenda21.pdf

United Nations. (2020a). United Nations Conference on Environment and Development (UNCED), Earth Summit. https://sustainabledevelopment.un.org/milestones/unced

United Nations. (2020b). Agenda 21—UNCED, 1992. https://sustainabledevelopment.un.org/index.php?page=view&nr=23&type=400&menu=35

Ward, B., & Dubos, R. (1972). *Only One Earth: The Care and Maintenance of a Small Planet*. Andre Deutsch.

WCED. (1987). Report of the World Commission on Environment and Development: Our Common Future. https://sustainabledevelopment.un.org/content/documents/5987our-common-future.pdf

5

The Automotive Industry Under Suspicion

5.1 Early Developments

The family three of the automotive industry may be rooted in very early developments, some of which considered landmarks of civilization. Dietsche and Kuhlgatz (2014), for instance, point out to the invention of the wheel by the Sumerians (3500 BC) as the starting point of this journey. Accordingly, nearly 5000 years were necessary for a further refinement of carriages, with the incorporation of new technologies such as steering wheels and suspensions only taking place around 1300 AD. After these initial innovations, a second period of relative inertia in technological development would have been established, while vehicles used for transportation did not present significant developments for nearly four centuries. From the second half of the eighteenth century, however, the development of new technologies gained considerable speed, with Joseph Cugnot (1725–1804) inventing the steam buggy in 1770, and Étienne Lenoir (1822–1900) creating the gas engine in the early 1860s. Following this innovation path, the first four-stroke internal combustion engine was built by Nikolaus Otto (1832–1891) in 1870, culminating with the invention of the first automobile by Carl Benz (1844–1929) in 1885.

M. Fracarolli Nunes, C. Lee Park, *Business Ethics and Environmental Fraud*,
https://doi.org/10.1007/978-3-030-73800-6_5

The patent granted to the German engineer set the era of vehicles powered by internal combustion engines.

Yet, the invention was far from unanimous, having divided public opinion. At the same time the automobile was seen as the epitome of progress by the proponents of the new age, most of the population showed discontent with several aspects associated with the first vehicles, including the annoyances of dust, noise, accident hazard, as well as inconsiderate drivers. These different perceptions on automobiles have accompanied them throughout the years, being the source of both the passion and the hatred they arouse until the present days. Still after Dietsche and Kuhlgatz (2014), despite all objections, its progress showed to be unstoppable. As pointed out by the authors, however, during its fresh years, the acquisition of an automobile was accompanied by a series of difficulties, being the lack of an appropriate infrastructure to its utilization among the most important ones. Road networks, for example, were nearly nonexistent, and repair shops were unknown. Fuel, in turn, was only available in drugstores, and spare parts were produced on demand, typically by the local blacksmith.

Regardless of all these difficulties, the first long-distance journey made with an automobile is believed to be that of Bertha Benz in 1888 (Dietsche & Kuhlgatz, 2014), who is also thought to have been the very first woman to drive a motorized vehicle. Accompanied by her two sons and without the knowledge of her husband, Carl Benz, Mrs. Benz drove the Benz Patentmotorwagen number 3 (i.e. patent motor car) between the southern German cities of Mannheim and Pforzheim, in a one-way route distance of more than 100 kilometers (approximately 65 miles) (Ziegler et al., 2014). As highlighted by Dietsche and Kuhlgatz (2014), the journey was not only an achievement on itself, but proved the reliability of the automobile. In face of the many obstacles and precarious conditions of the time, the fact that such a complex and, to some extent, fragile machine completed its mission must indeed have served as a demonstration of its robustness, possibly boosting sales and, by consequence, the growth of the automotive industry. On that regard, Ziegler et al. (2014) argue that, by demonstrating the maturity of Carl Benz's gasoline engine, Mrs. Benz's maiden voyage paved the ground for both the acceptance of automobile in society and the economic success of her husband. The historical and symbolic importance of this initial trip is translated by Mercedes-Benz's decision to go through the same route 125 years later; this time, however, for the debut of its autonomous vehicle the S-Class S 500 Intelligent drive.

Beyond having invented the internal combustion engine, Carl Benz seems to have been one of the few entrepreneurs to consider the potential of engine-powered vehicles on a worldwide scale, while the French also played an important role in the development of the industry (Dietsche & Kuhlgatz, 2014). In that direction, industrials such as Armand Peugeot (1849–1915), Louis Renault (1877–1944), and André Citroën (1878–1935) played a major role in the establishment of the automotive industry in the country, having founded the three companies that, until today, not only dominate the French market but also have an important participation in the industry around the world. Despite the apparent success, French automakers have experienced ups and downs throughout their history, with World War II being an important chapter in their path. Following accusations of collaboration with Nazi German, Renault went through a nationalization process during the governing of the then-French President General Charles de Gaulle (1890–1970). As a result, the company's ownership migrated from its founder to the French State, which, to this day, remains the largest shareholder of the company, with 15% of its shares (RFI, 2020). An important step in the consolidation of the French automotive industry also took place in 1976, the year in which Peugeot and Citroën merged to form PSA Peugeot Citroën (today PSA Group) (Britannica, 2020). The French State also appears as an important shareholder in the company, holding around 12% of its shares (France 24, 2020).

Similarly, in Japan, Kiichiro Toyoda established the bases of Toyota Motor Corporation in 1933 (Toyota, 2018), and, in 1948, Soichiro Honda and Takeo Fujisawa founded Honda Motor Co. Ltd. (Honda, 2020). Along with other companies like Mitsubishi and Nissan, the Japanese automotive companies stood as serious contenders to both European and American automakers, having conquered considerable portions of their market share between the 1960s and the 1980s (Cheney, 2015; Toyota, 2020). Among the factors that explain the Japanese success is the invention and dominance of operational practices such as

Just-In-Time and Lean Management, which have contributed enormously to the reduction of production costs, and consequently, to the competitiveness of these companies.

In view of the extremely challenging economic conditions that Japan faced in the period immediately after World War II, the development of production techniques capable of minimizing waste proved to be a key factor for the continuity of its industry. In addition to the difficulties in financing working capital, the limited supply of natural resources has led Japanese companies to optimize the use of their few resources, which, in many cases, has resulted in extremely efficient inventory management practices. With the synchronization of operations, the amount of buffer stock was gradually reduced, thus maximizing operational efficiency. The development and application of Just-In-Time and Lean Management, however, demanded great discipline and delegation of responsibility for employees who had the power to stop all production, should they face problems in the process. The fact that these conditions were apparently common in Japan but relatively rare in other locations (i.e. disciplined workers with high educational levels) ensured that the techniques developed there could not be fully copied by foreign companies, what partly explains the rapid development of the Japanese industry in the post-war decades.

A second factor that may have greatly contributed to the growth of the Japanese auto industry concerns the geopolitical tensions of the 1970s. More specifically, the oil crises of 1973 and 1979 acted as important agents for transforming the automobile market. With fuel prices rising rapidly, traditional American cars presented high operating costs for their owners, with the so-called muscle cars (i.e. large cars with powerful engines) gradually opening space for smaller and less powerful alternatives which, along with being cheaper, consumed less fuel. These were precisely the characteristics of most of the Japanese models who presented themselves at that time as an alternative to traditional American cars. Japanese companies have been able to take advantage of this window of opportunity, profiting from high oil prices to significantly increase their participation in the American market.

If, on the one hand, the procedural innovations implemented by Japanese companies after WWII were decisive in reshaping the automotive industry, perhaps no advance has been as revolutionary as those implemented years before by Henry Ford (1863–1947) in the United States. The introduction of the assembly line and the standardization of products allowed, among other things, the cost of automobiles to be drastically reduced. Based largely on Frederick W. Taylor's (1856–1915) ideas about Scientific Management, production processes greatly decreased the time required to manufacture an automobile, with the gains in scale further lowering production costs. The ideas of the French engineer Henri Fayol (1841–1925) also had a great influence on the development of the production processes that targeted cost reduction, being, to a certain extent, complementary to the proposals of Scientific Management. For some authors, the works of Taylor and Fayol form the basis of modern Management (e.g. Lama, 2018).

From a social point of view, the implementation of Taylor's "one best way" led to a revolution in labor relations. Excessive control of the time spent by each worker in performing tasks, for example, significantly increased the company's control over its employees. Likewise, the atomization of functions, that is, the maximum division of each operation into extremely simple tasks (e.g. tightening screws), contributed to a more favorable condition for companies. Indeed, the fact that each worker was responsible for an extremely small part of the process did not allow him or her to get to know it more widely, with factory managers being the only ones able to fully understand the complexities associated with the production methods. In this sense, the performance of simple tasks by employees greatly reduced their value, since they could easily be replaced by another employee without any specific skills or qualifications being required.

In addition to making employees "expendable", the fact that the tasks were simple eliminated the need for training, lowering even more the costs and speed of eventual replacements. Along with the benefits already described, the situation allowed Ford to make the most of its employees. Since there were not many employment alternatives in other companies, in most cases they had no choice but to submit to extremely difficult conditions, in which long working hours filled with repetitive movements were typical. In general, it shall be argued that Taylor's ideas aimed at the dehumanization of the worker, bringing their behavior closer to that of a machine. In times when industrial automation was still distant, the use of human beings as if they were robots was the solution found by Ford to achieve his goals.

In a way, the reduction of the human characteristics of workers in this initial phase of the automobile industry can be understood as a movement that follows a more profound social transformation, which would have its origin in the transition from an agricultural to an industrial and cosmopolitan society. As discussed by Brazilian philosopher Luiz Felipe Pondé (2016), the development of literary and artistic movements, such as Romanticism, would be based on the malaise generated by this transition, with the new forms of life generating a way of disenchantment and the search for a previous state, generally idealized. The author illustrates favoring the conception of man as a workforce by referring to the book *Die Verwandlung* (German for The Metamorphosis) by the Czech author Franz Kafka (1883–1924). Accordingly, when realizing that he had turned into a cockroach, the main character, Gregor Samsa, would have expressed as his main concern the fact that he would lose the tram that would take him to work, and consequently lose his job. In this sense, the character's reaction would be symptomatic of his overvaluation as a workforce, his concern in this sense prior to the effects of the transformation in his own condition. Thus, it can be argued that the dehumanization of workers promoted by Taylor and Ford is in fact the result of their time, reproducing a trend that marked a more comprehensive change in society. The search for the reestablishment of more equal conditions between employees and companies contributed to the formation of unions. Through collective organization, employees gradually improved both their working conditions and remuneration. In this sense, labor relations in the Ford era can be understood as a fundamental factor for the development of syndicalist activities in the following decades, what, in some cases, gave rise to ideological disputes between different currents of the political and economic spectrum, such as anarchists, communists, socialists, conservatives, and liberals, among others.

Although the application of Scientific Management had several social consequences, its contribution to the shaping of competition in the auto industry is the most relevant to the objectives of this book. It may be argued that the unrelenting search for operational performance is the genesis of an intense rivalry between carmakers. The offer of the famous model T in the United States, for example, has shifted the automobile status from a luxury equipment restricted to an extremely small portion of the society to becoming one of the most popular consumption items of the twentieth and twenty-first centuries. With the middle classes as part of the target market for car companies, the price of products took on a more relevant role, being often an order-winner factor. This dynamic was maintained for the following years and continues to condition competition between companies in the segment.

Cost-based competition is favored by the relatively low differentiation between the models offered by automakers (a specific analysis of the competitive environment of the automotive industry is proposed at the end of the chapter). In fact, the automobile industry cannot be considered a great example of innovation, since, in its essence, automobiles have changed little over a century. In addition to its basic constitution (i.e. four wheels, tires, steering, headlights), the engine technology used remained practically unchanged in this period, with improvements in consumption and performance occurring incrementally and organically. Only in recent years have internal combustion engines been replaced by electric motors, which represents, perhaps, the most significant change in the history of the industry. From the environmental point of view, this change is still subject to several criticisms, and may even increase the pressure of the automobile industry on the environment. This topic is covered in more detail in Chap. 11 ahead.

Among other explanations, technological inertia can be understood as the result of the success of cars and of their already great complexity. Likewise, the infrastructure built to allow its large-scale use (e.g. roads, pipelines, gas stations) represents long-term investments, not fostering incentives for the development of new applications. In addition, the very high volume of financial funds required for the construction of industrial plants works as an additional aspect of continuity, as well as the business model in general. This includes the development of relationships with a large number of suppliers and distribution channels. Thus, this great structure around the automobile industry makes it slow and, at times, unable to react adequately to the most profound changes that society requires.

Since the technologies and value propositions offered by companies are very similar, they have few alternatives for differentiation, with product design being one of them. In this context, companies in the automobile industry have been launched into a competition based on the price of their products, which, as discussed by Porter (1996), implies a constant search for cost reduction and gains in operational efficiency. This includes large-scale strategic moves such as mergers and acquisitions, whose main objective would be the gain of scale and the capture of operational synergies. This discussion on competitive dynamics is relevant because it constitutes an incentive to the practice of environmental fraud. In particular, the reduced options for differentiation and the exhaustion of the search for cost cuts are understood here as generating an environment conducive to criminal and illicit attitudes such as those occurring in the Volkswagen Dieselgate. This discussion is taken up in more detail in Chap. 6.

5.2 Economic Organization

Right after the end of WWII, the automotive industry was perceived as both a cause and a consequence of American economic achievements, being intrinsically associated with the development of the country (Cooney & Yacobucci, 2007). This view was expressed in the words of General Motors (GM) Chairman Charles Wilson in the 1950s, who claimed that "what's good for GM is good for America" (Patterson, 2013). By the time, the company produced more than half of the cars commercialized in the United States. According to Cooney and Yacobucci (2007), this success was largely due to the strategy adopted by GM, which, in opposition to mass production and standardization—Ford's original concept—proposed "a car for every purse and purpose" (The Henry Ford, 2020). General Motors, Ford, and Chrysler formed in the United States the group popularly known as the "Big Three", having dominated the American market for cars and light trucks for decades. Along with other smaller domestic manufacturers (e.g. American Motors, Studebaker-Packard, and Kaiser), these companies left no more than small niches to be occupied by foreign producers, among which Volkswagen and a few luxury and sports cars (Cooney & Yacobucci, 2007).

Since the mid-1980s, the automotive industry experienced a shift from relatively isolated groups of national industries to a model of greater integration among different players around the world (Sturgeon et al., 2008). Accordingly, the formation of global ties happened at the same time that strong regional patterns were formed at the operational level (Lung et al., 2004; Dicken, 2005, 2007). In that way, the dispersion of final assembly was motivated by factors such as the saturation of markets and political pressures that pushed automakers to "build where they sell", particularly in emerging countries such as Brazil, India, and China. As a result, in the space of 40 years—from 1975 to 2005—the number of countries controlling 80% of the global car production went from 7 to 11 (Automotive News, 2020). These global movements have caused several impacts on the organization of the industry, with some of their most important effects being felt in those regions of early development (e.g. United States). Cooney and Yacobucci (2007) stress that, by 2007, the Big Three's market share had declined to 60%, with the remaining lot being occupied by vehicles which were either imported or produced by foreign-based manufacturers in North American plants. These changes were also accompanied by a reduction in the workforce, having 600,000 jobs been shed by the companies since the 1980s. The metamorphosis of the American automotive industry had important effects in the structure and location of production in the country, with the state of Michigan being particularly affected by the loss of auto industry jobs. Still after the authors, beyond an increasing competition from foreign companies—particularly Japanese and German—critics have highlighted Big Three's resistance to environmental, safety, and social issues, not only opposing mandatory seat belt requirements in the past but also resisting the implementation of the Clean Air Act (CAA), and that of the Corporate Average Fuel Economy (CAFE) program. In addition, the progressive decline in Big Three's market share would be also explained by their lethargy with respect to the development of alternative fuel vehicles.

Regarding its economic distribution, the automotive industry seems to present some peculiarities, many of them resulting from the different understandings about the strategies to be adopted over time. On that regard, Sturgeon et al. (2008) argue that the industry would be neither fully global, nor tied to a narrow set of specific localities, with low labor-cost zones being the main destines of investments (e.g. South East Asia and China in Asia, the American south and Mexico in North America, Spain and Eastern Europe in Europe). When it comes to auto parts, however, the trade between regions is significantly more intense if compared to finished products. Still after the authors, within countries, the automotive production and employment would be typically clustered, comprehending one or a few industrial regions. In some cases, these clusters are centered on specific aspects of the business, including design, final assembly, or the manufacture of parts.

The expansion of car manufacturers in Europe illustrates the idea. In the attempt to meet the increasing competitiveness of the industry, at the end of the twentieth century Western European automakers broadened their production into former socialist countries in Central and Eastern Europe (CEE) (Nagy & Jámbor, 2018). Coherently with Sturgeon et al.'s (2008) views, this expansion was not accompanied by the transferring of innovation activities or the transferring of high value-added production. Instead, while these Western automakers profited from the favorable conditions of the CEE region (e.g. skilled workers, low wages, and the geographic proximity to consumer markets), they kept control of more critical activities. Beyond that, with the improvement of living standards, CEE regions ended up becoming relevant consumer markets themselves (Pavlínek, 2015; Jürgens & Krzywdzinski, 2009). In fact, that formula is still largely applied today. The Audi and Volkswagen groups, for example, have a considerable portion of their engines produced in Hungary since 1994, in what is considered the world's largest engine factory (Audi Hungaria, 2020). Accordingly, 8800 engines are produced daily in the city of Győr, accounting for a total production to date of more than 35 million engines.

In face of the considerable investments in capital equipment and skills that their structure demands, regional automotive clusters have a tendency to be long-term formations (Sturgeon et al., 2008). In summarizing the complex economic geography of the automotive industry, the authors argue that, while global integration has experienced a strong development at the buyer-supplier relationship level, production itself is typically organized nationally or regionally, with the manufacturing of bulky, heavy, and model-specific parts normally happening close to the final assembly plants. Among other reasons, that would be intended to assure timely delivery. Generic parts, in turn, would be more commonly produced at distance, so that companies could profit from economies of scale and low labor costs. Lately, vehicle development would be concentrated in few design centers, what, along with the other conditions approached, makes local, national, and regional value chains to be nested within the important dimensions of large firms' business models (e.g. global organizational structures, business relationships).

As discussed by Nagy and Jámbor (2018), the organization and the geography of automobile production have suffered considerable changes in the last decades. In this direction, issues such as the introduction of modular production, the contraction in the number of direct suppliers, and the organization of production networks in a macro-regional scale would appear as the most important tendencies in this period (Pavlínek, 2015). Before that, distinct regions were associated with different competitive potentials, with automotive manufacturers and their suppliers typically clustered in industrial cities (e.g. Detroit), which, beyond concentrating a strong local base of specialized suppliers (Krugman & Venables, 1993; Sturgeon et al., 2008), were attractive due to its geographic proximity to consumer markets. Currently, Nagy and Jámbor (2018) propose a division of the industry in five macro geographic regions: Europe (excluding Russia); North America; Japan and South Korea; the BRICs (Brazil, Russia, India, and China); and the rest of the world.

5.3 Car Culture and Society

For McShane (2017, p. 11), the modern automobile cannot be seen as a sheer machine. Instead, it must be discussed as an important factor in what the author calls a "social revolution". At the simplest level, this revolution would be geographic, as the shape of metropolitan areas changed dramatically while they seek to incorporate cars. In that way, complex social phenomena such as the development of suburbs (i.e.

suburbanization), the appearance of cities without centers, as well as an important portion of populational migration in the twentieth century would be products of this conjecture. Still after the author, the car holds functions that go beyond its initial purposes, standing as a powerful cultural symbol and an expression of wealth and status.

In line with this view, Sheth et al. (1991) propose that consumers' choice behavior is influenced by five distinct forms of value: functional, social, emotional, epistemic, and conditional. The functional value of a product or service would be linked to its perceived utility, referring to its capacity to perform functionally, utilitarianly, or physically. Based on the Economic Utility Theory (Marshall, 1890; Stigler, 1950)—which is popularly associated with the notion of an ideal "rational economic man"—the concept of functional value shall be derived from the characteristics and attributes of an alternative (Ferber, 1973), including its reliability, durability, and price. When it comes to the purchase of a car, for example, that may translate into decision-making based on fuel consumption and maintenance record (Sheth et al., 1991). Other characteristics of the vehicle such as the number of passengers it can take, its load capacity (weight and volume), and its ability to cross different types of terrain (e.g. off-road vehicles) shall be also included in this category.

In turn, the idea of social value derives from its association with one or more specific social groups. In that way, positive or negative social value would be linked to the way these groups are perceived, with demographic stereotypes, socioeconomic characteristics, and their cultural-ethnic aspects being important in this direction (Sheth et al., 1991). Accordingly, consumers' decisions involving highly visible products (e.g. clothes, jewelry), as well as goods and services that are shared with others (e.g. gifts), would be commonly driven by their social worth. It seems that the purchasing or consumption decisions based on social value are embedded in buyers' expectation to influence the way they are perceived by observers, absorbing, at least partially, the status of the product or service in question. This type of value transmission from one element to another (i.e. from an alternative to the consumer) may be seen as a type of spillover. While it may be difficult to measure the extent to which someone absorbs the value of a product, it seems that consumers' decisions in some cases are indeed driven by that pursuit. Within this view, the possession of a car would work as driver of diverse social labels.

Emotional value refers to the feelings and affective states that are associated with an alternative (Sheth et al., 1991). Accordingly, some consumers are said to have "love affairs" with their cars, what denotes the extent to which relationships between consumers and products may be complex. Likewise, epistemic value would be associated with an alternative's capacity to trigger curiosity, to provide novelty, and to satisfy the desire for knowledge. In this sense, it may be understood as the power of a product or service to call the attention of observers, eventually making them more willing to interact with their owner. That function seems to be very well performed by sports cars which, in addition to be noisy, are generally painted in very striking colors such as red and yellow. Finally, conditional value is linked to the set of circumstances or specific situations which the choice makers may be facing upon their purchasing decisions.

Along with these functions, cars also offer a sense of security, serving as a kind of "turtle shell". The feeling of being wrapped in an exoskeleton or in a metal armor gives drivers a sense of protection and distance from the reactions that are typical of the outside world. While this feeling may contribute to the well-being of car users, it can also give rise to aggressive behaviors, as the perception of being oblivious to an eventual retaliation shall favor harmful attitudes toward other drivers, cyclists, and pedestrians. The notion of security can also be applied from the point of view of the certainty that a means of transport will be readily available in the event of an emergency or unforeseen need.

It is also necessary to differentiate the relevance of the car in urban and rural areas. While large cities tend to offer a range of transport alternatives for their citizens (e.g. buses, subways, cycle paths, taxis, and Über), rural areas are generally poorly served in this regard. The lack of alternatives usually leads to a greater appreciation of cars in these regions, with the benefits discussed earlier being even more relished. In these cases, more than a symbol of status or personal worth (i.e. social and emotional value), the car functions as a tool that allows people to move around (i.e. functional value), and, at the limit, to integrate themselves into society. In more isolated areas such as farms, for example, the automobile may be the only means of access to local commerce, hospitals, schools, and churches, working as an important mechanism of social conjunction. The complex relationship between car use, its importance to people living outside urban centers, and environmental issues can lead to major social upheavals. This seems to be the case with the movement that became popularly known as yellow vests (*gilets jaune*) in France.

Broadly, the automobile may be said to have played a crucial role in social organization, having in many cases taken a leading role in the definition of public policies. Indeed, a large part of collective life in the twentieth century was, to a greater or lesser extent, organized around the automobile and its industry. The opening of roads, for instance, was a critical step in the integration processes of several countries, especially those that have larger territorial dimensions. Likewise, projects in this regard have often been used as ways to encourage economic activity. In the period after the 1929 crisis, for instance, the policies implemented by then-American President Franklin Delano Roosevelt (1882–1945) were based on large public works, in which the State acted as the main economic agent (Kennedy, 2009). Given the gravity of the crisis and the extremely fragile financial situation of private players (e.g. investors, entrepreneurs, companies), the government would assume the lead in the economic recovery. In this context, it represented an opportunity to employ large masses of workers that the private sector could not absorb at that time (Fishback, 2016). Along with the greater integration between different locations and the economic benefits of these connections, this process resulted in an even greater appreciation for the automobile in the United States, a legacy that persists to the present day.

In addition to contributing to the dissemination of the cult of automobiles, American roads were also important in determining some of the most striking characteristics of the cars sold in the country. In this sense, the generally long and straight roads seem to have favored the production of cars with powerful engines, with the performance measure being linked to acceleration and final speed. In Europe, on the other hand, the winding and curvy roads would have encouraged the development of automobiles more adapted to these environments, which usually translated into lower engine power, but in a more adjusted balance, allowing them to develop higher cornering speeds. The different characteristics of the roads would therefore be a fundamental factor in the development of distinctive automobile cultures that still remain separate. In fact, these different concepts are still manifested in sports competitions. While the typically European modalities (e.g. Formula 1, rallies) favor mixed circuits (i.e. courses that contain different lines and curves that vary both in length and speed), American auto races (e.g. Formula Indy, NASCAR) tend to happen in oval circuits (i.e. tracks in shapes closer to a circle). It is possible that the different conceptions of automobiles explain the difficulty of American automakers in entering the European market, in the same way that European companies have had a historic difficulty to satisfy American consumers. As discussed in more detail in Chap. 6 ahead, these issues can be understood as an additional factor in favoring the environmental fraud perpetrated by Volkswagen in the United States.

The opening of roads and the consequent strengthening of the automobile culture also contributed decisively to social formations in other countries. Among them, Brazil is possibly the one that has its recent economic history more linked to the development of an industrial park dedicated to the production of cars. In an effort to industrialize the country, economic incentives were given to companies such as Volkswagen, Ford, and General Motors to enter the Brazilian market (Faillace Junior & Rego, 2014). In this sense, opening roads has been configured as a necessary condition for a car consumer market to consolidate. In addition to creating the conditions for the implantation of the automobile industry, these initiatives allowed for several economic regions of the country to connect, collaborating enormously for the economic development in the regional scope. Industrialization processes supported by the automobile industry also took place in other Latin American countries such as Argentina (Mattei & dos Santos Júnior, 2009) and Mexico (Baranson, 1969). The choice of governments to support the implementation of automobile production is probably due to the fact that it demands the development of a number of other industries. In fact, the complexity of an automobile requires the combination of a series of parts in each of its different systems. Thus, the creation of companies specializing in suspension parts, engines, electrical parts, glass, multimedia, and tires, among others, is necessary. Likewise, the use of different materials leverages the development of industries as diverse as plastics, rubbers, and metallurgy.

In this sense, the automobile industry can be understood as a locomotive that stimulates the growth of several other economic activities.

It is also possible to point to the development of the energy industry, with the creation of oil refineries being one of the main activities in this direction. In Brazilian case more specifically, the large number of automobiles combined with the global energy crises that resulted from the 1970s oil shocks enabled the development of alternative fuels such as ethanol. This topic is covered in more detail in Chap. 11. In addition to the creation of an industrial park that can generate a large amount of jobs, the auto industry ends up playing an important role in other economic aspects. The set of these impacts and the relevance of the auto industry as a whole may explain the car's resistance to the great volume of criticism and accusations that it has been facing in the last decades.

5.4 A Harsh Competition

Regarding the dynamics of the business, it may be said that the characteristics of the automotive industry make it a relatively hostile environment for firms. Beyond the difficulties in meeting the growing social and environmental demands, companies see their operational margins being progressively diminished, leading them to a constant and seemingly endless search for cost reduction. Along with continual decrease in the quality of products—especially on what relates to the materials used in modern cars—this often translates into an aggressive and non-collaborative relationship with supply chain partners, as well as in the practice of discounts of policies and promotions. Despite occasionally offering immediate relief in terms of sales volume, these practices end up pressuring financial margins. The combination of these factors seems to contribute to the creation of a scenario in which the search for illicit advantages can appear as an alternative in the eyes of unscrupulous business leaders. In this sense, a brief discussion on the aspects that influence the dynamics of the industry may be helpful.

In that direction, Nagy and Jámbor (2018) highlight three different levels of competitiveness. Accordingly, microlevel competitiveness is that on the firm level and is linked to a company's ability to make its outcome—either services or products—preferable in relation to those of its competitors (Wijnands et al., 2008). Meso-level competitiveness, in turn, extends the idea to a regional range, expressing regions' and cities' ability to compete among them (Kitson et al., 2004). Finally, macro-level competitiveness refers to the extent to which a national economy is capable of ensuring the continuous growth of its citizens' welfare, as well as the sustainable growth of its productivity. That would be met through the changing of social norms and the maintenance of an appropriate environment for companies and other institutions to create, use, and sell goods and services that meet the standards of global competition (Chikán, 2008).

In the case of the automotive industry, these three levels seem to merge more acutely than in other contexts. In fact, many of the companies that today compete on a global level started their activities facing regional rivals, with this situation persisting in many cases. The low degree of differentiation and the consequent cost-based competition seems to be the most determining factor in this direction. On that regard, Nagy and Jámbor (2018) argue that the maintenance of low production costs in the automotive industry depends on the reach of economies of scale. As discussed by the authors, that would be at the origin of policies adopted by underdeveloped countries, which, through import barriers, try to protect their industry. Likewise, state-initiated development programs would also be common, with these initiatives partially explaining the establishment of both the Japanese and the South Korean automotive industries.

Still on the extended impacts of cost-based competition, Chazan (2019) claims that in order to meet the strong investment needs, car companies have been implementing harsh cost reduction initiatives, negatively impacting the operations of upstream partners. Some of the biggest suppliers of the industry such as Continental and Shaeffler—an auto technology and auto parts suppliers, respectively—have been negatively revising production forecasts. Likewise, presses maker Schuler has announced the dismissal of employees, and Mahle—also an auto parts supplier—is closing a factory dedicated to the production of air management for combustion systems. Along with this general diagnosis, a more detailed discussion on the specific factors affecting competition in the automotive industry is necessary. In this sense, a brief analysis of the five forces that shape competitive strategy (Porter, 1979, 1980) can be useful for the identification of the main issues that make up this scenario.

5.4.1 Internal Rivalry

As anticipated, it may be said that the competitive rivalry in the industry is quite fierce, with a large number of companies disputing a relatively inelastic space. The most determining factor in that direction seems to be the low level of differentiation between the value propositions offered by carmakers. As discussed throughout the chapter, automobiles have changed little over more than a century, with technological improvements generally being the result of a slow and gradual process of incremental innovations. In this context, the search for differentiation would be largely restricted to issues such as product design, which in many cases ends up being easily replicable. In the impossibility of charging premium prices, competition would be then based on the price of products. As a result, financial returns would be constantly pressured. In that way, the search for operational efficiency (i.e. to produce faster and/or cheaper than competitors) would assume a critical role (Porter, 1996).

5.4.2 Threat of New Entrants

If, on the one hand, the auto industry is home to a large number of competitors, the fact that it depends on high-value physical assets (e.g. machines, factories, warehouses, headquarters, offices), and a relevant investment in working capital minimizes the threat that new companies will compete for this market. In this sense, the high volume of capital demanded would act as a barrier to entry which, just like a wall, keeps the competitive environment relatively stable (at least with regard to the number of competitors). As also discussed earlier, this rule is sometimes broken by new players such as Tesla. Differently from its immediate competitors, however, the company positioned itself as a producer of electric cars since its origins. Among other consequences, this may have allowed it to profit from an emerging market practically alone. In this sense, it may be argued that the company did not enter the automotive industry directly. Instead, its growth seems to be linked to the exploration of what, until then, was a very promising market niche (i.e. electric cars) that evolved to become mainstream.

5.4.3 Threat of Substitutes

Over the years, the automobile has practically not suffered competition from other products, with no alternative offering a similar value proposition. Yet, the increased restrictions on the use of cars (e.g. more strict environmental legislations, less parking slots, increased traffic) seem to have led consumers to consider other means of private transport, especially within large urban centers. In that way, products like motorcycles, bicycles, and electric scooters gained space. In addition to the possibility of these products replacing the car, new business models also present threats. This includes companies operating in the so-called sharing economy, in which the same item is used by several customers.

5.4.4 Bargaining Power of Suppliers

As discussed in more detail in Chap. 3, the idea of bargaining power is associated with the level of dependence between parties. The greater the dependence of A on B, the greater the bargaining power of B on A. The origins of this dependency can be diverse. It is possible, for example, that a supplier has a monopoly on the production of a particular input that is essential to its customers. If it is impossible or difficult to purchase a product or service from other companies, buyers will be subject to suppliers' bargaining power, which is usually exercised through the establishment of higher prices or disadvantageous payment terms. Within this view, bargaining power represents an important factor in capturing the value generated in business relations.In the specific case of the automotive industry, these questions arise in the most diverse ways, mainly according to the rarity of the product or service in question. While auto companies buy simple materials (e.g. screws, tires), they also purchase much more elaborate technologies (e.g. traction control software). In the second case, suppliers can represent an important source of pressure, contributing to greater hostility in the industry by decreasing their customers' operating margins. With the bargaining power of suppliers varying, carmakers must adapt their relationships.

5.4.5 Bargaining Power of Customers

The bargaining power of customers can be analyzed in a similar way to that of suppliers, with issues related to dependence among agents playing a fundamental role. Unlike the rarity of inputs, the volume of purchases generally exercised by a buyer seems to be one of the determining factors of its power. Companies such as Wal-Mart, for example, benefit from this issue to pressure their suppliers both for lower prices and for more favorable payment conditions. In this sense, the exercise of bargaining power allows the company to pass on its benefits to its customers, offering them products that are usually cheaper than those offered by the competition. This dynamic ensures a higher sales volume, closing a virtuous cycle with regard to the company's economic performance. In addition to purchases' volume, buyers' bargaining power also stems from their quantity (i.e. the number of players). The more buyers the less their power, with the simple existence of a greater number of alternatives to suppliers acting as an incentive to compete for inputs. Broadly, this means that a buyer's bargaining power will be inversely proportional to its degree of isolation in a given market. At the same time companies in the auto industry tend to have great bargaining power in relation to their suppliers; they also need to be concerned with the power of their consumers. In the case of individual customers (i.e. final consumer), this power is relatively small, being probably greater in the case of institutional ones (e.g. car rental companies, transportation companies).

5.5 The Automotive Industry as a Scapegoat

Blaming the use of cars for air pollution seems to be a common practice of mainstream media, academia, and international institutions. Despite the complexity of the theme and the multiple sources of pollution, the automobile industry is often considered to be largely responsible for the deterioration of natural conditions, as well as for the proliferation of various public health problems. In many cases, this translates into several attacks on the reputation of automakers, with particulate emissions such as CO_2 and NO_x being identified as the main causes of these issues. In general, it may be argued, for instance, that no other industry has been so blamed for global warming. Yet, many of the criticisms directed at the automotive industry end up being justified. In addition to the consumption of fossil fuels and the emission of pollutants, one may point out to the high demand for natural resources (e.g. iron, aluminum), the large amounts of plastic used in vehicles, the environmental liability generated by old tires that are not being recycled, and the use of oil products in the asphalt of streets and roads, among many others. More recently, the problems arising from the use of batteries in electric models have entered the list. This includes the mining processes of raw materials (e.g. lithium), the accelerated wear of parts (e.g. brakes, suspension) and asphalt due to the greater weight of these vehicles, and the high polluting potential of batteries when they are disposed of in the environment.

This concentration of attacks in automakers may be convenient for companies in other industries, especially for the most polluting ones. In fact, with the attention of the media and the population focused on the debate on emissions, other forms of pollution remain largely unnoticed. This seems to be the case for considerable environmental damage caused by industries such as pharmaceuticals, food, and fashion, among many others. Likewise, the environmental aspects related to planting, harvesting, transport, storage, and distribution of food would be treated only marginally. This includes the use of pesticides and fertilizers, the development of genetically modified seeds, the consumption of fossil fuels, the use of large amounts of aluminum, cardboard, and plastic in packaging. With regard to the fashion industry, the environmental impacts arising from the cultivation of cotton (e.g. use of considerable amounts of water) do not seem to receive due attention, as well as the impacts of plastic fibers on clothing (e.g. polyester). Likewise, the environmental damage that comes from transporting raw materials and finished products over long distances is, in general, neglected. It cannot be said, however, that players from other activities consciously encourage this situation. Nevertheless, it is possible that the attacks on the automobile industry are, at least in part, directed and motivated by values less noble than the concern with environmental preservation. In this sense, carmakers would be an ideal scapegoat, concentrating not only their own sins but also those of a number of other industries.

It is also possible that the familiarity that consumers have with companies in the automotive sector leads media companies (e.g. televisions, radios, newspapers, magazines) to give greater prominence to the issues surrounding them. Just as celebrity-related news often draws the public's attention—however banal they may be—the fact that people know and identify with companies can serve as a stimulus for them to be placed at the center of debates. In this sense, the corporate scandals involving these firms would be very useful in creating headlines. A third possible reason behind the focus on the automotive industry concerns deep ideological issues, especially those related to the conflict between collectivism and individualism. As discussed in other contexts throughout the book, the car represents an expression of freedom, offering its owner the possibility to move according to their will, at any time, and in any direction. Owning a car, therefore, represents a kind of emancipation of the individual, greatly diminishing his dependence on public transport. If, from the individual freedoms' point of view, this movement is welcome and virtuous, then from the collectivist perspective it may come to be understood as a threat to social cohesion. In fact, a free individual escapes state control. It is natural to imagine, for example, that a socialist/communist dictatorship prefers its citizens to travel in trains or buses.

Still within the ideological question, it is possible that the automobile is attacked for its potential for social differentiation. As an important symbol of economic status, car ownership would reinforce mechanisms of inequality, leading those with a more left-wing worldview to be naturally inclined to a more critical eye. In this sense, bicycles would be more symbolic of an alleged equality between people, which may explain the large investments in the modification of world metropolises to accommodate long cycle paths during the terms of socialist, communist, social democrats, and left-wings mayors in general (e.g. São Paulo, Paris). It is possible to imagine that, in these and in other cases, noble purposes such as the reduction of pollutant emissions have served as a pretext for the advancement of an obscure agenda that, in the last case, aims at population control through the elimination of cars. Thus, little by little, the streets of large cities are becoming an inhospitable environment for the use of cars, with a series of restorations making their use practically impossible. In addition to transforming streets and avenues into cycle paths, this includes drastically decreasing traffic speed limits, imposing high fines for infractions with low offensive potential, the lack of maintenance of the infrastructure dedicated to cars, and the high prices of parking, even on public roads. Along with these measures, the high taxes on the purchase and use of cars, as well as fuel, make the financial burden of their owners even heavier. In some cases, high taxes are accompanied by subsidies for public transport that may even include exemption from payment for certain segments of society.

In a way, these mechanisms of taxing those who own cars (generally the middle class), and the relaxation of costs for more popular strata can be understood as a slow and gradual distribution of income, which contributes to the perspective that the war on automobiles has in fact a markedly ideological bias disguised as environmentalism. As an added benefit for politicians who adopt these strategies, populist income distribution policies such as those discussed here tend to pay important political dividends, often leading to electoral success. The efficiency of these strategies contributes to their maintenance, which makes the lives of both car owners and manufacturers increasingly difficult.

References

Audi Hungaria. (2020). *Engine Production*. https://audi.hu/en/profile/engine-production/

Automotive News. (2020). *Automotive News Data Center*. https://www.autonews.com/section/data-center

Baranson, J. (1969). Uma indústria automobilística integrada para a América Latina. *Finanças & Desenvolvimento*, pp. 58–66.

Britannica. (2020). *PSA Group*. https://www.britannica.com/topic/PSA-Peugeot-Citroen-SA

Chazan, G. (2019, August 1). Car Industry Woes Weight on Germany's Prospects. *Financial Times*. https://www.ft.com/content/0e477fae-b383-11e9-8cb2-799a3a8cf37b

Cheney, P. (2015, November 5). The Rise of Japan: How the Car Industry Was Won. *The Globe and Mail*. https://www.theglobeandmail.com/globe-drive/adventure/red-line/the-rise-of-japan-how-the-car-industry-was-won/article27100187/

Chikán, A. (2008). National and Firm Competitiveness: A General Research Model. *Competitiveness Review: An International Business Journal, 18*(1–2), 20–28. https://doi.org/10.1108/10595420810874583

Cooney, S., & Yacobucci, B. D. (2007). *US Automotive Industry: Policy Overview and Recent History*. Nova Science Publishers.

Dicken, P. (2005). *Tangled Webs: Transnational Production Networks and Regional Integration*. SPACES 2005-04. Phillips-University of Marburg.

Dicken, P. (2007). *Global Shift: Reshaping the Global Economic Map in the 21st Century* (5th ed.). Sage Publications.

Dietsche, K. H., & Kuhlgatz, D. (2014). History of the Automobile. In K. Reif (Ed.), *Fundamentals of Automotive and Engine Technology*. Springer.

Faillace Junior, J. E. M., & Rego, M. L. (2014). *A implantação da indústria automotiva no brasil sob a ótica do gerenciamento de projetos*. II Simpósio Internacional de Gestão de Projetos (II Singep) / Simposio Internacional de Inovação e Sustentabilidade (I S2IS).

Ferber, R. (1973). Consumer Economics, a Survey. *Journal of Economic Literature, 11*(4), 1303–1342.

Fishback, P. V. (2016). New Deal. In G. Jones (Ed.), *Banking Crises* (pp. 241–250). Palgrave Macmillan.

France 24. (2020). *Macron Announces Plan to Rescue French Auto Industry*. https://www.france24.com/en/20200526-macron-announces-plan-to-rescue-french-auto-industry

Honda. (2020). The *Honda Time Machine*. https://www.honda.com/history

Jürgens, U., & Krzywdzinski, M. (2009). Changing East–West Division of Labour in the European Automotive Industry. *European Urban and Regional Studies, 16*(1), 27–42. https://doi.org/10.1177/0969776408098931

Kennedy, D. M. (2009). What the New Deal Did. *Political Science Quarterly, 124*(2), 251–268.
Kitson, M., Martin, R., & Tyler, P. (2004). Regional Competitiveness: An Elusive Yet Key Concept? *Regional Studies, 38*(9), 991–999. https://doi.org/10.1080/0034340042000320816
Krugman, P., & Venables, A. (1993). Integration, Specialization and Adjustment. *National Bureau of Economic Research*. Working paper #4559. pp. 1–32.
Lama, K. (2018, January 14). Taylor et Fayol, toujours d'actualité? *Contrepoints*. https://www.contrepoints.org/2018/01/14/307252-taylor-fayol-toujours-dactualite
Lung, Y., Van Tulder, R., & Carillo, J. (Eds.). (2004). *Cars, Carriers of Regionalism?* Palgrave Macmillan.
Marshall, A. (1890). *Principles of Economics*. London: Macmillan.
Mattei, L., & dos Santos Júnior, J. A. (2009). Industrialização e substituição de importações no Brasil e na Argentina: uma análise histórica comparada. *Revista de Economia, 35*(1), 93–115.
McShane, C. (2017). *The Automobile: A Chronology of Its Antecedents, Development, and Impact* (Vol. 6). Taylor & Francis.
Nagy, J., & Jámbor, Z. (2018). Competitiveness in Global Trade: The case of the automobile industry. *Economic Annals, 63*(218), 61–84.
Patterson, R. W. (2013, July 1). What's Good for America...'. *National Review*. https://www.nationalreview.com/2013/07/whats-good-america-robert-w-patterson/
Pavlínek, P. (2015). Foreign Direct Investment and the Development of the Automotive Industry in Central and Eastern Europe. In B. Galgóczi, J. Drahokoupil, & M. Bernaciak (Eds.), *Foreign Investment in Eastern and Southern Europe After 2008. Still a Lever of Growth?* (pp. 209–255). ETUI.
Pondé, L. F. C. S. (2016). *A arte de refletir. Luiz Felipe Pondé conversa com Beny Schmidt*. https://www.youtube.com/watch?v=dQe8vWXADk8
Porter, M. E. (1979, March–April). How Competitive Forces Shape Strategy. *Harvard Business Review*. pp. 137–145.
Porter, M. E. (1980). *Competitive Strategy: Techniques for Analyzing Industries and Competitors*. Free Press.
Porter, M. E. (1996). What Is Strategy? *Harvard Business Review, 74*(6), 61–78.
RFI. (2020). *French Government Confirms 5 Billion Euro Loan for Renault, with Conditions*. https://www.rfi.fr/en/business/20200604-french-government-confirms-5-billion-euro-loan-for-renault-conditions-economy-business-car-industry-coronavirus

Sheth, J. N., Newman, B. I., & Gross, B. L. (1991). Why We Buy What We Buy: A Theory of Consumption Values. *Journal of Business Research, 22*(2), 159–170.

Stigler, G. J. (1950). The Development of Utility Theory. *Journal of Political Economy, 58*(4), 307–327–373–396.

Sturgeon, T., Van Biesebroeck, J., & Gereffi, G. (2008). Value Chains, Networks and Clusters: Reframing the Global Automotive Industry. *Journal of Economic Geography, 8*(3), 297–321.

The Henry Ford. (2020). *Advertisement for General Motors, 'A Car for Every Purse and Purpose', 1925*. https://www.thehenryford.org/collections-and-research/digital-collections/artifact/192114/

Toyota. (2018). *Toyota Motor Corporation Founder Kiichiro Toyoda Inducted into Automotive Hall of Fame*. https://global.toyota/en/newsroom/corporate/23493360.html

Toyota. (2020). *Our European Journey*. https://www.toyota-europe.com/world-of-toyota/feel/operations

Wijnands, J. H. M., Bremmers, H. J., Van Der Meulen, B. M. J., & Poppe, K. J. (2008). An Economic and Legal Assessment of the EU Food Industry's Competitiveness. *Agribusiness, Vol. 24, 4*, 417–439. https://doi.org/10.1002/agr.20167

Ziegler, J., Bender, P., Schreiber, M., Lategahn, H., Strauss, T., Stiller, C., Dang, T., Franke, U., Appenrodt, N., Keller, C. G., & Kaus, E. (2014). Making Bertha Drive—An Autonomous Journey on a Historic Route. *IEEE Intelligent Transportation Systems Magazine, 6*(2), 8–20.

6

Dieselgates: VW, FCA, Renault, and PSA

6.1 The Volkswagen Dieselgate

Considered one "of the most outrageous white-collar crimes and corporate scandals of recent times" (Kottasova, 2015), the case known as the Volkswagen Dieselgate is the finest example of environmental fraud ever reported. Incorporating numerous elements that allow situations, events, and corporate practices to be classified as such, the fraud perpetrated by the German company aggregates several aspects of corporate criminology (e.g. misinformation, the cover-up of negative environmental impacts), taking the deceptive search for profits, power, and privileged competitive positions to a new level. In addition to the technical issues related to the case, it comprises a series of unethical matters, ranging from the deliberately dishonest approach adopted by Volkswagen, to its negligence regarding the impact of its illicit practices for the environment and for public health. In this sense, it may be argued that the Volkswagen Dieselgate thoroughly illustrates the search for an *improper competitive advantage*, as the company not only betrayed the belief of its stakeholders but also took advantage of the values embedded in the *age of green*. Given the representativeness of the case for the ideas developed throughout the

M. Fracarolli Nunes, C. Lee Park, *Business Ethics and Environmental Fraud*,
https://doi.org/10.1007/978-3-030-73800-6_6

book, a more detailed discussion on the sequence of events that resulted in the Dieselgate as well as the motivations behind it becomes critical.

6.1.1 The Dieselgate in America

Through the implementation of illegal software in its vehicles, Volkswagen circumvented emission tests in the United States, making its customers believe that the pollution generated by its cars was significantly lower than it actually was. In response to the stricter U.S.' Environmental Protection Agency (EPA) Tier 2 emission standards, the company commercialized supposedly "clean" turbocharged direct injection (TDI) diesel models in the American market (Bovens, 2016), totaling 590,000 units between the years 2009 and 2016 (EPA, 2020a). More specifically, in search to meet the NO_x emission limits established by the American government, Volkswagen developed the EA 189 engines, a special category of diesel motors which, unlike conventional models, did not use urea in its water mix (Atiyeh, 2015). Along with other improvements, the novelty was intended to decrease the damages from gas emissions. Despite the investment in the new engine, the company was unable to reach the limits imposed by the authorities.

This increased rigor in the environmental legislation proved to be a challenge to Volkswagen, as the company's strategy was largely dependent on the success of its diesel engines in the United States. By way of comparison, from mid-1990s to mid-2000s, NO_x Tier 1 emission standards applicable to diesel cars was 1.25 g/mile at 100,000 miles, while NO_x Tier 2 emission standards—to which Volkswagen Jetta was certified—was 0.07 g/mile at 120,000 miles (EPA, 2016). The use of the cheating software appeared then as an alternative, which, despite immoral, was adopted by the company. In this sense, EPA alleged that Volkswagen vehicles were "equipped with 'defeat devices' in the form of computer software designed to cheat on federal emissions tests" (EPA, 2020a). Still after the organ, "the major excess pollutant at issue in this case is oxides of nitrogen (NO_x) and is a serious health concern". After years of successful application of the illegal practice, the fraud was discovered by a group of researchers and investigators. Following the notification from local authorities and the disclosure of the case, the company's adulterous activities triggered what configured a huge corporate scandal, which, beyond costing Volkswagen billions of dollars in market values losses (La Monica, 2015) and court settlements (Shepardson, 2016), caused great damage to its reputation (Le Figaro and Agence France Press, 2019).

Along with more restrictive environmental legislation, the definition of ambitious short-term goals appears to be a determining factor in the development of the case. Volkswagen's stated objectives were indeed very challenging, and arguably detached from the harsh reality imposed on automobile manufacturers. Back in 2008, the company's main executive, Martin Winterkorn, announced its plans to become the biggest player in the global automotive industry by 2018 (Muller, 2013). As pointed out by the author, a couple of years before the scandal, however, "[…] skeptics may snicker that Winterkorn's grandiosity is delusional, especially his plan for the USA, where VW would need to triple its 2008 volume to meet his target of one million cars a year (800,000 Volkswagens and 200,000 Audis). Competitors like Toyota, Honda and Hyundai aren't about to yield; neither will the domestics."

Inserted in the competitive logic of the automobile industry discussed in the previous chapter, the search for gains of scale seemed to be among Volkswagen's strategic priorities, with the growth of its participation in the American market being key in this regard. As highlighted by Muller (2013), however, "VW had ignored the USA market for decades after stumbling badly in the 1980s and remains saddled with a reputation here for high prices, mediocre quality and a tin ear for American tastes". In an attempt to change the way it was perceived in the country, Volkswagen conducted a "large-scale promotion of diesel vehicles in the USA in 2005" (Volkswagen, 2015a).

Among the efforts made in this direction was a "Dieselution Tour to educate USA consumers and lawmakers about the advantages of clean diesel" (Bernestein, 2007). According to Volkswagen of America's CEO by the time, Stefan Jacoby, the Dieselution Tour would be a critical source of information for all those concerned about the environment, particularly on what relates to the improvement of fuel economy standards. In this sense, it would be intended to change obsolete perceptions regarding the diesel technology (Bernestein, 2007). Despite these heavy investments in the improvement of diesel's image, by 2014, Volkswagen's sales in the American market were limited to 366,970 units per year (Volkswagen, 2015b), well below the 1 MM units target for 2018.

Regardless of its relatively poor performance in terms of sales volume in the American market, the fact that Volkswagen's cars regularly passed emission tests—particularly in California—arose the curiosity, and even the mistrust, of its competitors. These included companies like General Motors, Mazda, and Honda, all of which searching to strengthen their position in the diesel segment (Kiley, 2016). Accordingly, even though there was intense scrutiny in Volkswagen cars, General Motors' engineers, for example, were unable to decipher the puzzle. On this issue, the vice chairman of the company Robert Lutz stated that "our people told me that they had studied the Volkswagen products and that they could not get the hardware to perform the same way to satisfy California's emissions standards. And I asked if their people were just smarter than ours" (Zhang, 2016). Additional investigations were then financed by the International Council on Clean Transportation (ICCT). After an extensive period of tests conducted by West Virginia University's researchers, significant differences between actual emissions and those indicated in the tests were detected. The analyses were carried out on a VW Jetta, a VW Passat, and a BMW X5, on a course of more than 1200 miles (1931 km) connecting the cities of San Diego, in California, and Seattle, in Washington (Neate, 2015b). These initial studies were confirmed by the EPA, as well as by the California Air Resource Board (CARB), contributing to the scandal (Morgan, 2015).

At first, Volkswagen questioned the results, claiming that deviations were probably due to methodological flaws. Despite taking a defensive stance, the company decided to conduct a "white recall", that is, a recall carried out spontaneously to repair a problem that poses no immediate risk to users. This process resulted in the first reassessment of nearly 500,000 cars sold in the United States (Neate, 2015a). Despite Volkswagen's efforts, the emissions enigma remained unresolved, with EPA and CARB continuing to investigate the issue. The insistence of the agencies ultimately led to the discovery of the software installed in the cars' electronic central in 2015. According to the EPA, the software administered a highly complex mechanism which was based on a series of vehicle operating data. That included the position of the wheels, the speed of the car, the duration of the process (i.e. time elapsed since the engine was ignited), and barometric pressure, among others. The analysis of these data allowed the software to identify situations that would be common to tests, so that emissions were adjusted to levels below the maximum limits allowed. Shortly after the criminal scheme's revelation, Volkswagen admitted that nearly 11 million cars around the world were equipped with the software, further announcing a recall of 8.5 million cars in Europe.

Despite gaining notoriety for the way it was applied by Volkswagen, the software was originally developed by Bosch, a German company whose history is closely linked to the development of technologies for Diesel engines. In fact, Robert Bosch—the founder of the company—himself personally worked in the enhancement of Diesel injection pumps since 1922 (Dietsche, 2014). Although responsible for the software design, the firm denied any participation in what it judged to be an inappropriate use of its product by Volkswagen. However, the charges against Bosch did not end until it agreed to pay the US $327.5 million settlement to American Justice (McGee, 2017).

Following the results of different studies, Volkswagen was criminally prosecuted by the American government, with the charges initially pointing out that 482,000 units sold in the United States between 2009 and 2015 had been illegally equipped with the software. The case included five different models: Jetta, Beetle, Golf, Passat, and Audi A3 (Hotten, 2015). As a result of these initial events, Volkswagen's CEO Martin Winterkorn presented his resignation (Farrell & Ruddick, 2015), with several other company executives being suspended. Among them were the head of brand development, Heinz-Jakob Neusser, the head of Audi's research and development, Ulrich Hackenberg, and the head of Porsche research and development Wolfgang Hatz (Chaboud, 2016). The company also announced that it intended to spend around US $7.3 billion on repairing vehicles affected by the fraud, and that it was provisioning financial resources to deal with legal proceedings conducted both in the United States and in Europe. Only in the United States, the cost of the Volkswagen Dieselgate scandal is estimated to have reached up to US $24 billion, including vehicle buybacks, compensations, and fines, among other expenses (Brunsden & McGee, 2017), along with a loss of US $6.44 billion in the American firms only (Fracarolli Nunes & Lee Park, 2016).

6.1.2 Settlements in the United States

EPA's accusations against Volkswagen were based on two main axes: (1) the use of defeat devices by the company, and (2) its authority to require manufacturers to issue recalls. Regarding the first, the EPA (2016) clarifies that Section 203 (a)(3)(b) of the Clean Air Act (CAA), 42 U.S.C. Sec. 7522(a)(3)(b) "prohibits the manufacture, selling, or installation of any device that intentionally circumvents EPA emission standards by bypassing, defeating, or rendering inoperative a required element of the vehicle's emissions control system", and that Section 203(a)(1) of the CAA "also prohibits the sale of motor vehicles or engines that are not covered by valid certificates of conformity". Around the second, under the Section 207(c)(1) of the CAA, EPA has the authority "to require a manufacturer to issue a recall when EPA determines that a substantial number of vehicles do not conform to EPA regulations". Section 203(a)(4)(B) of the CAA makes clear that it is a "prohibited act for manufacturers to fail or refuse to comply with an ordered recall by EPA". These accusations started a complex legal process in which the company sought to minimize its financial damage. After years of dispute, the cases were closed with the company basically recognizing its responsibilities by pledging to repair the damage caused by its fraudulent conduct.

Regarding the outcomes of the lawsuits in the United States, the EPA (2020b) informs that "through a series of three partial settlements, the EPA has resolved a civil enforcement case against Volkswagen AG, Audi AG, Dr. Ing. h.c. F. Porsche AG, Volkswagen Group of America, Inc., Volkswagen Group of America Chattanooga Operations, LLC, and Porsche Cars North America, Inc. (collectively 'Volkswagen')". On October 25, 2016, the United States District Court for the District of Northern California approved the first partial settlement with some of these Volkswagen entities addressing vehicles containing 2.0 liter diesel engines (known as the "2.0 liter partial settlement"). On May 17, 2017, the court approved the second partial settlement addressing vehicles containing 3.0-liter diesel engines (i.e. the "3.0 liter partial settlement"). Finally, on April 13, 2017, the court approved the third partial settlement addressing civil penalties and injunctive relief to prevent future violations (i.e. the "third partial settlement"). These settlements resolve allegations that Volkswagen violated the CAA by the sale of approximately 590,000 model year 2009 to 2016 diesel motor vehicles equipped with defeat devices. Among the obligations assumed by the company in the first partial settlement is the interruption of marketing of 2.0 engines affected by the fraud by June 2019, in the United States. Alternatively, the company could carry out approved emissions modifications on at least 85% of these engines, with the same criteria applying in a separate California recall. In case the company fails to achieve these goals, it must pay additional funds into the mitigation trust in the amount of US $85 million for each percentage point below the national recall target and US $13.5 million for each point below California recall target.

Still, in the pursuit of these recall rates, Volkswagen should offer vehicle owners and lessees the opportunity to sell their cars to the company at a fair price that refers to the day immediately preceding the disclosure of the scandal (i.e. as of September 17, 2015), or to have their lease terminated with no additional cost. Both options should be available for consumers for the period of two years. The company is not authorized to export these vehicles before making the appropriate emission modifications, and in case it fails to properly fix them, they must be recycled or scrapped. If the company chooses to offer a modification to the vehicles so that they reach the emission levels authorized by the EPA and CARB, it must offer this option to the owners.

Following a determination by the Federal Trade Commission (FTC), Volkswagen has agreed to pay eligible consumers compensation for any damages related to the sale and marketing of the defrauded 2.0 liter vehicles. According to the company's estimates, the cost of reaching the recall rates stipulated by the CAA 2.0 partial settlement and the concurrent meeting of the FTC order is US $10.033 billion. In addition, under the CAA 2.0 partial settlement, the company was required to create a US $2.7 billion mitigation trust fund, as well as to invest US $2 billion in Zero Emission Vehicle (ZEV) charging infrastructure, as well as in the promotion of the technology. This value would be intended to partially correct the damage caused by the fraud. In this sense, the EPA (2020b) argues that "the ZEV investments required by the CAA 2.0 liter partial settlement are intended to address the fact that consumers purchased these illegal vehicles under the mistaken belief that such vehicles were lower-emitting than others". In order to meet these requirements, Electrify America, LLC, was created by the Volkswagen group.

Likewise, under the CAA 3.0 partial settlement, Volkswagen compromised to withdraw from the American market "or perform an approved emissions modification on at least 85 percent of the affected 3.0 liter vehicles", in addition to meet a separate recall rate of 85% in the state of California. Similar to the first partial settlement, the company agreed to pay additional funds in case it fails to reach the recall levels stipulated. These extra fines vary depending on the technology generation of the vehicles; for generation 1 cars, Volkswagen must pay US $5.5 million for each percentage point it fails to reach regarding the national recall target, and US $900,000 in the case of the California recall target. In turn, for generation 2 cars, the values account for US $21 million and US $5.5 million, respectively. FTC sanctions regarding consumers' compensations also apply, as well as the possibilities that Volkswagen has to offer its customers in terms of buyback in the case of car owners, or the termination of leasing operations at no additional costs. The company was also required to create a US $225 million mitigation trust fund. Unlike the first partial settlement, however, the CAA 3.0-liter partial settlement did not include any additional requirement regarding ZEV investments.

Finally, for the third partial settlement, Volkswagen agreed to pay a US $1.45 billion civil penalty. Furthermore, the company must ensure that the personnel engaged in the testing of its vehicles are separate from those who design them, as a measure to avoid similar issues in the future. In line with these measures, Volkswagen must also establish a steering committee with the aim of assuring compliance with the Clean Air Act. The company must also perform Portable Emission Measurement Systems (PEMS) on its cars—including gasoline ones—as well as follow strict procedures upon the development of new models. Volkswagen must also establish a whistle-blower system, and monitor its employees to safeguard compliance with American environmental laws. Lastly, under the third partial settlement, Volkswagen agrees to be thoroughly assessed by an independent auditor.

6.1.3 The Dieselgate in Europe

Following the eruption of the scandal in the United States, the European Anti-Fraud Office (*Office Européen de Lutte Antifraude*, OLAF) initiated an investigation into a loan made by the European Investment Bank (EIB) to Volkswagen (ECA, 2019). Accordingly, despite arguably intended to push the development of fuel-efficient and environmentally friendly engine components, allegations were made that the loan also encompassed the development of the defeat devices used by Volkswagen on its scope. As pointed out by the EIB (2019, p. 1) itself,

> On 19 November 2015, OLAF opened an investigation regarding alleged misuse of EIB loans by Volkswagen AG for the development and/or implementation and/or purchase of devices aiming at deceiving the regulatory bodies on the real level of gas emissions of vehicles and automotive components manufactured by Volkswagen AG; and alleged misrepresentations created by representatives of Volkswagen AG in order to obtain these EIB loans.

Still after EIB, the "VW Antrieb RDI" project, which comprehended research and development activities held by Volkswagen in the drive train areas (i.e. engine and transmission), was granted by the bank with a EUR 400 million loan in February 2009, based on 12 sub-projects (e.g. automotive lightweight construction, double-clutch gears, onboard diagnostic concepts, new technologies to improve fuel efficiency with the reduction of CO_2, NO_x, and other particles emissions for both diesel and petrol engines). From these 12 sub-projects, one—the "Dieselmotoren nach EUV und ULEV standards"—was found to be related to the technology used in the EA 189 engines. Upon the approval process of the transaction, in October 2008 EIB requested Volkswagen to provide relevant information concerning the environmental impact of the sub-project, as well as the pertinent circumstances and risks believed to possibly influence the operational results of the project, such as changes of environmental regulation or in the company's research and development strategy.

In that way, OLAF established that, at the moment the EIB loan was disbursed, Volkswagen was aware of the serious difficulties of the EA 189 engines to meet emission standards and that a defeat device was being used to overcome these complications in a fraudulent manner. Yet, the investigation also established that Volkswagen did not inform EIB about these situations, with both the difficulties and the use of the defeat devise not being found in the information provided by the company. That would have hold true for the entire duration of the loan, from February 24, 2009, to February 24, 2014, facts that were not contested by Volkswagen in response to OLAF's invitation to comment on the issue, having the company, however, denied to have committed a criminal offense or acted against the financial interests of the European Union (E.U.).

In conclusion, OLAF claimed that Volkswagen also deceived the EIB by omitting these pertinent facts in order to obtain and maintain the loan. The behavior of the company characterizes then a prohibited conduct. OLAF recommends that, on its actions toward Volkswagen, EIB also takes into consideration "the possible financial advantage VW benefitted from, by obtaining the loan at an advantageous interest rate compared to the market conditions applicable at the time of the conclusion of the finance contract" EIB (2019, p. 3). As previously discussed, the advantage obtained in a dishonest manner also composes what is here called *improper competitive advantage*, which, in this case, seems to have been reached by a classic case of "environmental fraud". Despite not a sustainable competitive advantage, as it does not represent a strategic resource or does not lead to a unique and differentiated position, the access to more advantageous loan rates increases the return rates of the company in the short and middle term.

Yet, at the same time, Volkswagen admitted to have installed deceive devices in diesel vehicles in the United States, the company maintained that it broke no European Union law, ruling out paying compensations to its European consumers upon the scandal (Brunsden & McGee, 2017). On that matter, in a letter addressed to the chair of the transport committee of the United Kingdom Parliament House of Commons, Ms. Lilian Greenwood, in June 2017, Mr. Paul Willis—Managing Director of the Volkswagen Group United Kingdom Limited at the time—affirms the understanding of the company. In his words:

> I can confirm that it remains our Group position that there is no basis for compensation within the European Union arising out of the issue. The situation regarding the issue is materially different in the US compared to the situation in Europe. (…) We do not consider that our customers have suffered any loss as a result of the issue. (United Kingdom Parliament, 2017)

During months of pressure and discussion with Volkswagen, members of the European Commission expressed their frustration for not getting the company to pay cash compensation to its European customers, with only a two-year extended warranty being offered instead (Reuters, 2017a). Within what was labeled by Volkswagen the "Trust Building Measure", that would refer to the consideration of "any complaints that are established to have arisen as a result of the implementation of the technical measure on vehicles with EA189 diesel engines and that relate to certain parts of the engine and exhaust treatment system" (United Kingdom Parliament, 2017). As specified by Mr. Paul Willis in the same document, "the Trust Building Measure applies for a period of 24 months from when the vehicle receives the technical measure and only to vehicles with mileage under 160,000 miles at the time the Trust Building Measure is implemented (whichever comes first)".

Despite not directly expressed, the mentioned "technical measure" would refer to the actions expected to be taken within the recall program imposed on the company, among which the update of the software controlling the exhaust system of the vehicles affected by the scandal (ECA, 2019). The initiative was also adopted by other companies within the Volkswagen Group. As stated by Audi, for example,

> With the Trust Building Measure, Audi is sending a clear signal that the update has no negative effects on vehicle durability. This measure should serve to strengthen customer confidence in the technical measure and should encourage more customers to have their cars updated. (Audi, 2020)

The application of the Trust Building Measure to all Volkswagen, Volkswagen Commercial Vehicles, Audi (2020), Škoda (2020), and Seat (2020) models equipped with EA 189 type diesel engines has a worldwide reach, with the exception of the United States, Canada, and South-Korea, countries which are subject to different regulations (Audi, 2020).

6.1.4 General Outcomes of the Dieselgate

As expected for a case of such magnitude, the Dieselgate received considerable attention from the media, with the case yielding a negative exposure for Volkswagen. By the time, traditional vehicles like Reuters, for example, claimed that, in addition to the damage to the company or the auto industry, the discovery of the fraud posed a major threat to the entire German economy (Reuters, 2017b). Likewise, Deutsche Welle (2015) pointed out to the "tsunami lawsuit" that Volkswagen would have to face, as well as to the harsh consequences that the case could have on German's psyche. Accordingly, the scandal represented a serious threat to the value of the "Made in Germany" brand. Popular Mechanics magazine, in turn, classified the case as the worst recall ever in the auto industry, since Volkswagen had been clearly dishonest (Dyer, 2015). Likewise, countless television shows approaching the issue were broadcasted, as well as a considerable number of videos accessible on platforms such as YouTube, Daily Motion, or Vimeo. To further compound the company's problems, Dieselgate has received a lot of attention from social media (e.g. Facebook, Twitter), with consumers openly discussing the firm's dishonesty. That includes a range of memes that still circulate, constantly reviving stakeholders' memory about the crimes committed by the company.

The fraud perpetrated by Volkswagen is configured as a typical case of corporate hypocrisy, representing a damage to the trust of several groups with which the company exchanges. The fact that it admitted dishonest behavior puts in doubt all of its corporate communication, which includes not only messages addressed to consumers through advertising but also the more technical aspects related to reliability, security, and performance of its automobiles. Likewise, the fraud can raise questions about the company's entire strategy, especially with regard to its management of environmental aspects. Indeed, the scandal may make it difficult for Volkswagen to convince its public that, despite having incurred a major environmental fraud, Volkswagen has a sincere appreciation for environmental preservation. Among other consequences, this can mean the total loss of credibility of the diverse forms of institutional communication routinely used by the company, such as its sustainability reports, for example.

Interestingly, Volkswagen's fraud did not cause a significant impact on sales of diesel-powered vehicles in the American market. In April 2017—15 months after the scandal—the company resumed the commercialization of diesel-powered cars, which accounted for 12% of its sales in that month (Shepardson, 2017). Yet, within a broader perspective, the scandal may have caused a serious damage to diesel's reputation, possibly condemning its use in light vehicles to its disappearance in the short future. On that regard, Frost and Guillaume (2016) stress that Volkswagen's fraud led Renault's executives to expect diesel engines to disappear from the majority of European models commercialized by the company. Accordingly, the tighter emission standards established after the case would make the production of certain diesel motors economically inviable. Coherently with this view, media channels such as The Economist (2016) argued that "the damage done by Volkswagen's cynical and ethically challenged behavior could well prove fatal to the future of the diesel technology in the USA". Likewise, VW of America's Chief Executive, Mr. Hinrich Woebcken, confirmed that the company had no plans to bring in new diesel models in the United States, focusing instead, on offering extra electric vehicles and Sport Utility Vehicles (SUVs) (Shepardson, 2017). The specific impact of Dieselgate on the future of the diesel technology is further discussed in Chap. 11 ahead.

Still on the consequences of the case, Hachenberg et al. (2018) point out the impacts of the Dieselgate on Volkswagen's leasing operations, with the company executing an extraordinary EUR 353 million (US $391 million) write-down to cover a possible decline in the residual value of the vehicles composing its leasing portfolio (Reuters, 2016). Accordingly, that would be necessary as the admission that Volkswagen cheated on emission tests had severe consequences on the resale value of its cars, pushing VW financial services to promote the adjustment. On that regard, Hachenberg et al. (2018) argue that consumers were hit by the scandal both in terms of their exposition to further restrictions on diesel vehicles in city centers (Tsang & Schuetze, 2018) and the possible capital loss from the expected decline on their cars' residual value (Isidore, 2015).

6.2 Fiat Chrysler Automobiles (FCA)

Despite defining the modern scandal over diesel engine emissions, Volkswagen was not the only company cheating on the issue (Kiley, 2019). On May 23, 2017, the United States Justice Department, on behalf of the EPA, filed a civil complaint against Fiat Chrysler Automobiles (FCA), claiming the company equipped vehicles with illegal and undisclosed software to manipulate emission control tests (EPA, 2019). Accordingly, at the same time emission control systems would be reduced or deactivated in real world driving—ultimately lessening their effectiveness—they would be fully activated upon compliance tests. Discovered by the EPA during emission tests performed at the National Vehicle and Fuel Emissions Laboratory in 2015 and 2016, the utilization of these software features in the configuration of FCA's vehicles led to the allegations that they would be defeat devices. More specifically, the complaint represents a

> civil action brought pursuant to Sections 204 and 205 of the Clean Air Act ("Act"), 42 U.S.C. §§ 7523 and 7524, and the regulations promulgated pursuant to Section 202 of the Act, 42 U.S.C. § 7521, and codified at 40 C.F.R. Part 86. (Control of Emissions from New and In-Use Highway Vehicles and Engines)

with FCA US LLC, V.M. Motori S.p.A., V.M. North America, Inc., and Fiat Chrysler Automobiles N.V. being implied in the sale of approximately 103,828 diesel-fuelled new noncompliant motor vehicles (EPA, 2017a, pp. 1–2).

As stated by The United States Department of Justice (2017), the fault would be based on the fact that, among the requirements of the CAA, is the need of manufacturers to obtain a certificate of conformity (COC) before commercialization, what demands the demonstration to EPA that the vehicles in question will meet applicable federal emission standards to control air pollution. In this sense, manufacturers must disclose all auxiliary emission control devices, including computer software capable to affect the performance of emission controls in reflex to the operating parameters of the vehicle. Also, the eventual presence of such devices must be justified, and an explanation for why those mechanisms capable to reduce the effectiveness of emission controls should not be classified as defeat devices.

As pointed out in the civil complaint, FCA's COC application for model years 2014–2016 Ram 1500 and Jeep Grand Cherokee vehicles sold in the United States between 2013 and 2016 would not have disclosed at least eight software-based features that affect emission control systems, which, individually or in combination, would bypass, defeat, and/or render the emission control systems of the vehicles inoperative (EPA, 2017a, 2017b). As a result, vehicles that meet emission standards during regulatory testing would emit air pollutants—including NO_x—at a substantially higher rate than those allowed by the EPA and California emission standards (EPA, 2019). The complaint was filed in a federal court in Detroit, Michigan, and is consistent with the allegations set forth in the notice of violation issued by the EPA to FCA US LLC and FCA NV on January 12, 2017 (The United States Department of Justice, 2017). In the document addressed to Mr. Kyle, M.H. Jones, Senior Counsel of the Environment, Health and Safety Office of the General Counsel of FCA US LLC, and to Mr. Jonathan S. Martel and Mr. Joel M. Gross from the lawyers' firm Arnold and Porter LLP (Arnold & Porter, 2020), the EPA informs that it had been investigating and should continue to investigate FCA for compliance with the CAA and its implementing regulations (EPA, 2017a, 2017b).

In January 2019, the U.S. Department of Justice, the EPA, and the State of California jointly announced a settlement with Fiat Chrysler Automobiles N.V., FCA US, and affiliates (FCA) in face of alleged violations of the CAA and California law (EPA, 2019). Accordingly, that would relate to claims of FCA's use of defeat devices, or, "design elements (in this case, software functions) installed in vehicles that reduce the effectiveness of the emission control system during normal on-road driving conditions" (EPA, 2019). In order to "settle claims of cheating emission tests and failing to disclose unlawful defeat devices" (EPA, 2019), the company agreed to pay a civil penalty of US $305 million and implement a recall program to repair over 100,000 noncompliant diesel vehicles sold or leased in the United States, comprehending model years 2014, 2015, and 2016 Ram 1500 and Jeep Grand Cherokee equipped with allegedly "EcoDiesel" 3.0-liter engines.

Beyond that, FCA compromised to offer an extended warranty on repaired cars, as well as to implement a program to mitigate excess pollution from the concerned vehicles. The joint cost of the recall and the program is expected to reach up to US $185 million. Separately, the company settled to pay additional US $19 million to California to mitigate excessive emissions from more than 13,000 of the irregular vehicles commercialized in the state. In addition, FCA and the State of California have initiated another settlement to resolve alleged violations to California consumer protections laws linked to the affected vehicles. Likewise, in an independent agreement with the United States Customs and Border Protection, the company concurred to pay a US $6 million civil penalty to end allegations around the illegal importation of 1700 noncompliant vehicles.

As stated by EPA Acting Administrator Andrew Wheeler,

> Fiat Chrysler deceived consumers and the federal government by installing defeat devices on these vehicles that undermined important clean air protections (…) the settlement sends a clear and strong signal to manufacturers and consumers that EPA will vigorously enforce the nation's laws designed to protect the environment and public health. (EPA, 2019)

Principal Deputy Associate Attorney General, Jesse Panuccio, in turn, claimed that the "Department of Justice is committed to the full and fair enforcement of the laws that protect our nation's environment. Fiat Chrysler broke those laws and this case demonstrates that steep penalties await corporations that engage in such egregious violations" (EPA, 2019).

Still after EPA (2019), the settlement does not resolve potential criminal liabilities, claims from consumers and individual owners, nor lessees those who may have asserted claims in the then-ongoing multidistrict litigation.

As discussed by Balsamo and Krisher (2019), in January 2019, FCA agreed to pay a US $300 million fine to the U.S. government to settle allegations that it defrauded emissions tests. The deal with the Justice Department and EPA provides that the company must recall and repair more than 104,000 noncompliant Jeep SUVs and Ram pickup trucks. Separately, FCA and Bosch—which supplied the emission control software used to cheat the tests—agreed to pay US $307.5 million to settle lawsuits brought by vehicle owners, with the companies accounting for US $280 million and US $27.5 million, respectively (Shepardson, 2019). Beyond that, FCA signed the payment of US $19 million to the state of California to settle similar regulatory allegations (Balsamo & Krisher, 2019). After the authors, despite FCA not admitting wrongdoing and maintaining that it did not deliberately scheme to cheat, U.S. federal officials allege that vehicles equipped with diesel engines produced between 2014 and 2016 were programmed to run pollution controls during tests, being these commands, however, turned off under certain road conditions.

In the words of Jesse Panuccio, "by concealing this software, Fiat Chrysler deceived regulators and violated environmental law" (CBS News, 2019). Following Volkswagen agreements, FCA's settlement is only the second between an automaker and the U.S. government over allegations of fraud on diesel emission tests (Balsamo & Krisher, 2019). On top of that, in February 2019, FCA and Bosch agreed to pay US $66 million in fees and costs to lawyers representing owners of U.S. diesel vehicles (US $7 million in costs and US $59 million in attorney's fees), with FCA being expected to disburse 90% of that value (Shepardson, 2019).

6.3 Renault and PSA (Opel)

In addition to the cases involving Volkswagen and FCA, the controversies surrounding the use of software in emission tests also affected two of the largest French companies in the automotive sector. In this sense, Williams (2016) points out to a French government report concluding that the NO_x emissions of some of the Renault models were 9–11 times higher than European Union limits. In respect to an order issued by the French Justice in October 2017, the Institut Supérieur de l'Automobile et des Transports (Higher Institute of Automobile and Transport, ISAT) conducted a series of complementary tests on Captur and Clio IV, two models commercialized by the company (Mandard, 2019). Following the examination, ISAT's conclusion were unequivocal, pointing out to the modification of depollution devices that allowed for adaptations to homologation procedures, in such a way that the behavior of the vehicles in these occasions was different from those observed in actual conditions of use.

Still after Mandard (2019), ISAT argued that the two depollution systems used by Renault—the valve EGR and the NO_x trap—would not be functional in certain conditions. While the former would only operate within a given range of temperatures, the latter would operate with a low frequency at commonly used speeds, beyond being inoperant below 50 km/h. More specifically, emission controls would be turned on between 17 °C (62.6° Fahrenheit) and 35 °C (95° Fahrenheit), while emission tests would be typically conducted in ambient temperatures ranging from 20 °C (68° Fahrenheit) to 30 °C (86° Fahrenheit) (Bovens, 2016). Temperature-related shutdowns, however, would be permitted by E.U. law as a way to prevent engine damage, an argument frequently used by carmakers in the justification of such cut-offs (Williams, 2016). South Korean environmental officials have also alleged that Nissan vehicles equipped with Renault motors used cheating mechanisms to fraud emission tests (Sang-Hun, 2016). Despite strongly denying any wrongdoing, in February 2017 Nissan was found guilty of using a defeat device in its SUV Qashqai, as ruled by the Seoul Administrative Court (Jin, 2017).

With regard to PSA, problems appear to have been inherited from the acquisition of the German brand Opel, which in October 2018 was also accused by the Kraftfahrt-Bundesamt—the German federal motor transport authority—of commercializing vehicles equipped with an illegally manipulated software (Capital, 2018). Along with Vauxhall, in March 2017 PSA acquired the company from General Motors in a EUR 2.2 billion (US $2.3 billion) transaction (Frost & Taylor, 2017), positioning the French group in second place in the European Market by the time, with 17% of market share (PSA, 2017). German authorities would be investigating Opel since July 2018, after the identification of the supposedly fraudulent software in three of the brand's models (Cascada, Insignia, and Zafira), with the manipulations possibly concerning around 95,000 cars in Europe (Capital, 2018).

6.4 General Considerations

As discussed throughout the chapter, the gap between Volkswagen's messages (e.g. Dieselution tour) and the reality revealed in the scandal increases the perception that the company not only was punctually dishonest but that the development of fraudulent schemes was part of its strategy. By selling the idea that it was capable of producing a superior diesel technology—from the perspective of its environmental performance—Volkswagen created false expectations, contributing to the general disappointment of its stakeholders upon the exposure of the fraud. In addition to the sequence of events that led to this outcome, a debate around its possible reasons may be useful. In fact, the Dieselgate—as well as the other cases discussed above (FCA, Renault, and PSA)—seems to bring together a range of different issues which, jointly, created a favorable context for the occurrence of environmental fraud.

Within this view, Treviño and Nelson (2016, p. 2) stress what seems to be a collective and contributive nature of corporate public embarrassment, particularly on what relates to wrongdoing. As argued by the authors, serious ethical scandals would often be the result of small or large contributions of multiple parties, each individually adding to the creation of a catastrophe. The responsibility of Enron's collapse in 2001, for example, would not be limited to the executives and employees of the company, but also to those responsible to audit it, to the bankers who provided financial resources, and to lawyers who never signaled Enron's dishonest activities. Regarding the Dieselgate, a similar analysis may be developed, as, even though Volkswagen is to be considered the main responsible for the fraud, several other actors contributed to it, even if unintentionally. As previously pointed out, this includes the developer of the software (Bosch), financial institutions that supported the projects (e.g. European Investment Bank), and, in a broader view, the inability of the inspection bodies to detect the criminal schemes set in motion by the company. In addition to these secondary actors, the general characteristics of the context in which the fraud occurred were arguably decisive for the observed results. In this sense, one may point to the evolution of the regulatory context, the harsh competition in the automotive industry, and the company's inability to achieve its bold objectives. Adds to that the apparent moral fragility of the top executives of the company who, despite possible hesitations, end up carrying out the option for a devious competition.

In that way, the tripartite model developed in Chap. 1 may be used for a more detailed analysis of Dieselgate's moral and ethical issues. Considering the aspects related to human nature, for example, it may be argued that the decision to defraud the tests is probably linked to the managers' disproportionate ambition. In fact, the search for accelerated growth in the company's activities may be associated with short-term financial gains (e.g. bonus), but also with the search for greater social status. The pursuit of grandiose goals such as becoming the largest automaker in the world can also suggest the manifestation of some of the pathologies previously discussed. Among them, the possible narcissism of those occupying positions of command.

In addition to unreasonable ambitions, other aspects of the case reinforce this hypothesis. With the technology used in environmental analyses being constantly improved, it would be natural to assume that, sooner or later, the gap between the levels of emissions observed in the tests and those presented in the practice would be detected. Nevertheless, Volkswagen managers apparently doubted that their criminal conducts would be discovered. It is possible that this belief in impunity is due to a perception that they were intellectually superior to those whose mission was to monitor their activities, which, to some extent, is consistent with narcissism.

The very slogan used by the company for years can be understood as representing a possible belief in its superiority. As discussed in more detail in Chap. 9, the famous "Das auto" (i.e. the car) seems to seek to position the company as one that can determine the very nature of the automobile. After the Dieselgate scandal, this slogan was abandoned in what seems to be an effort by the company to reposition itself within a less arrogant attitude. The belief in impunity may also be the result of a long and progressive construction in which immoral practices have been shown to be rewarding over time. As the unethical individual realizes that s/he is not punished for their actions, s/he may develop an exaggerated confidence in their ability to deceive. To some extent, this rationale can explain the audacity of Volkswagen's managers.

Issues related to power dynamics in organizations can also offer important clues for understanding the case. As previously discussed, disputes over hierarchical positions in companies tend to be aggressive. In addition to issues more directly related to the performance of employees and their ability to assume roles of greater responsibility, political criteria often have a considerable influence on these choices. Thus, it is possible that the environmental fraud was motivated by internal disputes at the company, with the risk of losing hierarchical positions leading executives to take more risky positions, and the search for spectacular results may have been interpreted as critical for the maintenance of their positions. In this sense, the distribution of dividends would keep investors satisfied and probably make them more favorable to seal the group of executives at the head of the company. Once again, the consideration of these issues is merely speculative. For a better understanding of the real influence of these factors, a detailed empirical research would be necessary.

Although the two analyzed dimensions (i.e. human behavior and dynamics of power) are possible explanations of the fraudulent behavior adopted by Volkswagen, it is possible that the third dimension (i.e. business dynamics) is the most relevant in this direction. As discussed in the previous chapter, the automobile industry has some characteristics that may favor the search for undue advantages. Among them are the various sources of pressure suffered by carmakers, which may lead them to consider the use of illicit means (e.g. environmental fraud) as an alternative in the search for operational and financial performances.

In dealing with the dynamics of Dieselgate's decisions, the consumers reports' director of Automotive Testing, Jake Fisher, explained them within the logic of trade-offs (Watch Mojo, 2015). Accordingly, three dimensions would have to be considered when making decisions about vehicle motorization: performance, consumption, and the level of environmental pollution. Although different in their essence, these dimensions would be related in a way so that gains in one would normally require sacrifice in the other(s). Consistent with its differentiation strategy, Volkswagen would have sought to deceive its consumers by giving them the impression that its diesel technology (allegedly more advanced) was capable of delivering higher performance in all dimensions. As is now known, in reality, the German company not only sacrificed the environmental dimension but sought to mask this fact, benefiting from its dishonesty.

In this context, the environmental fraud that the company incurred can be understood as an attempt to create an illusion that the basic engine trade-off was solved, with Volkswagen being the only company that knew the formula (i.e. differentiation). This logic dialogs with the discussions in Chap. 3, particularly with the concept of *improper competitive advantage*.

References

Arnold & Porter. (2020). About the Firm. https://www.arnoldporter.com/en/about/firm

Atiyeh, C. (2015, November 25). Volkswagen Details Fix for EA189 Diesel in Europe, but It'll Be More Complex for U.S. *Car and Driver*. https://www.caranddriver.com/news/a15351089/volkswagen-details-fix-for-ea189-diesel-in-europe-but-itll-be-more-complex-for-u-s/

Audi. (2020). EA189 Service Action – Trust Building Measure. https://www.audi.co.uk/owners-area/emissions/trust-building-measure.html

Balsamo, M., & Krisher, T. (2019, January 10). Fiat Chrysler Reaches Settlement in Emissions Cheating Cases. *Associated Press*. https://apnews.com/ed2de574d9064450bf8a8e85f1d4834c

Bernestein, M. (2007, September 28). Start Your Diesels. *Bloomberg*. www.bloomberg.com/news/articles/20070928/Startyourdieselsbusinessweekbusinessnewsstockmarketandfinancialadvice

Bovens, L. (2016). The Ethics of Dieselgate. *Midwest Studies in Philosophy, 40*(1), 262–283.

Brunsden, J., & McGee, P. (2017, June 14). Volkswagen Clarifies Repair Terms for EU Diesel Owners. *Financial Times*. https://www.ft.com/content/1ba7857a-5117-11e7-bfb8-997009366969

Capital. (2018, July 14). Bild: Problèmes d'émissions chez Opel, selon la KBA. https://www.capital.fr/entreprises-marches/bild-problemes-demissions-chez-opel-selon-la-kba-1298035

CBS News. (2019, January 11). Fiat Chrysler Settles Emissions-Cheating Case with U.S. https://www.cbsnews.com/news/fiat-chrysler-settles-emissions-cheating-case-with-u-s/

Chaboud, I. (2016, September 13). Volkswagen un an après le scandale des moteurs diesel truqués: qui savait? qui a décidé? *The Conversation*. https://theconversation.com/volkswagen-un-an-apres-le-scandale-des-moteurs-diesel-truques-qui-savait-qui-a-decide-65213

Deutsche Welle. (2015, September 24). Lawsuit Tsunami Headed for Volkswagen. https://www.dw.com/en/lawsuit-tsunami-headed-for-volkswagen/a-18737417

Dietsche, K. H. (2014). History of the Diesel Engine. In K. Reif (Ed.), *Fundamentals of Automotive and Engine Technology*. Springer Vieweg.

Dyer, E. (2015, September 21). This VW Diesel Scandal Is Much Worse Than a Recall. *Popular Mechanics*. https://www.popularmechanics.com/cars/a17430/ezra-dyer-volkswagen-diesel-controversy/

ECA. (2019). The EU's Response to the "Dieselgate" Scandal. *European Court of Auditors*. https://www.eca.europa.eu/lists/ecadocuments/brp_vehicle_emissions/brp_vehicle_emissions_en.pdf

EIB. (2019). Summary of the European Anti-Fraud Office (OLAF) Report on the European Investment Bank (EIB) Loan "Antrieb RDI" to Volkswagen AG. https://www.eib.org/attachments/press/summary-olaf-report-antrieb-rdi-volkswagen-ag.pdf

EPA. (2016). Laws and Regulations Related to Volkswagen Violations. https://www.epa.gov/vw/laws-and-regulations-related-volkswagen-violations

EPA. (2017a). 2017-05-23 FCA US Complaint as Filled. https://www.epa.gov/sites/production/files/2017-05/documents/2017-05-23_fca_us_complaint_as_filed.pdf

EPA. (2017b). Notice of Violation for Model Year 2014–2016 Diesel Light-Duty Vehicles (Dodge Ram and Jeep Grand Cherokee). https://19january2017snapshot.epa.gov/sites/production/files/2017-01/documents/fca-caa-nov-2017-01-12.pdf

EPA. (2019). In Civil Settlements with the United States and California, Fiat Chrysler to Settle Allegations of Cheating on Federal and State Vehicle Emissions Tests. https://www.epa.gov/newsreleases/civil-settlements-united-states-and-california-fiat-chrysler-settle-allegations

EPA. (2020a). Learn About Volkswagen Violations. https://www.epa.gov/vw/learn-about-volkswagen-violations

EPA. (2020b). Volkswagen Clean Air Act Civil Settlement. https://www.epa.gov/enforcement/volkswagen-clean-air-act-civil-settlement

Farrell, S., & Ruddick, G. (2015, September 23). Volkswagen CEO Martin Winterkorn Quits over Diesel Emissions Scandal. *The Guardian*. https://www.theguardian.com/business/2015/sep/23/volkswagen-ceo-martin-winterkorn-quits-over-diesel-emissions-scandal

Fracarolli Nunes, M., & Lee Park, C. (2016). Caught Red-Handed: The Cost of the Volkswagen Dieselgate. *Journal of Global Responsibility, 7*(2), 288–302.

Frost, L., & Guillaume, G. (2016, September 6). Exclusive: Renault Sees Diesel Disappearing from Most of Its European Cars. *Reuters*. https://www.reuters.com/article/us-renault-diesel-exclusive-idUSKCN11C1MF

Frost, L., & Taylor, E. (2017, March 6). PSA Targets Opel Turnaround as GM Exits Europe. *Reuters*. https://www.reuters.com/article/us-opel-m-a-psa/psa-targets-opel-turnaround-as-gm-exits-europe-idUSKBN16D0J1

Hachenberg, B., Kiesel, F., & Schiereck, D. (2018). Dieselgate and Its Expected Consequences on the European Auto ABS Market. *Economics Letters, 171*, 180–182.

Hotten, R. (2015, December 10). Volkswagen: The Scandal Explained. *BBC News*. https://www.bbc.com/news/business-34324772

Isidore, C. (2015). Volkswagen Emission Scandal Could Dent Car Prices. https://money.cnn.com/2015/09/24/autos/volkswagen-emission-scandal-resale-values/index.html

Jin, H. (2017, February 9). South Korean Court Rules Against Nissan in Emissions Case. *Reuters*. https://www.reuters.com/article/us-nissan-southkorea/south-korean-court-rules-against-nissan-in-emissions-case-idUSKBN15O0EW

Kiley, D. (2016, February 16). Bob Lutz: GM Knew VW's Vehicles Couldn't Pass California Emissions Tests. *Forbes*. http://www.forbes.com/sites/davidkiley5/2016/02/16/boblutzgmknewvwsvehiclescouldntpasscaliforniaemissionstests/#314fbad82e54

Kiley, D. (2019, January 10). FCA Settles with U.S. Regulators Over Its Own "Dieselgate". *Forbes*. https://www.forbes.com/sites/davidkiley5/2019/01/10/fca-settles-with-u-s-regulators-over-its-own-dieselgate/?sh=1eafc6dc7557

Kottasova, I. (2015, October 14). 7 of the Biggest Corporate Scandals. *CNN Money*. https://money.cnn.com/gallery/news/2015/10/14/biggest-corporate-scandals/

La Monica, P. R. (2015). Volkswagen Has Plunged 50%. Will It Ever Recover? *CNN Business*. https://money.cnn.com/2015/09/24/investing/volkswagen-vw-emissions-scandal-stock/

Le Figaro and Agence France Press. (2019). Volkswagen: chronologie du scandale du dieselgate. https://www.lefigaro.fr/societes/dieselgate-chronologie-d-un-scandale-20190930

Mandard, S. (2019, May 13). «Dieselgate»: l'expertise qui met en cause Renault. *Le Monde*. https://www.lemonde.fr/planete/article/2019/05/13/dieselgate-l-expertise-qui-met-en-cause-renault_5461406_3244.html

McGee, P. (2017, February 1). Bosch Reaches $328m Settlement in VW Emissions Scandal. https://www.ft.com/content/964a2f72-e898-11e6-967b-c88452263daf

Morgan, D. (2015, September 23). West Virginia Engineer Proves to Be a David to VW's Goliath. *Reuters*. http://www.reuters.com/article/ususavolkswagenresearchersidUSKCN0RM2D720150924

Muller, J. (2013, April 17). How Volkswagen Will Rule the World. *Forbes*. http://www.forbes.com/sites/joannmuller/2013/04/17/volkswagensmissiontodominateglobalautoindustrygetsnoticeablyharder/#5c3030f11ab6

Neate, R. (2015a, September 18). Volkswagen Under Investigation over Illegal Software That Masks Emissions. *The Guardian*. http://www.theguardian.com/business/2015/sep/18/epacaliforniainvestigatevolkswagencleanairviolations

Neate, R. (2015b, September 26). Meet John German: The Man Who Helped Expose Volkswagen's Emissions Scandal. *The Guardian*. https://www.theguardian.com/business/2015/sep/26/volkswagen-scandal-emissions-tests-john-german-research

PSA. (2017, August 1). Birth of a European Champion: Opel and Vauxhall Join Group PSA. https://www.groupe-psa.com/en/newsroom/corporate-en/birth-of-a-european-champion-opel-and-vauxhall-join-groupe-psa/

Reuters. (2016). VW Financial Services Takes Writedown for Emission Scandal. https://www.reuters.com/article/us-volkswagen-financialservices-idUSKCN0WH1BO

Reuters. (2017a, June 14). UPDATE 2-VW to Offer EU Diesel Car Owners Extended Warranty but No Money Back – EC. https://fr.reuters.com/article/volkswagen-emissions-idUSL8N1JB4UC

Reuters. (2017b). Emissions Scandal Is a Risk to German Economy: Ministry. https://fr.reuters.com/article/idUSKCN1B00U5

Sang-Hun, C. (2016, May 16). South Korea Accuses Nissan of Cheating on Emissions Tests. *The New York Times*. https://www.nytimes.com/2016/05/17/business/south-korea-nissan-emissions-cheating.html

Seat. (2020). EA189 NOx Issue. Trust Building Measure. https://www.seat.co.uk/owners/diesel-engines/trust-building-measure.html

Shepardson, D. (2016). U.S. Judge Approves $14.7 Billion Deal in VW Diesel Scandal. *Reuters*. https://www.reuters.com/article/us-volkswagen-emissions-idUSKCN12P22F

Shepardson, D. (2017). VW Resumes U.S. Diesel Sales After Emissions Scandal. *Reuters*. https://www.reuters.com/article/us-volkswagen-emissions-idUSKBN17Z2ET

Shepardson, D. (2019, February 7). Fiat Chrysler, Bosch Agree to Pay $66 Million in Diesel Legal Fees: Filing. *Reuters*. https://www.reuters.com/article/us-fiat-chrysler-emissions-idUSKCN1PW080

Škoda. (2020). Trust Building Measure. D'leteren Auto répond aux préoccupations de ses clients. https://fr.skoda.be/concernant-skoda/trust-building-measure

The Economist. (2016, January 12). The Dieselgate Dilemma. https://www.economist.com/science-and-technology/2016/01/12/the-dieselgate-dilemma

The United States Department of Justice. (2017). United States Files Complaint Against Fiat Chrysler Automobiles for Alleged Clean Air Act Violations. https://www.justice.gov/opa/pr/united-states-files-complaint-against-fiat-chrysler-automobiles-alleged-clean-air-act

Treviño, L. K., & Nelson, K. A. (2016). *Managing Business Ethics – Straight Talk About How to Do It Right* (5th ed.). John Wiley & Sons.

Tsang, A., & Schuetze, C. F. (2018). In a First for Germany, Hamburg Bans Diesel Engines. *On 2 Roads*. https://www.nytimes.com/2018/05/30/business/energy-environment/hamburg-germany-diesel.html#:~:text=that%20is%20changing.-,On%20Thursday%2C%20Hamburg%20became%20 the%20first%20city%20in%20Germany%20to,to%20prohibit%20older%20diesel%20engines

United Kingdom Parliament. (2017). Letter from the Managing Director of Volkswagen Group United Kingdom Limited, Mr. Paul Willis to the Chair of the Transport Committee of the United Kingdom Parliament House of Commons, Ms. Lilian Greenwood. https://www.parliament.uk/documents/commons-committees/transport/Letter-from-Paul-Willis-to-Chair-re-Volkswagen-Group-UK-recent-activities-30-November-2017.pdf

Volkswagen. (2015a, December 10). Volkswagen Making Good Progress with Its Investigation, Technical Solutions, and Group Realignment. *Volkswagen*. http://www.volkswagenag.com/content/vwcorp/info_center/en/news/2015/12/VW_PK.html

Volkswagen. (2015b, January 5). Volkswagen Reports December 2014 Sales and 2014 Year-End Results. *Volkswagen*. Retrieved April 15, 2016, from http://media.vw.com/release/907/

Watch Mojo. (2015). 10 Volkswagen Scandal Facts WMNews Ep. 47. https://www.youtube.com/watch?v=E7UaX2HzSGU

Williams. (2016, August 22). Report on France's Renault Emissions Probe Omitted Crucial Details. *Financial Times*. https://www.ft.com/content/15e40ef8-63cc-11e6-a08a-c7ac04ef00aa

Zhang, B. (2016, February 16). GM Suspected VW Was Cheating on Diesel Emissions. *Forbes*. https://www.businessinsider.com/gm-suspected-vw-was-cheating-on-diesel-emissions-2016-2?IR=T

7

Not a "Privilege": Environmental Fraud Beyond the Automotive Industry

7.1 Initial Thoughts

Moral and ethical deviations are certainly not restricted to the automotive industry. With the popularization of the environmentalist debate, it seems that all firms are, to some extent, pressured to build and maintain positive environmental images. In this set, the need to appear sustainable creates a fertile ground to environmental fraud, with organizations not only exaggerating their environmental performance but also hiding or dissimulating their impacts. That includes companies lying, deceiving, and even operating environmental solutions only in specific parts of their processes—usually those that are visible to stakeholders. While some companies do seek to be sustainable—and base their environmental reputations on real sustainability efforts—others are limited to the building of environmental façades (Fracarolli Nunes & Lee Park, 2017). Nevertheless, as discussed in Chap. 2, there is a gray area between environmental fraud, corporate hypocrisy, and greenwashing. The analysis of cases of environmental fraud in industries other than the automotive one allows for a better understanding of the relationship between these concepts.

M. Fracarolli Nunes, C. Lee Park, *Business Ethics and Environmental Fraud*,
https://doi.org/10.1007/978-3-030-73800-6_7

7.2 Environmental Fraud in Fast Fashion

Fashion has undergone an intense transformation in recent years, reshaping the way clothes are produced and consumed. By offering well-designed cheap garments, companies such as Zara and H&M conquered a legion of faithful and frequent consumers. Their business model, however, seems to be based on an implicit and silent agreement between companies and consumers: as long as the former continues to offer accessible good-looking clothes, the latter will not ask many questions about the social and environmental impacts needed to do so. That includes an unusual tolerance to the amount of resources used in the production of clothes, the large amounts of waste, the volumes of fossil fuel dispensed over long distances between production and consumption, and the often poor working conditions offered to employees, among others.

As discussed by Sweeny (2015), fashion is a rather complex business which involves long and varied supply chains. That includes a multitude of players tangled in the production of raw material, textile manufacture, sewing clothes, transportation, distribution, use, and, ultimately, disposal. Among other consequences, this intricacy makes the determination of its carbon footprint extremely difficult. Beyond the more obvious pollutants (e.g. pesticides applied in cotton crops, toxic dyes used in manufacturing, and the great amount of waste created by discarded clothes), a general assessment in that direction must also take into account the excessive amounts of natural resources consumed in the different phases of the production processes. Along with the primary part of the business (i.e. extraction, farming, and harvesting), that also includes its industrial (i.e. processing and manufacturing) and logistic aspects (i.e. shipping). With all that considered, it is estimated that the fashion industry responds for 10% of all anthropogenic carbon emissions (more than all maritime shipping and international flights combined), being the second-largest consumer of the world's water reserves (McFall-Johnsen, 2019).

On that regard, Sweeny (2015) points out that more than 18,927 liters (5000 gallons) of water may be necessary to produce the cotton used in just a T-shirt and a pair of jeans. Leahy (2015), in turn, argues that the water used to grow the cotton exported by India in 2013 would be sufficient to supply 85% of its population (i.e. more than 1 billion people) with a daily amount of 100 liters of water every day. The numbers, however, would be extraordinarily bad in the country, as, due to a series of operational inefficiencies, it ends up having a water footprint more than twice higher than that of the global average. While the production of 1 kilogram of cotton demands, in general, 10,000 liters of water, that same output would require 22,500 liters in India. At the same time, synthetic fibers do not seem to be an adequate response to the issue (Sweeny, 2015). Although not as water-intensive, their use in clothes means that 500,000 tons of microfibers—what corresponds to 50 billion plastic bottles—are released into the ocean each year when clothes are washed (McFall-Johnsen, 2019). Accordingly, much of those fibers are made of polyester, a sort of plastic present in 60% of the clothes currently produced, and which production releases two to three times more carbon emissions than that of cotton. In addition, the material does not decompose in the ocean, meaning it may pollute natural environments indefinitely. It is estimated that 31% of all plastic pollution is composed of microplastic, 35% of which would come from the laundering of synthetic textiles (Boucher & Friot, 2017).

Several other environmental issues are associated with the fast fashion business model. As highlighted by McFall-Johnsen (2019), while garment sales grew 60% between 2000 and 2014, consumers kept their clothes for half as long. Besides denoting the relative poorer quality of the goods sold, these figures illustrate the considerable problem that clothes waste represent, particularly if all the resources used to manufacture them are contemplated. The strategies adopted by fashion companies seem to stimulate this decrease in the clothing lifecycle. As pointed out by the author, European brands went from two collections a year in 2000 to an average of five in 2011. Some companies like H&M and Zara go even further in this process, offering between 12 and 24 collections per year. Additionally, as the water leftover from text dyeing is commonly discarded into ditches, streams, and rivers, the process is considered to be the world's second-largest polluter of water. Altogether, these numbers position the fashion industry as one of the most harmful to the environment.

In this sense, the claims of fast fashion companies that their operations are truly sustainable could be classified as classic cases of corporate hypocrisy. In the most acute events, in which the real impact of businesses is concealed or hidden from the general public, the practices could be classified as a sort of environmental fraud. On its annual report, Inditex (2019) (Zara's parent company) approaches the issue of plastic pollution, but curiously, in a very superficial manner. The company focuses, for example, on issues related to the reduction of single-use plastic cutlery by employees, the replacement of plastic containers in vending machines, the elimination of plastic bags in stores and online shipment. The pollution caused by the microplastics on its products, in turn, is presented quite timidly, with the company limiting itself to reporting that it is working with a university (*Universitat Politècnica de Catalunya*) in research that seeks to find ways to minimize the environmental impact caused by the material used on its products. Indeed, the word "microplastic" appears only twice in the 472 pages of the document, both occasions referring to the same matter.

In addition to the pollution caused by the manufacturing of clothes itself, the long distances between production and consumption stand as a main environmental issue within the fast fashion business model. The delocalization of garment production to low labor-cost zones is inserted in a macro business trend that has dominated much of the strategic thinking in recent decades. Following important geopolitical changes in the second half of the twentieth century (e.g. the end of the Cold War), regions previously isolated from the dynamics of market capitalism were gradually integrated. In this process, countries such as China, India, Bangladesh, Pakistan, and Vietnam, among others, became common destinations for factories, basically due to the relatively low cost of labor force they offered. The fashion industry, specifically, became an important part of the economy of some of these countries. In Bangladesh, for example, it accounts for 80% of exports (Suhrawardi, 2020) and 16% of the countries' GDP, providing more than 5 million direct jobs (Rahman et al., 2017).

The sudden drop in production costs transformed competitive dynamics, with an increasing number of companies seeking to benefit from it. In a sort of herd behavior, the transfer of production to low labor-cost zones grew exponentially, with many American, Japanese, European, and even Latin American companies partially or entirely transferring their production to the other side of the world. This geographic relocation was operationalized in the most diverse ways. While some companies opted to close their plants in their home countries and build new ones in the targeted regions, others chose to outsource their production. In the case of China, specifically, joint ventures between foreign investors and Chinese citizens were common. Regardless of the type of arrangement used, the fact is that the reduction in production costs was achieved at the sacrifice of environmental performance. In addition to the usually looser environmental legislation in these regions—which in itself favors a higher level of poorly treated waste and pollution—the distance between producers and consumers generates significant additional consumption of fossil fuels in transportation.

From a social perspective, in turn, these changes caused several impacts, many of which negative. Among the most direct is the unemployment of less-qualified workers in developed countries. With the closing of the factories, the working class in former industrial areas progressively saw their jobs disappear. As the job market for low-skilled professionals became less welcoming, the standard of living of the most popular strata decreased. With income levels falling, the quality of life of these populations was gradually reduced and, as the problems intensified, social welfare programs were pressured. The situation generated frustration and growing unsatisfaction among the most popular levels, what partially explains the electoral triumph of politicians who openly oppose globalization. With his discourse praying "America First", the 45th president of the United States, Mr. Donald John Trump, is, perhaps, the best example of the issue. Among the pillars supporting the slogan "Make America Great Again" is his attempt to reverse the evasion of American factories toward emerging countries. Using a series of protectionist measures, such as the reduction of specific taxes for goods produced in the United States (BBC, 2019), his policies have been to some extent successful, with several companies transferring their production back to the country. These measures have generated tensions with China, as it concentrates a large portion of all the factories in the world.

If, on the one hand, the migration of factories led to important social upheavals in developed countries, then, on the other hand, it was responsible for much of the advances in the quality of life in underdeveloped ones. With the rapid warming of the labor market, Chinese workers, for example, saw their average income significantly increase. Yet, several cases of disrespect for human rights have been reported in Chinese factories, among the most common practices of modern slavery and child labor. In 2012, for example, riots broke out in Foxconn—the largest electronics manufacturer of the world—arguably due to the constant use of violence against employees and the extreme conditions of work they were offered. The case caught the attention of the international press, fueling the debate on the matter. Similar problems were also observed in other industries, in particular fashion. Tragic episodes such as the collapse of the Rana Plaza building in 2013, killing 1134 workers (Safi & Rushe, 2018), illustrate the issue. Likewise, the various cases of fire in sewing workshops in the region victimized thousands of workers. In response to these issues, campaigns such as "Who made my clothes?" (Omotoso, 2018) emerged.

7.2.1 Organic Cotton

Despite not setting up fraudulent practices themselves, the severe social and environmental impacts generated by the fast fashion business model discredit the positioning of its composing companies as sustainable enterprises. Nevertheless, fraudulent components can be more easily identified in other practices of the industry. Back in 2010, clothing chains H&M and C&A, for example, were accused by media reports and consumer groups of using genetically modified cotton in their allegedly eco-friendly range (Deutsche Welle, 2010). In the occasion, several organisms spoke out against what was seen as a negligent practice by both firms. According to a representant of the German Federal Consumer Affairs Agency (*Verbraucherzentrale Bundesverband*), the companies were not vigilant enough, and should adopt measures so that such situations do not recur. That includes the disclosure of their supply chains and the development of more robust controls of their certifiers, with the conduction of random checks being a basic measure in that direction. Likewise, a representant of

Germany's Green Party in the European Parliament called for stricter controls on organic textiles produced in developing countries.

In addition to this seemingly milder analysis, accusations that genetically modified cotton was being commercialized as organic were treated by some entities as a way to deceive consumers, with the environmentalist group Greenpeace classifying the practice as consumer fraud. An agricultural expert of the group also called for the punishment of those involved in the practice, even with the issue being likely to be unintentionally caused. Accordingly, at the origin of the problems would be the small structure of the farming sector in India, what would favor the formations of production clusters. With producers geographically close to each other and cultivating a variety of distinct crops (e.g. organic, conventional, and genetically modified), contamination from one field to the other would be relatively common. Still after Deutsche Welle (2010), large volumes of genetically modified cotton from India had been commercialized as organic, according to the German newspaper *Financial Times Deutschland*. The publication also pointed out that Indian authorities would have learned of the problems in 2009, with the then-Indian agricultural authority claiming to be facing a fraud of gigantic proportions.

As it has also been the case in other situations of environmental fraud discussed (e.g. Volkswagen Dieselgate), the cotton used by H&M and C&A was certified as organic by two European companies. As stressed by the newspaper, it remained unclear whether the certifiers—one Dutch and one French—were aware that genetically modified cotton was falsely labeled as organic. In its defense, a representative of H&M acknowledged to news agency AFP that the company was aware of the issue, claiming, however, that one could not rule out the possibility that the contaminated cotton has accidentally landed in the organic range used by it. C&A, in turn, announced it planned to conduct a thorough investigation on the matter (Deutsche Welle, 2010). The issue was particularly risky to the operations of both firms, as, by the time, companies were particularly interested in increasing their profits by positioning themselves as valid alternatives for consumers in the middle of the "organic bandwagon". H&M, in particular, was set to launch its spring collection, which it literally claimed to be "made using organic and recycled materials" (Deutsche Welle, 2010).

7.3 Food and Beverage Industry

Similarly, the commercialization of conventional products as organic seems to be spread within the food and beverage industry. Among the factors that make the practice particularly attractive in food manufacturing are the low margins associated with the production of agricultural goods. With products like soybeans, corn, rice, sugar, and orange juice having little or no differentiation, competition in commodities markets is often based in the price of products. The fact that equal (or very similar products) are offered by a relatively large number of producers tends then to put downward pressure on prices, as no other alternative is available for producers who wish to improve their offer to potential buyers. That typically translates into low operational margins. In that way, the premium prices organic products carry end up encouraging both their production—which also entails "premium costs"—and the improper commercialization of conventional products as organic, situation in which margins may be particularly high.

The value associated with an organic product can be inferred by the treatment that some international entities grant them. The European Commission (2019), for instance, assigns a distinction to all organic goods produced by the European Union. Among them are all pre-packaged EU food products that are produced and commercialized as organic within the EU, imported products that conform to EU standards on the import of organics, and EU organic products that are placed on third countries markets (European Commission, 2020). By stamping the EU organic logo in these products, a coherent visual identity would be created. In turn, the logo cannot be used for products that contain less than 95% of organic ingredients, mass catering operations (e.g. restaurants, hospitals), products that are not included in the scope of organic rules (e.g. cosmetics, products from hunting and fishing), and products in the transition to organic or, as put by the agency, in conversion. That includes situations in which organic methods have just been introduced, as non-organic substances must still be found in the soil or animal chain. In that way, the European Commission (2019) calls misleading practices intended to circumvent these and other standards as organic fraud, with the practice standing as a serious threat to the credibility of its EU organic logo.

That seems to be the case of one of the largest criminal schemes involving the production of food in U.S. history (CBS News, 2019). According to the United States Department of Justice (2019), Randy Constant, a 61-years-old Missouri farmer, "fraudulently sold millions of dollars' worth of non-organic grain as thought it was organic". Following the judiciary procedures, the disclosure of organic fraud earned him more than ten years in federal prison. Likewise, three farmers from the state of Nebraska were also sentenced for their participation in the scheme to defraud American customers. At their plea hearings, they admitted knowing that the conventional grain they produced was being falsely marketed and sold as organic. The admission of guilty, however, did not release them from serving their sentences of 20 and 24 months for two of them, and 3 months for the other, as he was recognized by the judge as "a legitimate war hero" for his action in Vietnam. In addition, each of the farmers was ordered to forfeit US $1,000,000 in proceeds. Mr. Constant, in turn, admitted that the scheme comprehended at least US $142.4 million in grain sales, most of which fraudulent. The criminal also recognized to have falsely told customers that his grain was grown on his certified organic fields, while it was either purchased from other uncertified producers, mixed with non-organic grains, or sprayed with unauthorized chemicals. In addition to his prison sentence, Mr. Constant agreed to forfeit more than US $128 million that resulted from the scheme. Still after the United States Department of Justice (2019), in 2016, the fraudulent producer was responsible for approximately 7% of all comparable organic cotton grown in the United States, as well as for 8% of all organic soybeans grown in the country. In total, Constant would have sold more than 312,979 tons (11,500,000 bushels) of grain, with 90% of which having been falsely commercialized as organic.

Beyond the damage to the image, finances, and, as in the case reported, freedom of those who practice it, organic fraud seems to have a particular potential to disseminate in supply chains. As pointed out by the United States Department of Justice (2019), Constant's grain was mostly used as animal feed, mainly for chickens and cattle, with the livestock or derived products being sold as organic. The fraud reaches consumers as they pay premium prices for what is believed to the outcome of an organic production. In that way, the deception in the early tiers of the chain (i.e.

grain producer) extends to other players, who, in one way or another, are harmed. In line with the fraud dissemination processes discussed in Chap. 2, organic fraud seems to be a typical trigger of supply chain contamination.

While the losses caused by the practice of organic fraud seem to be more evident, the combat to such deviations still seems to be far from being up to the task. Among the possible reasons for the gap, one must consider the still incipient recognition of organic products as a distinct category, as well as the lack of universally accepted standards to define it. The lack of these definitions and of a consensus on acceptable inputs and production techniques difficult inspections and end up making the life of those who intend to take advantage of the good faith of consumers—even corporate ones—easier. The hardship in fighting organic fraud may also be associated with the difficulties in distinguishing an organic product from a conventional one. Without specialized tests, or with an effective control of origins, the differentiation between products can be nearly impossible to the naked eye. Even if organic products appear to have some specific characteristics due to their no exposure to chemicals (e.g. smaller, less shining), a clear and reliable distinction between organic and non-organic products on the part of the end consumers seems unlikely.

Likewise, the high volumes produced, and the long extensions of land used for the cultivation of agricultural commodities, represent additional adversities. Similarly, the large numbers of geographically spread producers, as well as the high number of intermediary processes (e.g. planting, harvesting, transportation, processing, and distribution) and actors (e.g. farmers, traders, conveyors) between production and consumption may significantly increase the chances of misconducts. On that regard, Spink et al. (2010) argue that consumers and manufacturers are exposed to counterfeiting, contamination, and adulterations, particularly in supply chains. Companies of the pharmaceutical, manufacturing, technology, and food and beverage industries would be under constant risk of having their brands harmed, as criminals become involved in the relationship they maintain with their consumers. While some products do not pose risks to the health of consumers—despite financially damaging them—others may have serious implications in this regard. As pointed out by the authors, it is estimated that 30% of pharmaceutical products sold in developing countries are counterfeit. Since the long-term effects of ingesting pesticides, fertilizers, as well as other chemicals used in large-scale food production are not yet fully understood, it is possible that the dissimulation of conventional food as organic also comes to have consequences as negative as those of consuming falsified drugs, possibly worse.

Despite the difficulties, several actions have been taken in the attempt to minimize, or, at least, decrease the cases of misconducts in food production. Among the measures adopted by the European Commission to combat organic fraud is a targeted action launched in 2018, in the framework of the OPSON VIII operation (European Commission, 2019). Resulting from a joint effort between Europol and Interpol, the OPSON VIII operation is focused on fake and substandard food and beverage (Europol, 2020). Along with the identification of vulnerable points within supply chains (particularly within complex and international ones), the actions investigate suspicious of fraud and false certification, mostly on imported products destined to be redistributed under the EU organic label. In that way, the aim of the operation is to preserve the reputation of the EU organic logo and protect the confidence that consumers have in it (European Commission, 2019).

Unexpectedly, the entity claims that organic fraud does not present food safety risks, with products discovered to be noncompliant with the organic rules simply being downgraded and commercialized as conventional ones. In a sense, this contradicts the value added by organic production, which, as discussed, is largely based on the idea that organic food would be free from the possible harm that chemicals could cause to the health of consumers. In addition to the investigation, the efforts of the body also include the development of the Electronic Certificate of Inspection, which would have significantly improved the traceability of organic products that are imported from non-EU countries. As pointed out by Manning and Soon (2016), food-related frauds may be specifically combated through measures such as the use of unique numbers either at batch, product, or lot level, and the increase in traceability through the employment of technologies such as Radio Frequency Identification Devices (RFID), as well as features on the package of individual items (e.g. special inks, holograms), particularly on products or on every single pallet (Spink et al., 2010).

7.4 Logistics

The fast development of e-commerce radically altered the way products are marketed and sold (Scott Matthews et al., 2001). Among the main changes is the fact that consumers are no longer obliged to travel to traditional points of sale to have access to products. Instead, they may order and receive them in the place of their choice, often within a reasonable price and delay. Although arguably trivial to younger consumers, such transactions were unthinkable until recently. Business models based on online exchanges were only possible because of the magnificent development that information technology has gone through in the last decades. That includes the extension of communication networks, the creation of new products (e.g. smartphones), the increased access to the internet, and the development of means of payment, among other related matters. The materialization of e-commerce, however, depended on the development of logistics services, which, although less glamorous, were equally important in that path. Firms' capacity to make goods transit from one point to another in the most efficient way possible is the very essence of successful e-commerce. In this sense, in order to keep up with the digital revolution, logistic service providers (LSPs) also had to significantly improve their capacity to process data, with the high investment in technology becoming one of the main features of the current logistics industry. This metamorphosis in the way goods are distributed ended up boosting the operations of large LSPs, with some players considerably expanding their business. That seems to be the case of companies such as FedEX, whose stocks appreciated 291% from January 1, 2000, to December 31, 2019 (Yahoo Finance, 2020a) (considering the close price adjusted for both dividends and splits). By way of comparison, the Dow Jones Industrial Average Index appreciated 151% in the same period (Yahoo Finance, 2020b). Likewise, the revenues of the company grew from US $18.2 billions (FedEX, 2000) to US $69.7 billions (FedEX, 2019) in the same 20 years.

From a broader perspective, the consolidation of e-commerce represented far more than a sheer change in the way products are distributed. In fact, it has created what seems to be the convenience economy

(Dickinson, 2020), in which practicality and speed are often more important than factors such as price or quality. In analyzing this trend, Fromm (2019) points out to the new meaning that the idea of convenience has gained, moving from consumers' access to products or experiences within a reasonable walk or drive, to an expectation that things shall be readily available, at anytime and anyplace. Accordingly, this notion would be particularly popular among millennials and generation Z customers—loosely, those born between 1980 and 1994, and between 1995 and 2010, respectively (Francis & Hoefel, 2018). Driven by technology and by an on-demand culture, they would be under the "Amazon Effect" (Fromm, 2019), with this unrelenting desire for convenience becoming the main challenge faced by modern supply chains.

As discussed by Brin (2016), by offering an easy remote purchasing and a quick and low-priced shipping, e-commerce became a dominant disruptor in the U.S. market. In this set, the development of the means allowing products to be delivered faster and at lower costs turned into LSPs' main objectives, and, ultimately, sources of competitive advantage. It is not by chance that these companies account for significant investments in research and development, and are, in many cases, seen as technology companies above all. The words of Amazon Chief Technology Officer Werner Vogels illustrate the view, in which he states: "Amazon is a technology company. We just happen to do retail" (McCarty, 2011).

Economies of scale, in turn, depend on the operation of large volumes that, in the case of LSPs, demand the administration of a considerable set of physical assets. That includes warehouses, airport terminals, offices, trucks, ships, and airplanes, among others. Regarding the dynamics of the industry, technological innovation, and the operation of heavy physical structures constitute significant barriers to entry (Porter, 1979, 1980), what basically explains why the logistics industry is dominated by a small number of large firms. Like most companies, LSPs have traditionally focused on the generation of profits, with the interests of investors and customers being often privileged over those of other groups. Indeed, the tangibility of the operational success of these companies (i.e. goods being delivered in the right place, at the right time, and at a competitive price) contributed for their focus on the minimization of their operational cycle, as well as of the cost of the services provided. From a more strategic point of view, the fact that logistics services do not offer great sources of differentiation makes competition less sophisticated. In this sense, the impossibility of charging premium prices puts pressure on operational margins, which, in turn, creates a constant need for cost reduction. These dynamics justify the need for LSPs to obtains gains of scale, as well as the search to diminish their operational cycle (and cost) through high investments in information technology.

Within a trade-offs perspective, it appears that LSPs have traditionally understood that the meeting of social and environmental performance would demand unaffordable sacrifices in their operational performance. On the other hand, the pressure they suffered to incorporate these new demands increased to the point that they could not be ignored. The incongruity between low operational margins and the extra expenses that the adoption of sustainable models impose makes the logistics industry a fertile ground for environmental hypocrisy, and, eventually, for the practice of environmental fraud. From an environmental viewpoint, the effects of e-commerce are ambiguous (Scott Matthews et al., 2001) as, at the same time reductions in inventory levels and returns provide significant environmental savings, the energy consumed as well as all the packaging material used in product fulfillment and delivery raise major environmental concerns. Likewise, the fuel balance is unclear. As discussed by the authors, the integration between e-commerce and logistics services causes less environmental damage than the private automobile travels for shopping that they avoid.

It is necessary to point out that issues related to social and environmental responsibilities of companies arise at a time when LSPs' business models are already strongly consolidated. Just as the large-fixed asset base of these firms proved to be difficult, expensive, and slow to modernize, the corporate culture of their leaders also offered resistance. Among the reasons for such difficulties may be the profile of managers who traditionally led these companies and their eventual incapacity to understand that the new challenges faced by firms could no longer be solved in a purely technical way. Likewise, consumers' expectations on logistics services were already set, with time and cost being at the very top of their priorities. It seems then that the *age of green* spread at a speed that some industries simply could not keep up with. In addressing these tensions, LSPs have invested in looking sustainable, mainly by employing green alternatives in their last-mile urban deliveries. The practice may be seen as a sort of tip-of-the-iceberg strategy. Basically, that means that the portion which is visible to consumers often hides a much larger one that may not be as environmentally friendly. In the case of logistics companies, this is translated in the massive use of fossil fuels in most of the long distances traveled by airplanes, ships, and trucks, contrasting with bicycles and other arguably low-emission vehicles (e.g. electric and natural gas-powered vehicles). The creation of positive environmental images through the camouflage of environmental impacts shall be framed as a particularly complex and nuanced type of environmental fraud. Differently from the illicit adulteration or manipulation of products—as is the case in the fraudulent installation of deceiving software in the automotive industry—tip-of-the-iceberg strategies deal with the administration of perceptions, resting, therefore, within the intangible resources arena.

One must not affirm, however, that logistics companies are consciously deluding consumers, or Machiavellianly fooling them. Instead, it is very possible that they are sincerely aiming to minimize CO_2 emissions of their operational processes, with efforts concentrated on the last-mile delivery being an initial step in that direction. It is also imaginable that environmentally friendly alternatives are still restricted to parts of the process due to technological or financial constrictions, as, in the current state of affairs, the use of renewable or less-pollutant fuels in large scale may not be viable. At the same time that the available means of transport (e.g. airplanes, ships, trucks) are mostly powered by oil derivates (e.g. kerosene, diesel, gasoline), the utilization of alternative fuels may significantly impact the cost of freight, and ultimately, that of the final product.

The move toward a greener logistics *de facto* would depend then on the concertation of the interests of a range of industries (e.g. aviation, naval, automotive, oil), which may explain the modest development in that direction. Yet, even if logistics companies are indeed moved by an honest desire to minimize the impact of their operations, the perils of tip-of-the-iceberg strategies must be considered, as they may hide severe social and environmental damages while creating an illusion in the mind of customers, who may be willing to pay premium prices for what they believe to be a form of green transportation. In that way, potentially malicious managers may take advantage of the relative ignorance that consumers generally have of the integrity of transportation and distribution processes. In light of this reasoning, we briefly examine Amazon and UPS, two of the main players of the industry.

7.4.1 Amazon

Incorporated by American entrepreneur Jeff Bezos in 1994 and headquartered in Seattle, Washington, Amazon is an internet-based company that commercializes a range of products and services (e.g. books, music, electronics, movies, toys, housewares), either directly or intermediating the operations between other retailers and its customers (Britannica, 2020). Currently, it ships products internationally to 190 different countries and regions dispersed in Africa and Middle East, Europe, Americas, Australia, Asia, and Pacific (Amazon, 2020a). The company also operates more than 175 fulfillment centers around the globe, comprehending more than 13.94 million square meters (150 million square feet) of space (Amazon, 2020b). In 2019 Amazon's net sales accounted for more than US $280 billion (Amazon, 2020c), placing it ahead of large-technology companies such as Apple (US $260 billion—Apple, 2019), Google's parent company Alphabet (US $162 billion—Alphabet, 2020), Microsoft (US $126 billion—Microsoft, 2019), and Facebook (US $71 billion—Facebook, 2020). The success of the company is also clear when the evolution of its market share is considered. In 2016, Amazon's participation in the American e-commerce market was 34% in terms of gross merchandise volume, with the figure being projected to be around 50% by 2021 (Statista, 2020).

Its rapid growth was reflected in the profits of those who believed in its potential since the beginning. According to Investopedia (2020), US $10,000 invested in the company upon its initial public offering would be worth more than US $12 million as of May 2020, representing a 120,000% growth. Accordingly, that is also reflected in Amazon's market value, which surpassed US $1 trillion by 2018. Among the factors influencing the company's success would be its ability to add differentiated services to products sales, such as its personalization tools which recommended products to customers, and the publishing of customers' reviews of products, creating a sort of consumers' community who would support each other upon their purchasing experiences (Britannica, 2020). The relationships with and among consumers are still managed by the company, within what is now called Amazon Community. In a dedicated space on its website, Amazon gathers customers' reviews, offering them the possibility to manage their interaction and to have access to contribution rewards (Amazon, 2020d).

In face of all its uniqueness, Bezos did not position Amazon as a retailer, but rather as a technology company. In support of this view, in early 2000s the company launched a series of data-driven services such as Amazon Web Services, offering data on internet traffic patterns. Likewise, with the launch of its Elastic Compute Cloud and the Simple Storage Service in 2006, Amazon started to operate the rent of computer processing power and data storage. These services supported the popularization of the idea that the possession of computational resources was not indispensable, with companies and individuals being able to rent them on the internet, or "in the cloud" (Britannica, 2020). As part of its business model, Amazon has kept close relationships with some of the largest logistics service providers in the world, such as United Parcel Service (UPS), Federal Express (FedEx), and DHL, among others.

7.4.2 UPS

Founded in 1907 as a private messenger and delivery service in Seattle, Washington, UPS has grown to become "the world's largest package delivery company, a leader in the U.S. less-than-truckload industry and a premier provider of global supply chain management solutions" (UPS, 2019a, p. 1). Counting on more than 2500 worldwide operating facilities, 125,000 vehicles, and 572 airplanes in its fleet, the company has an annual delivery volume of 5.5 billion packages and volumes, which translates to more than US $74 billion a year. As one of the largest LSPs in the world, UPS has its operations constantly monitored, its environmental impacts being a favorite subject of environmentalist groups and NGOs. On its "click clean scorecard" report, Greenpeace (2015), for example, negatively evaluates the company for its arguably low energy transparency (i.e. providing consumers with information about energy demands and energy footprint) and commitment to renewable sources (i.e. the extent to which companies rely on renewable sources of energy).

In the attempt to improve its environmental image, the company has adopted a series of measures over the years, focusing mainly on the introduction of low-emission vehicles on its fleet. As of 2019, alternative fuels represented 24% of UPS' total ground fuel use. By the time, the company counted with more than 10,300 low-emission vehicles, including pure and hybrid electric vehicles (UPS, 2019b, 2019c), natural gas-powered trucks (UPS, 2019d), and bicycles (UPS, 2018). UPS' environmental efforts, however, seem to concentrate on its urban operations. That includes a range of different projects using conventional and electric bicycles, in cities such as New York (Hu & Haag, 2019) and Seattle (UPS, 2018).

7.5 Electronics

Along with the deliberate goal of deceiving consumers about the environmental attributes of their products, companies' misconducts may also be classified as cases of environmental fraud according to their indirect consequences. Back in 2018, Apple and Samsung—the two largest electronic companies of the world—were fined for deliberately slowing down phones, arguably for pushing new purchases (Gibbs, 2018). Accordingly, an investigation launched early that year by Italy's competition authority found that software updates negatively impacted the operational performance of smartphones with the aim of encouraging consumers to buy new devices. The practices were classified as dishonest by the Italian institution, which imposed the maximum fine of €5 million in each of the companies. Yet, Apple was also fined an additional €5 million for not providing consumers with clear information about the basic characteristics of lithium batteries (e.g. average life expectancy, maintenance, and replacing advice).

Still after Gibbs (2018), in December of the previous year Apple had already recognized it had intentionally slowed smartphones through software updates. The company denied, however, to have done so to shorten the life cycle of the product, being the measure intended to avoid the sudden shutdown of iPhones equipped with degraded batteries. Following the episode, Apple not only apologized for its actions but also reduced the cost of battery replacement. In addition to this Italian process, the practices of the company were also investigated by French authorities and questioned by the U.S. senate. Likewise, the argued fraud has been the object to more than 60 separate lawsuits in the United States. In February 2020, the investigations in France resulted in Apple being fined €25 million by the country's competition and fraud authority (BBC, 2020a). Weeks later, the company agreed to settle the case in the United States for US $500 million (BBC, 2020b). Samsung, in turn, had never had its software updates questioned before, denying the accusations it was facing in Italy.

Along with the economic damage caused to consumers, the artificially accelerated obsolescence of electronic devices has serious environmental consequences. As pointed out by Greenpeace (2017, p. 3), "behind this innovative [twenty-first]-century technology lie supply chain and manufacturing processes still reliant on [nineteenth]-century sources of energy, dangerous mining practices, hazardous chemicals, and poorly designed products that drive consumption of the Earth's resources". The arguments raised by the environmental group set the base for judging the impacts that the companies' dishonest practices have from the environmental point of view. Meanwhile, both forms displayed their environmentally friendly initiatives, arguing for the sustainability of their operations. On its 2018 sustainability report, Samsung, for instance, stated to be committed to the reduction of its footprint, with resource efficiency being a central goal for the company (Samsung, 2018). Similarly, on its 2018 environmental responsibility report, Apple (2018, p. 3) claimed to be engaged in the conservation of precious resources "so we all can thrive". Thus, even if Samsung's and Apple's arguably misleading practices were primarily intended to increase their sales, the fact that the fraudulent practices have a significantly negative environmental impact, coupled with an environmental communication that is at least inexact, puts the conducts of the company in the gray area between corporate hypocrisy and environmental fraud.

The same logics may be applied to other cases, as, while some companies seem to proudly highlight their environmentally friendly practices, they are said to be largely responsible for critical pollution situations. Coca-Cola, for example, often depicts the arguably environmental practices within its policies for a "sustainable packaging" (Coca-Cola, 2020), while it is named the worlds' most polluting brand in a plastic waste audit (Nace, 2019). The conclusion was reached after 848 cleanup events were held in 51 countries, in which more than 72,000 volunteers collected over 475,000 pieces of plastic waste on beaches, cities, and waterways. The waste gathered was then attributed to the company of origin. Coca-Cola is followed in the ranking by other large multinational companies, with firms of the food and beverage sectors being strongly represented in the top positions (Nestlé in 2nd, Pepsico, Mondeléz International in 3rd, Unilever in 4th, Mars in 5th, Procter & Gamble in 6th, Colgate-Palmolive in 7th, Philip Morris International in 8th, and Perfetti van Melle in 10th).

In fact, it seems that regardless of the results of the analysis, these companies are, in general, comfortable in calling their business models sustainable. As pointed out by Nestlé's CEO, Peter Brabeck-Letmathe in the company's sustainability review, "As we move ahead in the [twenty-first] century, we believe that a business strategy based on high-quality food and beverage products can only be maintained by business practices based on the principles of long term sustainable development" (Nestlé, 2020, p. 3). Curiously, the word "plastic" is not mentioned in the document.

References

Alphabet. (2020). Alphabet Announces Fourth Quarter and Fiscal Year 2019 Results. https://abc.xyz/investor/static/pdf/2019Q4_alphabet_earnings_release.pdf?cache=79552b8

Amazon. (2020a). AmazonGlobal Export Countries and Regions. https://www.amazon.com/gp/help/customer/display.html?nodeId=201910800

Amazon. (2020b). Our Fulfillment Centers. https://www.aboutamazon.com/amazon-fulfillment/our-fulfillment-centers

Amazon. (2020c). 2019 Annual Report. https://s2.q4cdn.com/299287126/files/doc_financials/2020/ar/2019-Annual-Report.pdf

Amazon. (2020d). Amazon Community. https://www.amazon.com/gp/help/customer/display.html?nodeId=GHPQCG33U7WM883N

Apple. (2018). Environmental Responsibility Report. https://www.apple.com/environment/pdf/Apple_Environmental_Responsibility_Report_2018.pdf

Apple. (2019). Annual Report Pursuant to Section 13 or 15(d) of the Securities Exchange Act of 1934 for the Fiscal Year Ended September 28, 2019. https://s2.q4cdn.com/470004039/files/doc_financials/2019/ar/_10-K-2019-(As-Filed).pdf

BBC. (2019). Trade Wars, Trump Tariffs and Protectionism Explained. https://www.bbc.com/news/world-43512098

BBC. (2020a, February 7). Apple Fined for Slowing Down Old iPhones. https://www.bbc.com/news/technology-51413724

BBC. (2020b, March 2). Apple Settles iPhone Slowdown Case for $500m. https://www.bbc.com/news/technology-51706635

Boucher, J., & Friot, D. (2017). Primary Microplastics in the Oceans: A Global Evaluation of Sources. *International Union for Conservation of Nature*. https://portals.iucn.org/library/sites/library/files/documents/2017-002-En.pdf

Brin, D. E. (2016, August 21). How e-commerce sparked a logistics boom. *Supply Chain Dive*. https://www.supplychaindive.com/news/ecommercelogistics-boom-real-estate/424829/

Britannica. (2020). Amazon.com. https://www.britannica.com/topic/Amazoncom

CBS News. (2019). Four Farmers Face Sentencing in U.S. Largest Organic Fraud Case. https://www.cbsnews.com/news/organic-food-fraud-four-farmers-to-be-sentenced-for-defrauding-organic-customers/

Coca-Cola. (2020). Sustainable Packaging. https://www.coca-colacompany.com/sustainable-business/packaging-sustainability

Deutsche Welle. (2010, January 24). European Clothing Chains Hit by 'Fake' Organic Label Controversy. https://www.dw.com/en/european-clothing-chains-hit-by-fake-organic-label-controversy/a-5164495#:~:text=European%20clothing%20chains%20hit%20by%20'fake'%20organic%20label%20controversy,in%20their%20eco%2Dfriendly%20range

Dickinson, G. (2020). *The Convenience Economy. B2B: Adapt Now or Pay*. Dreamstarters.

European Commission. (2019). Commission Takes Action Against Fraud in Organic Products. https://ec.europa.eu/info/news/commission-takes-action-against-fraud-organic-products-2019-jun-21_en

European Commission. (2020). The Organic Logo. https://ec.europa.eu/info/food-farming-fisheries/farming/organic-farming/organics-glance/organic-logo_en

Europol. (2020). Operation Opson. https://www.europol.europa.eu/activities-services/europol-in-action/operations/operation-opson

Facebook. (2020). Facebook Reports Fourth Quarter and Full Year 2019 Results. https://investor.fb.com/investor-news/press-release-details/2020/Facebook-Reports-Fourth-Quarter-and-Full-Year-2019-Results/default.aspx

FedEX. (2000). FedEX Corporation 2000 Annual Report. https://s1.q4cdn.com/714383399/files/doc_financials/annual/2000annualreport.pdf

FedEX. (2019). FedEX Corporation 2019 Annual Report. https://s1.q4cdn.com/714383399/files/doc_financials/annual/2019/FedEx-Corporation-2019-Annual-Report.pdf?utm_source=InvestorRelations&utm_medium=Referral&utm_campaign=AnnualReport2018&utm_content=FinancialInformationAnnualReports

Fracarolli Nunes, M., & Lee Park, C. (2017). Self-Claimed Sustainability: Building Social and Environmental Reputations with Words. *Sustainable Production and Consumption, 11*, 46–57.

Francis, T., & Hoefel, F. (2018). 'True Gen': Generation Z and Its Implications for Companies. *Mckinsey*. https://www.mckinsey.com/industries/consumer-packaged-goods/our-insights/true-gen-generation-z-and-its-implications-for-companies#

Fromm, J. (2019, January 4). Marketing Convenience to the Modern Consumer. *Forbes*. https://www.forbes.com/sites/jefffromm/2019/01/04/marketing-convenience-to-the-modern-consumer/?sh=680b4539127f

Gibbs, S. (2018, October 24). Apple and Samsung Fined for Deliberately Slowing Down Phones. *The Guardian*. https://www.theguardian.com/technology/2018/oct/24/apple-samsung-fined-for-slowing-down-phones

Greenpeace. (2015). Click Clean Scorecard: Key Findings & Scores Explained. https://www.greenpeace.org/usa/wp-content/uploads/2015/08/2015ClickCleanScorecardKeyFindings.pdf

Greenpeace. (2017). Guide to Greener Electronics 2017. https://www.greenpeace.org/usa/reports/greener-electronics-2017/

Hu, W., & Haag, M. (2019). Park It, Trucks: Here Come New York's Cargo Bikes. https://www.nytimes.com/2019/12/04/nyregion/nyc-cargo-bikes-delivery.html

Inditex. (2019). Annual Report 2019. https://www.inditex.com/documents/10279/645708/2019+Inditex+Annual+Report.pdf/25aa68e3-d7b2-bc1d-3dab-571c0b4a0151

Investopedia. (2020). If You Invested Right After Amazon's IPO. https://www.investopedia.com/articles/investing/082715/if-you-had-invested-right-after-amazons-ipo.asp

Leahy, S. (2015, March 20). World Water Day: The Cost of Cotton in Water-Challenged India. *The Guardian*. https://www.theguardian.com/sustainable-business/2015/mar/20/cost-cotton-water-challenged-india-world-water-day

Manning, L., & Soon, J. M. (2016). Food Safety, Food Fraud and Food Defense: A Fast Evolving Literature. *Journal of Food Science, 81*(4), R823–R834.

McCarty, B. (2011). Amazon's CTO: "Amazon Is a Technology Company. We Just Happen to Do Retail". *The Next Web*. https://thenextweb.com/insider/2011/10/05/amazons-cto-amazon-is-a-technology-company-we-just-happen-to-do-retail/

McFall-Johnsen, M. (2019, October 18). The Fashion Industry Emits More Carbon Than International Flights and Maritime Shipping Combined. Here Are the Biggest Ways It Impacts the Planet. *Business Insider*. https://www.businessinsider.nl/fast-fashion-environmental-impact-pollution-emissions-waste-water-2019-10/

Microsoft. (2019). Annual Report 2019. https://www.microsoft.com/investor/reports/ar19/index.html

Nace, T. (2019, October 29). Coca-Cola Named the World's Most Polluting Brand in Plastic Waste Audit. *Forbes*. https://www.forbes.com/sites/trevornace/2019/10/29/coca-cola-named-the-worlds-most-polluting-brand-in-plastic-waste-audit/#2282bb3774e0

Nestlé. (2020). The Nestlé Sustainability Review. https://www.nestle.com/sites/default/files/asset-library/documents/reports/csv%20reports/environmental%20sustainability/sustainability_review_english.pdf

Omotoso, M. (2018, December 5). "Who Made My Clothes" Movement – How It All Began. *Fashion Insiders*. https://fashioninsiders.co/features/inspiration/who-made-my-clothes-movement/#:~:text=Who%20Started%20the%20%E2%80%9CWho%20Made,opinion%20leader%20in%20sustainable%20fashion

Porter, M. E. (1979, March–April). How Competitive Forces Shape Strategy. *Harvard Business Review*, 137–145.

Porter, M. E. (1980). *Competitive Strategy: Techniques for Analyzing Industries and Competitors*. Free Press.

Rahman, M. T., Habibullah, M., & Abdullah-Al-Masum, M. (2017). Readymade Garment Industry in Bangladesh: Growth, Contribution and Challenges. *Journal of Economics and Finance, 8*(3), 1–7.

Safi, M., & Rushe, D. (2018). Rana Plaza, Five Years On: Safety of Workers Hangs in Balance in Bangladesh. https://www.theguardian.com/global-development/2018/apr/24/bangladeshi-police-target-garment-workers-union-rana-plaza-five-years-on

Samsung. (2018). Samsung Electronics Sustainability Report 2018. https://www.samsung.com/us/smg/content/dam/samsung/us/aboutsamsung/2017/Sustainability_Report_2018_v2.pdf

Scott Matthews, H., Hendrickson, C. T., & Soh, D. L. (2001). Environmental and Economic Effects of e-Commerce: A Case Study of Book Publishing and Retail Logistics. *Transportation Research Record, 1763*(1), 6–12.

Spink, J., Helferich, O. K., & Griggs, J. E. (2010). Combating the Impact of Product Counterfeiting. *Distribution Business Management Journal, 6*, 60–64.

Statista. (2020). Projected Retail e-Commerce GMV Share of Amazon in the United States from 2016 to 2021. https://www.statista.com/statistics/788109/amazon-retail-market-share-usa/

Suhrawardi. (2020, March 30). Collapse of Bangladesh's Garment Industry During Coronavirus Leaves Its Workers More Vulnerable Than Ever. *Forbes*. https://www.forbes.com/sites/rebeccasuhrawardi/2020/03/30/collapse-of-bangladeshs-garment-industry-leaves-its-workers-more-vulnerable-than-ever-during%2D%2Dcoronavirus/#5bf5830f27e0

Sweeny, G. (2015). Fast Fashion Is the Second Dirtiest Industry in the World, Next to Big Oil. *Ecowatch*. https://www.ecowatch.com/fast-fashion-is-the-second-dirtiest-industry-in-the-world-next-to-big%2D%2D1882083445.html

United States Department of Justice. (2019). Field of Schemes Fraud Results in Over a Decade in Federal Prison for Leader of Largest Organic Fraud Case in U.S. History. https://www.justice.gov/usao-ndia/pr/field-schemes-fraud-results-over-decade-federal-prison-leader-largest-organic-fraud

UPS. (2018). Pressroom. https://www.pressroom.ups.com/pressroom/ContentDetailsViewer.page?ConceptType=PressReleases&id=1540482965617-103

UPS. (2019a). 2019 Annual Report. http://www.investors.ups.com/static-files/e4d06ff9-8dcd-45a7-a8f5-b400c944455e

UPS. (2019b). 2019 Corporate Sustainability Highlights. https://sustainability.ups.com/media/sustainability-report-highlights-brochure-us_en.pdf

UPS. (2019c). Pressroom. https://pressroom.ups.com/pressroom/ContentDetailsViewer.page?ConceptType=PressReleases&id=1567522217503-928

UPS. (2019d). Pressroom. https://www.pressroom.ups.com/pressroom/ContentDetailsViewer.page?ConceptType=PressReleases&id=1570546455953-427

Yahoo Finance. (2020a). FedEx Corporation (FDX). https://finance.yahoo.com/quote/FDX/history?period1=946684800&period2=1577750400&interval=1d&filter=history&frequency=1d

Yahoo Finance. (2020b). Dow Jones Industrial Average (^DJI). https://finance.yahoo.com/quote/%5EDJI/history?period1=946684800&period2=1577750400&interval=1d&filter=history&frequency=1d

8

The Intangible Costs of Environmental Fraud: Impacts for Brands, Trust, Corporate Identity, Image, Credibility, and Reputation

8.1 Constructs

The association of companies to misconducts and corporate crimes may significantly harm their esteem among its stakeholders. The disclosure of unethical behavior may impair the faith that people have in an organization's ability or willingness to comply with good business practices. If an aura of mistrust is installed around a firm, its relationship with its environment becomes particularly difficult, with economic actors being reticent or even refusing to engage in commercial transactions. The discomfort with a company's conducts may reflect in negative expectations of its future behavior, pushing customers, investors, employees, suppliers, and governments to consider other alternatives. With the overall perception around a company depending on the signals it sends to observers, its credibility among its publics becomes critical. In this sense, such damages may put the continuation of cheating companies at risk.

Consumers, for example, may be hesitant to buy a product or a service when they doubt the honesty of the firm providing it, either because they do not believe that the quality announced is verifiable in practice or because they do not consider that the company is being transparent. The

M. Fracarolli Nunes, C. Lee Park, *Business Ethics and Environmental Fraud*,
https://doi.org/10.1007/978-3-030-73800-6_8

reasoning may be extended to basically all other classes of stakeholders. Suppliers may avoid selling to a company perceived as deceitful, fearing that they will not be properly paid for their offerings. Investors, in turn, shall keep their distance of firms reputed for unethical behavior, as, along with possible moral issues, misconducts may have a high financial cost (e.g. product recalls, indenizations, legal fees). The possibility that such problems take place may significantly increase investment risks, eventually making transactions impracticable. Likewise, in case employees' trust is eroded, they are expected to look for repositioning in other companies, eventually competitors, and applicants in the job market may not wish to integrate such companies, what may significantly compromise the quality of workforce.

Broadly, it seems that the association of a company to unscrupulous conducts damages its competitiveness. Although such outcome is not surprising, the mechanism through which it takes place may be of great complexity, as the study of the nature and dynamics of intangible resources involves some of the most intricate constructs in Management literature. Among them are the concepts of brand, trust, corporate identity, corporate image, corporate credibility, and corporate reputation, each of which is worthy of attention. The difficulties in studying these constructs come from their very nature—unlike physical resources (e.g. machines, equipment, buildings), intangible ones are not in companies' possession and depend on the opinions, beliefs, feelings, expectations, perceptions, and emotions of observers. In a sense, it must be argued that intangible resources have the minds of stakeholders as their habitat. This explains the high investments of companies in advertising, sponsorship, and institutional communication (e.g. sustainability reports), among others. Basically, these activities represent attempts to control, or at least influence the space that companies occupy in the life of their different audiences.

Still on the contrast between tangible and intangible resources, one should note the differences in the ways which each of these groups is obtained. While tangible resources can be acquired (e.g. land, buildings, machines), intangible must, in general, be built. This means that they are not easily accessible and often demand long periods to be fabricated. Also, intangible resources usually cannot be transported or transferred from one company to another. This partially expounds their high strategic value, as discussed later in the chapter. In addition to their immateriality, the investigation of intangible resources' dynamics is difficult because they usually get confused with each other. It is not possible, for example, to determine a clear point where issues related to trust end and those around the credibility of companies begin. In reality, these two notions deal, in many cases, with the same issues, although representing different ideas. Because of their similarities, they often end up complementing each other, with the differences between them being nuanced. To a greater or lesser extent, the same occurs with other intangible resources, which ultimately contribute to forming the way in which a company is seen, as well as what is expected of it. In search to offer a better comprehension on the specificities of the different intangible resources discussed here each is explored in greater detail.

8.2 Brand

As pointed by van Riel and Fombrun (2007), for

> (...) practitioners 'a brand is a mixture of attributes, tangible and intangible, symbolized in a trademark, which, if managed properly, creates value and influence' (see www.brandchannel.com). The Dictionary of Business and Management similarly defines a brand as 'a name, sign or symbol used to identify items or services of the seller(s) and to differentiate them from goods of competitors'. Advertising guru David Ogilvy positioned a brand more expansively as 'the intangible sum of a product's attributes: its name, packaging, and price, its history, its reputation, and the way it's advertised'. (van Riel & Fombrun, 2007, p. 39)

Accordingly, these and other common definitions would all indicate that brands create images in the minds of observers. That would be due to their power to communicate a combination of verbal, visual, and emotional hints that push targeted observers to identify with it. While the large scope of these definitions indicates the intricacy of the concept, it also denotes its importance for companies' success. On that regard, Aaker (2009) argues that the product's origin would be signed to the costumer by the brand, in such a way that both the costumer and the producer would be protected from competitors offering products that seem to be identical. Coherently with the previous views discussed, brands would stand then as tools allowing the identification of goods and services of a seller (or group of sellers), and hence distinguishing them from those of competitors. Still after the author, the notion of brand equity would encompass a set of brand assets and liabilities which might be grouped in five categories: brand loyalty, name awareness, perceived quality, brand associations, and other proprietary brand assets (e.g. patents, trademarks, channel relationships). Thus, brand equity would create value for both customers and firms. Regarding the former, the value creations would be associated with an enhanced interpretation/processing of information, higher confidence in purchase decision, and use satisfaction. For firms, value would come from a greater efficiency and effectiveness of marketing programs, brand loyalty, higher prices and margins, brand extensions, trade leverages, and finally, competitive advantage.

Kapferer (2008) also stresses the strategic importance of brands. Accordingly, along with Research and Development, real consumer orientations, efficiency cultures, employee involvement, and a firm's capacity to change and react rapidly, brands would represent one of the few strategic assets capable to provide long-lasting competitive advantage. Accordingly, these would compose the mantra of firms such as Wal-Mart, Starbucks, Apple, and Zara. Strong brands would be a key element for companies' growth, leading to high product penetration rates and high purchase frequency per buyer. In this set, brand loyalty would be the utmost sort of loyalty, ahead of price or bargain-related ones. The name and the visual symbol of a brand comprehends all the goodwill generated by clients' positive experiences or prospects, as well as its products, channels, stores, communication, and people, being the management of these issues the core skill needed for a competent brand management. As pointed out by van Riel and Fombrun (2007), the creation of more general positive perceptions around a company would be inserted in the concept of corporate branding.

Although naturally associated with producers and distributors operating fast-moving consumer goods, branding has become a strategic issue in basically all sectors, including non-governmental and non-for profit organizations, pharmaceutical laboratories, commodities, utilities, and business-to-business (B2B), among others (Kapferer, 2008). In fact, even people are being managed like brands, with football players like David Beckham illustrating the practice, as the US $250 million invested by the Los Angeles Galaxy to contract the player are expected to be recovered through the commercialization of products using his name, face, or signature, composing the "Beckham brand".

In organizing the debate on brand equity, Kapferer (2008, p. 14) proposes three main sub-constructs composing it: brand assets, brand strength, and brand value. While brand assets relate to a brand's patents and sources of influence (e.g. awareness/saliency, type of relationship with consumers, image), brand strength would be associated with the outcomes of brand equity, often captured by behavioral competitive indicators such as loyalty rates, market share, market leadership, and, occasionally, premium prices. Brand value, in turn, translates a brand's ability to deliver profits. The author also alerts to what he calls the "intellectual temptation" to evaluate brands apart from its business objectives, as, although certain brands may indeed be analyzed through sociological, psychological, semiotics, anthropological, and philosophical lenses, they are historically associated with the generation of profits. In that way, saying that "lack of profit is not a brand problem but a business problem is to separate the brand from the business", what would end up corrupting the original motives of brand management.

As discussed by Cobb-Walgren et al. (1995), back in the 1990s, the cost of bringing a new brand to market was estimated to be around US $100 million (Ourusoff, 1992), with a probability of failure of 50% (Crawford, 1993). While it may be hard to give some practical meaning to figures such as this one—as brands, companies, and contexts may change dramatically, and so may the cost of branding—they portray the idea that the creation of a brand may be expensive, complex, and risky investments for companies. Although traditionally seen as a way to create positive product perceptions among consumers, brand principles are also argued to apply to other groups of stakeholders (e.g. employees, communities, environmental groups) (van Riel & Fombrun, 2007).

In addressing the sociological impact of brands, Muniz Jr. and O'Guinn (2001) introduce the idea of brand community. As discussed by the authors, admirers of a brand may organize in specialized, non-geographically bound communities, which, through the structuration of a set of social relationships, develop a shared consciousness, rituals, traditions, and a sense of moral responsibility. In that way, along with participating in a brand's larger social construction, brand communities form an important part of its legacy. The formation of brand communities would be coherent with the idea of a neo-tribalism (Maffesoli, 1996) which, among other things, points to reaggregations of hyper individualist societies (Shields, 1996). Different from the classic anthropological conceptions associated to tribalism (Muniz Jr. & O'Guinn, 2001), these neo-tribes would be characterized by their fluidity, meaning that their relationships would be marked by occasional gatherings and dispersals (Maffesoli, 1996). Although unbound to physical co-presence, members of these neo-tribes would still exhibit "a local sense of identification, religiosity, syncretism, *and* group narcissism" (Cova, 1997, p. 300), being, however, consumption practice the fact that, among the different things, holds these neo-tribes together is (Muniz Jr. & O'Guinn, 2001). That seems to be the case of Harley-Davidson consumers, who typically gather to share their experiences.

8.3 Trust

Business relationships are driven by the most distinct motives, varying greatly, however, in terms of duration and strength. The relationship between a large food company and a conventional soy producer, for example, does not necessarily need to be built to last. The fact that soy is a commodity (i.e. a product with no differentiation) reduces the dependence of the food company, once it may obtain an identical or a very similar product from a range of farmers. Likewise, the existence of a large consumer market for soybeans (e.g. animal food, human consumption) allows the producer to sell his output to other interested buyers in case he is not satisfied with the conditions proposed by the large firm. Since mutual dependence between the parties is virtually nil, there are no incentives for the creation and development of a solid relationship. Adds to that the fact that the technological challenges associated with the production of soybeans are relatively overcome in such a way that there is no need for collaboration between buyers and suppliers to augment productivity. In these cases, exchanges are closer to the dynamics of free markets, as discussed in Chap. 3.

On the other hand, business models based on production outsourcing of technology products tend to strengthen ties between companies, particularly if the manufacturing and assembling of innovative products are transferred to suppliers (Schoenherr et al., 2015). In these cases, it is not rare that partners work in close collaboration, being common for companies to develop products together, optimizing the capabilities of both, and maximizing the value generated. The exchange of critical information and the sharing of know-how that are necessary in this type of relationships make trust even more important in the search for competitive advantage.

Between these extremes there is a long variety of relationships. In practice, the same company applies different relationship strategies depending on the characteristics of its suppliers and customers, as well as on the perceived value of each relationship. Companies like Volkswagen, for instance, count on nearly 40,000 suppliers worldwide (Volkswagen, 2020), ranging from office material provisioners to software developers, including those used to cheat environmental inspections within the Dieselgate scandal. Clearly, these two types of suppliers require different sorts of relationship. While the impact of the former on the performance of the company is probably modest, the latter was at the heart of the company's strategy, allowing it to enjoy an *improper competitive advantage* (see Chap. 6). Moreover, at the same time an office material provisioner offers little to no differentiation—and by consequence competes on costs and may be easily substituted—software developers shall grant the company with a tailor-made product which counts on great doses of intellectual capital. It may be argued then that the relationship between Volkswagen and its office material suppliers is fragile and is closer to those between soybeans producers and food companies, while the companies' bonds with its software developers must be managed in a way to ensure that the relationship is long-lasting and satisfying for both parts.

In fact, long-term buyer-supplier relationships are relatively common in other industries, particularly in those where the parties need to share valuable information. That includes sectors such as aeronautics, military, as well as a series of activities related to information technology. The use of e-mail providers (e.g. Microsoft Outlook), or the implementation of enterprise resource planning software (e.g. SAP, Oracle), for instance, is necessarily based on the development of mutual confidence. Regardless of the type of relationships, they seem to be all based on some level of trust between the parties. The nature of trust explains its value, as its establishment usually depends on a timely sequence of interactions. Despite the typical difficulties to be built, trust between parties can be quickly destroyed. Just like a cracked crystal, once broken, trust will hardly be restored. The preservation of trust stands then as a strategic issue for companies, particularly for those which seek to develop solid relationships with their partners. In that regard, Ha et al. (2011) stress the importance of trust in the establishment of close relationships within supply chain contexts. In face of the personal characteristics of trust, however, the notion would be less applicable to inter-organizational relationships (in comparison to interpersonal ones). The idea of reliance—as a complementary construct to trust—would be more indicated to treat firm-to-firm relationships (Mouzas et al., 2007).

It is possible, however, that the relationships between people and companies are even more complex than the ones discussed so far. Similar to bank accounts, individuals and organizations would build trust accounts (Covey, 1989), as one could draw on these accounts and eventually even make mistakes, given that the reserve is maintained. That would allow individuals and organizations the necessary flexibility and freedom to act in the absence of scrutiny, making all sorts of relationships more efficient in terms of time and energy invested on them. Alike marriages in which partners do not need to constantly check on each other's fidelity—and may thus be free to focus on their day-to-day activities—trust-based business relationships profit from similar benefits, with a handshake sealing a deal and words standing as factual contracts (Treviño & Nelson, 2016). On that regard, Belk (1988) points out to the important role that organizations can play in people's life. Accordingly, as brands and products become part of people's lives, they turn into a part of their affective memories, in such a way that a sort of an extended self is formed. In line with these views, Berry (1996) sees trust as, perhaps, the most powerful relationship marketing tool companies can count on. The exchanges between financial institutions and their clients, for example, are largely built on the faith that one has in the other. When depositing their savings, one believes that the money can be withdrawn at any moment. Clients suppose that the treasury will custody their money and eventually pay them the agreed interest. Likewise, credit operations are structured around banks' beliefs that customers will not only be able to return the principal plus interest, but also will have good faith to do so. If, by any chance, the confidence in either of these two poles is compromised, activities immediately end, what, depending on the magnitude of the problem, may lead to serious economic crises.

Within this view Evans and Krueger (2009, p. 1003) define trust as a "mental construct with implications for social functioning and economic behavior", with psychologists of assorted backgrounds identifying "interpersonal trust as a social construct of far-reaching significance". Erikson (1950, p. 221), in turn, positions trust as "the first task of the ego", with the notion playing a major role in the development of social interaction. In the absence of trust, one could not tolerate the continuous perspective of being attacked or somehow harmed by others, what would ultimately prevent the constitution of social relationships (Evans & Krueger, 2009). Analogously, Rotter (1971) claims that trust is in the basis of our entire social fabric, with nearly all of one's day-to-day decisions involving trusting someone else (e.g. paying taxes, flying to a convention, going to the dentist). As argued by Treviño and Nelson (2016, p. 27) trust would be a more elusive benefit resulting from ethical conduct, having economic and moral values. As highlighted by the authors, in studying what seems to be the "biology of trust", neuroscientists have found that the hormone oxytocin is released in trusting relationships, granting those involved in cooperation with a pleasant feeling. Trust would be notably relevant in the context of a service economy, in which reputations for dependability and satisfactory service would account for a great portion of companies' resources. When it comes to firms operating in e-commerce that may be particularly important, as the transaction is, to a great extent, based on consumers' belief that the company will physically hand in what it has sold them.

On that view, Glaeser et al. (2000) classify trust as a pivotal component of social capital, which, in turn, has been argued to influence sundry significant economic and political phenomena. Building a parallel with the concepts of physical and human capital—understood as the "tools and training that enhance individual productivity", Putnam (1995, p. 67) defines social capital as those "features of social organization such as networks, norms, and social trust that facilitate coordination and cooperation for mutual benefit". Accordingly, in communities counting with substantial stocks of social capital life would be easier, as networks of civic engagement tend to foster norms of reciprocity, not only encouraging the emergence of social trust but also facilitating coordination and communication, amplifying reputations, and allowing dilemmas of collective action to be resolved. Beyond that, economic and political impasses embedded in networks that promote dense social interaction would have the incentives to opportunistic behavior reduced.

Complementing these views, Tyler and Kramer (1995) discuss trust in the lenses of the rational choice model. Based on individual gains (Stigler, 1950) and the exchange of material resources (Laver, 1981), the model argues that, when faced with forms of social interaction, people would be motivated by self-interest (i.e. maximization of personal gains and minimization of personal losses), reacting in a self-interested and instrumental manner. In this set, Axelrod (1984) claims that cooperation is based on the "shadow of the future", meaning that trust in the actions of a counterpart is sustained by the expectation of an ongoing relationship (Tyler & Kramer, 1995). As highlighted by Ha et al. (2011), however, trust comprehends emotional aspects such as beliefs and sentiments between individuals, with further consideration at a personal level being necessary. The relevance of trust as a critical element in human relationships is also approached by some of the most influential thinkers of the West. In his classic *The Theory of Moral Sentiments*, Adam Smith (1976 [1759], p. 86), for example, discusses how conformity to a given expected behavior shall influence the development of positive interactions, even among those who would not be particularly adherent to social norms. Accordingly, "if there is any society among robbers and murderers, they must at least (...) abstain from robbing and murdering one another". As pointed out by Gambetta (2000), Smith's passage reinforces the perception that basic forms of cooperation would be inevitable in the constitutional process of viable societies.

Based on the discussion above, it may be said that the disclosure of unethical conducts may seriously compromise companies' capacity to establish positive relationships with its stakeholders. Beyond damaging a firm's capacity to engage in long-term collaboration with its supply chain partners, the loss of trust may also have a direct impact in consumers' willingness to buy. Among other things, these effects may translate into a lesser capacity for innovation, as well as in serious harms in terms of customers' loyalty to brands.

8.4 Corporate Identity

As put by Gray and Balmer (1998) corporate identity refers to the essence of an organization (i.e. what it is, Balmer, 2001), encompassing its strategy, the philosophy of its leaders, its culture, and its organizational design. Accordingly, a company' strategy relates to its master plans, objectives, policies, and programs. Corporate philosophy, in turn, is linked to top executives' values and beliefs, while corporate culture comprehends the assumptions, values, and beliefs that are shared by the members of an organization. Lately, organizational design refers to the fundamental questions on the structure of an organization, including its degree of centralization, the number of hierarchical levels, and size of staff, among others. The interaction of these factors would make each firm different from all others, "making (…) its 'corporate brand' distinct" (Gray & Balmer, 1998, p. 695). For Gylling and Lindberg-Repo (2006, p. 3), despite a general definition on a theoretical level is still missing, the most common interpretation of the concept is that "corporate identity is a mix of characteristics that an organisation possesses as a subject".

Stuart (2002), however, highlights the confusion between the concepts of corporate identity and organizational identity. On that regard, Hatch and Schultz (1997) argued that, while the former is proper to the Marketing literature, the latter would have originated in the organizational one. Accordingly, the concepts would diverge, as, while top management has an explicit role in the definition of how a company is expressed to external audiences (i.e. in the bases of corporate identity), organizational identity would refer to a collectively shared understanding about an organization's unique values and characteristics. For Kiriakidou and Millward (2000), in turn, corporate identity would stand as the tangible representation of organizational identity. In this vein, Stuart (2002) argues that, depending on the stage of an organization's history, the relationship between corporate and organizational identities shall vary.

Corporate identity and organizational identity would be analogous in the early stages of an organization's development, as the expression of its core messages to external stakeholders (i.e. corporate identity) is likely to be based on the reality of the organization (i.e. organizational identity). Yet, in face of organizational growth and of eventual changes in leadership, it is possible that corporate identity and organizational identity come to diverge, particularly when organizations seek to reposition themselves as an answer to market forces. Still after the author, in such cases, the focus is on changing the visual identity—instead of the corporate one—with companies being expected to follow a new path in response. In that way, levels of juxtaposition between corporate and organizational identities would be common (Balmer, 2001; Stuart, 2002), varying from an ideal adjacency in which corporate identity is fully based on the organizational identity (Kiriakidou & Millward, 2000) to situations in which corporate and organizational identities are seen as distinct entities with no relationship—this later referring to situations in which the corporate identity that is projected is not primarily based on the organizational reality, but instead, on public relations and advertising (Kennedy, 1977).

In this sense, corporate identity would be linked not only to the reality of a company but also to its uniqueness (Gray & Balmer, 1998). The building of corporate identities may be seen as a way out of the Porter's (1996) operational effectiveness paradigm discussed in Chap. 3, even for companies in the automotive industry. The singular characteristics perceived in a company would work as the structural basis of its differentiation efforts, and ultimately, of its strategy. On that regard, Gylling and Lindberg-Repo (2006) point out to safety as a core attribute that makes Volvo special in the eyes of consumers, and the one on which the company builds its identity. Within this view, van Riel and Balmer (1997) argue that corporate identity management would be mainly driven to the establishment of favorable reputations among stakeholders, in such a way that these groups develop a higher propensity to (1) buy the products and services offered by the organization, (2) work for it, and (3) invest in it (Balmer, 2001; van Riel, 1995).

Building on this notion, Stuart (2002) gathers important points on the relationship between corporate identity and the behavior of employees. As pointed out by the author, the greater the identification of an employee with an organization, the more likely they are to support it (Mael &

Ashforth, 1992), to accept its premises, and to make decisions which are coherent with organizational objectives (Littlejohn, 1989). Employee identification would be thus linked to the extent to which the members of an organization define themselves by the attributes they believe the organization is defined by (Dutton et al., 1994). As shown by Eriksson (2004), companies' efforts to change their identities are associated with the development of emotional problems by employees, with issues such as depression, the loss of self-trust, lack of perspective, and emotional fatigue being common. Despite being a primary group of stakeholders, employees are often overlooked, with companies focusing their attention on external groups whose relevance for organizational survival are perceived as greater (Stuart, 2002). Meijs (2002), in turn, argues that corporate identity would be among the most important assets of organizations, deserving management's constant attention. The author, however, points out that multiple identities may co-exist within an organization, contradicting the idea of a unique and harmonious body. In face of the still poor understanding of the issue, the management of corporate identities would be actually a myth, with both processes of change and the co-existence of multiple identities contributing to organizational instability.

Considering the matters approached, the association of companies with immoral practices (e.g. environmental fraud) may significantly damage the way it is perceived by its internal stakeholders (e.g. employees). Along with the possible negative impacts of these connections in their perception about themselves, the emotional stress generated in such situations may harm their performance and even their willingness to keep their positions. In any case, these situations are likely to impair the operations, which could bring huge losses for companies involved in ethical scandal in the long run.

8.5 Corporate Image

From a macro perspective, corporate image refers to the set of feelings and perceptions associated with a company. Differently from the notion of corporate identity, however, it does not relate to internal stakeholders (e.g. employees), nor with the understanding that companies have about themselves. Instead, the construct would be better suited to address the reactions caused by companies' names and brands in external observers. That includes the most distinct groups such as consumers, suppliers, investors, governments, and local communities. In this sense, it may be argued that corporate image is one of the main intangible resources that a company can count on, with positive evaluations on that regard playing a major role in firms search or sustainable competitive advantage. In differentiating brand image and identity, Kapferer (2008) simplistically claim that the former is on the receivers' side, while the latter is on the senders' side. Differently put, it may be argued that, while image refers to the capacity of someone to interpret the signs received from a source, identity would relate not only to what this source is, but to what it seeks and believes to be. As put by the author, that would refer to a brand's meaning, aim, and self-image. Different definitions have been proposed during the years, most of which corroborating this view. Gray and Balmer (1998, p. 696), for example, claim that "[c]orporate image is the mental picture of the company held by its audiences—what comes to mind when on sees or hears the corporate name or sees its logo".

As discussed by Gotsi and Wilson (2001), however, early works described corporate image in such a way it seemed synonymous with corporate reputation. Martineau (1958), for instance, positioned the construct as the combination of functional qualities and psychological attributes that inhabit the mind of consumers, while for Boulding (1973) it stood as a subjective knowledge. These perspectives corroborate the view previously discussed that intangible resources would rest beyond companies' control. In fact, since intangible resources reside in stakeholders' minds, companies are left with the arduous task of influencing and shaping them in the best way possible, without ever being able to be sure of the result of their efforts. This partially explains both the high investments in advertising and the prominence of Psychology studies in the Marketing literature. All in all, one can be confident about the content and the meaning of a message sent, but can never be assured about the way it is going to be interpreted and absorbed by their interlocutors.

Depending on the nature of each business, as well as that of the markets they target, the images companies seek to project may greatly vary. For an aviation company, for example, attributes such as operational safety, punctuality, and comfort are crucial. For an electronics company, an image linked to innovation can be decisive in influencing customers looking for the latest technology available, just as a bank needs to build an image of solidity to convince people to entrust their savings to it. The strategic value of corporate image is reflected in several aspects, with distinct classes of stakeholders reacting to it. As pointed out by Kim et al. (2011), favorable corporate images may have a powerful impact on sales, as it positively affects customer satisfaction and loyalty. Gatewood et al. (1993), in turn, discusses the relevance of corporate image in influencing job choice decisions, while Hoffmann and Fieseler (2012) stress the role of corporate image in investment decisions. Accordingly, that would encompass a set of non-financial information equity analysts rely on, including the nature of the relationship companies keep with their stakeholders, corporate governance, corporate social responsibility initiatives, reputation, brand, the quality of management, and strategic consistency.

In parallel with all the specific corporate images exemplified above, it seems that virtually all companies seek to attach themselves to positive social and environmental images. In this sense, the creation of favorable images with regard to sustainability issues would not aim to convince stakeholders that companies are operationally capable of delivering the functional value they promise, neither that they can do that more efficiently than their competitors. Instead, the management of social and environmental images would feed the impression that the company is concerned with aspects that go beyond the generation of profits, thus being "for the good". Given the characteristics of corporate image, it is not surprising that scandals involving firms have the potential to seriously damage it.

8.6 Corporate Credibility

The notion of corporate credibility seems to be anchored in the faith stakeholders have in a company, whether concerning its ability to deliver the value they promise, or its good faith to do so. Within this notion, companies would be seen as sources of communication, with observers' beliefs depending on the combination of two sub-constructs: expertise and trustworthiness (Newell & Goldsmith, 2001). Accordingly, corporate credibility stands as "the extent to which consumers feel that the firm has the knowledge or ability to fulfill its claims and whether the firm can be trusted to tell the truth or not" (Newell & Goldsmith, 2001, p. 235). Although focused on consumers, the reasoning may be extended to all other classes of stakeholders. When it comes to suppliers, for example, the assumption that a buyer will effectively honor its commitments (i.e. pay for the inputs purchased, respecting both the amount and the conditions agreed) is crucial in the development of transactions. The lack of this credibility among suppliers may create several difficulties for a company, particularly for the good management of its working capital. Mistrust can actually prevent the company to profit from more favorable payment conditions (e.g. installment) and hamper inventory management. In addition to leading to operational problems, that usually translates into increased production costs and in a deterioration of financial performance.

Likewise, if a company lacks credibility with financial institutions and investors, it will have difficulties obtaining loans or capitalizing itself, which can be reflected in a series of short, medium, and long-term setbacks, and significantly increase the likelihood of insolvency. When it comes to employees, the loss of credibility may lead to a sudden interruption of operations (i.e. strikes) in case they believe that they will not be properly paid, or that the company will not comply with collective agreements (e.g. issues related to work safety, the implementation of career plans, pensions funds, employee stability). In this sense, cases of environmental fraud may harm both the expertise and trustworthiness aspects of corporate credibility. In such events, it is possible that stakeholders come to believe that the company has chosen an unethical path because it is unable to outperform, or at least match its competitors within legal limits. From this point of view, the incidence of any sort of fraud would stand as a strong sign of incompetence. Likewise, cases of environmental fraud represent a direct attack to stakeholders' trust. Once more, the Volkswagen Dieselgate scandal serves as an exemplary illustration of these issues.

8.7 Corporate Reputation

The concept of corporate reputation may be understood as the result of all the concepts previously discussed, representing the overall perception of companies among all the publics they interact with. Within this view, van Riel and Fombrun (2007, p. 38) propose corporate reputation as "a multi-stakeholder construct that is particularly appropriate for measuring the effectiveness of an organization's communication system". In turn, Dowling (1986) argues that corporate reputations have an important impact on stakeholders' choices, influencing not only their product preferences but also their investment and career decisions. Despite being now widely recognized as critical corporate assets, in the past, corporate reputation and corporate image were perceived as vague concepts, representing, at best, a peripheral concern to senior management (Gray & Balmer, 1998). The subject, however, has attracted the interest of both Marketing academics and practitioners since the 1960s (Gotsi & Wilson, 2001), being also a common object of investigation within other Management disciplines. Strategy scholars, for example, often position it as an intangible resource for the firm (Barnett et al., 2006).

In this set, Fombrun and Shanley (1990) position corporate reputations as the result of a competitive process among firms, in which they signal their main characteristics to maximize their social status (Spence, 1974). Accordingly, corporate reputations would denote how firms' products, jobs, strategies, and prospects compare to those proposed by competitors, with a series of benefits following from that. By inhibiting the mobility of rivals in an industry, for example, corporate reputations would generate excess returns for firms (Caves & Porter, 1977; Wilson, 1985). The charging of premium prices would be also possible, as positive reputations may indicate that companies' products are superior (Klein & Leffler, 1981; Milgrom & Roberts, 1986a). Likewise, positive corporate reputations would attract better applicants (Stigler, 1962) and investors (Milgrom & Roberts, 1986b), ultimately, consolidating the status of a firm within an industrial social system (Shrum & Wuthnow, 1988), and adding to the study of industrial stratification (Fombrun, 1986).

With the ensemble of discussions treated above and the context of the book, it is useful to understand that cases of environmental fraud will effect each construct differently. Table 8.1 summarizes this impact on the constructs discussed throughout the chapter:

Table 8.1 Impact of environmental fraud on companies' intangible resources

Construct	Impact of environmental fraud on construct
Brand	Compromise of messages sent by brands, with the disclosure of environmental fraud replacing positive perceptions with an association with illegal and/or immoral conducts.
Trust	Environmental fraud may represent a severe breach of trust, especially as it deals with an issue that tends to be very dear for a significant part of stakeholders (i.e. the environment). In addition, it is linked to dishonesty, what may lead stakeholders to no longer value a company's statements, not only regarding environmental issues but all others.
Corporate identity	With a company's employees embedded in its culture, the revelation that it incurs in crimes or ethically reprehensible behavior can cause an identity crisis, with honest personnel rejecting to adhere to the firms' corrupt values. In the case of environmental fraud specifically, this may even lead to a stamped of the employees most connected to the cause, as well as difficulties in recruiting new employees, especially the younger ones.
Corporate image	The association of companies with cases of environmental fraud may represent a permanent scratch in the way they are perceived by external observers. As such scandals usually have great repercussion, they tend to be remembered for a long time, and can be remembered through simple searches on the internet. Beyond that, competitors of companies involved in environmental fraud will probably take advantage of these episodes, attacking their positioning and labeling them as hypocrites.
Corporate credibility	Permanent or long-standing damage to all strategies aimed at positioning the company as an environmentally responsible enterprise. This would be mainly due to the loss of credibility, with past actions being used as a parameter for future expectations.
Corporate reputation	In a sense, the impacts of environmental fraud on corporate reputation synthesize all the negative effects caused in the constructs previously discussed. In fact, since reputation is, in a great measure, composed by all of them, it manifests the set of losses caused by the company.

Source: Author(s)

References

Aaker, D. A. (2009). *Managing Brand Equity: Capitalizing on the Value of a Brand Name*. The Free Press.

Axelrod, R. (1984). *The Evolution of Cooperation*. Basic Books.

Balmer, J. M. T. (2001). Corporate Identity, Corporate Branding and Corporate Marketing: Seeing Through the Fog. *European Journal of Marketing, 35*(3/4), 248–291.

Barnett, M. L., Jermier, J. M., & Lafferty, B. A. (2006). Corporate Reputation: The Definitional Landscape. *Corporate Reputation Review, 9*(1), 26–38.

Belk, R. W. (1988). Possessions and the Extended Self. *Journal of Consumer Research, 15*(2), 139–168.

Berry, L. L. (1996). Retailers with a Future. *Marketing Management, 5*(1), 39–46.

Boulding, K. E. (1973). *The Image*. The University of Michigan Press.

Caves, R. E., & Porter, M. E. (1977). From Entry Barriers to Mobility Barriers: Conjectural Decisions and Contrived Deterrence to New Competition. *The Quarterly Journal of Economics, 91*(2), 241–261.

Cobb-Walgren, C. J., Ruble, C. A., & Donthu, N. (1995). Brand Equity, Brand Preference, and Purchase Intent. *Journal of Advertising, 24*(3), 25–40.

Cova, B. (1997). Community and Consumption: Towards a Definition of the Linking Value of Product or Services. *European Journal of Marketing, 31*(Fall/Winter), 297–316.

Covey, S. R. (1989). *The 7 Habits of Highly Effective People*. Simon & Schuster.

Crawford, M. (1993). *New Products Management*. Irwin.

Dowling, G. R. (1986). Managing Your Corporate Images. *Industrial Marketing Management, 15*(2), 109–115.

Dutton, J., Dukerich, J., & Harquail, C. (1994). Organizational Images and Member Identification. *Administrative Science Quarterly, 39*, 239–263.

Erikson, E. (1950). *Childhood and Society*. Norton & Company, Inc.

Eriksson, C. B. (2004). The Effects of Change Programs on Employees' Emotions. *Personnel Review, 33*(1), 110–126.

Evans, A. M., & Krueger, J. L. (2009). The Psychology (and Economics) of Trust. *Social and Personality Psychology Compass, 3*(6), 1003–1017.

Fombrun, C. J. (1986). Structural Dynamics Within and Between Organizations. *Administrative Science Quarterly, 31*(3), 403–421.

Fombrun, C. J., & Shanley, M. (1990). What's in a Name? Reputation Building and Corporate Strategy. *Academy of Management Journal, 33*(2), 233–258.

Gambetta, D. (2000). Can We Trust Trust? In D. Gambetta (Ed.), *Trust: Making and Breaking Cooperative Relations*, Chapter 13 (pp. 213–237). Department of Sociology, University of Oxford. http://www.sociology.ox.ac.uk/papers/gambetta213-237.pdf

Gatewood, R. D., Gowan, M. A., & Lautenschlager, G. J. (1993). Corporate Image, Recruitment Image, and Initial Job Choice Decisions. *Academy of Management Journal, 36*, 414–427.

Glaeser, E. L., Laibson, D. I., Scheinkman, J. A., & Soutter, C. L. (2000). Measuring Trust. *The Quarterly Journal of Economics, 115*(3), 811–846.

Gotsi, M., & Wilson, A. M. (2001). Corporate Reputation: Seeking a Definition. *Corporate Communications: An International Journal, 6*(1), 24–30.

Gray, E. R., & Balmer, J. M. T. (1998). Managing Corporate Image and Corporate Reputation. *Long Range Planning, 31*(5), 695–702.

Gylling, C., & Lindberg-Repo, K. (2006). Investigating the Links Between a Corporate Brand and a Customer Brand. *Journal of Brand Management, 13*(4–5), 257–267.

Ha, B. C., Park, Y. K., & Cho, S. (2011). Suppliers' Affective Trust and Trust in Competency in Buyers. *International Journal of Operations & Production Management, 31*(1), 56–77.

Hatch, M. J., & Schultz, M. (1997). Relations Between Organizational Culture, Identity and Image. *European Journal of Marketing, 31*(5–6), 356–365.

Hoffmann, C., & Fieseler, C. (2012). Investor Relations Beyond Financials: Non-Financial Factors and Capital Market Image Building. *Corporate Communications: An International Journal, 17*(2), 138–155.

Kapferer, J. N. (2008). *The New Strategic Brand Management: Creating and Sustaining Brand Equity Long Term*. Kogan Page Publishers.

Kennedy, S. H. (1977). Nurturing Corporate Images. *European Journal of Marketing, 11*(3), 119–164.

Kim, K. H., Jeon, B. J., Jung, H. S., Lu, W., & Jones, J. (2011). Effective Employment Brand Equity Through Sustainable Competitive Advantage, Marketing Strategy, and Corporate Image. *Journal of Business Research, 64*(11), 1207–1211.

Kiriakidou, O., & Millward, L. J. (2000). Corporate Identity: External Reality or Internal Fit? *Corporate Communications: An International Journal, 5*(1), 49–58.

Klein, B., & Leffler, K. B. (1981). The Role of Market Forces in Assuring Contractual Performance. *Journal of Political Economy, 89*(4), 615–641.

Laver, M. (1981). *The Politics of Private Desire: The Guide to the Politics Of Rational Choice*. Penguin.
Littlejohn, S. (1989). *Theories of Human Communication*. Wads Worth.
Mael, E., & Ashforth, B. E. (1992). Alumni and Their Alma Mater: A Partial Test for the Reformulated Model of Organizational Identification. *Journal of Organizational Behavior, 13*, 103–123.
Maffesoli, M. (1996). *The Time of the Tribes: The Decline of Individualism in Mass Society*. Sage.
Martineau, P. (1958). The Personality of the Retail Store. In A. M. Findlay & L. Sparks (Eds.), *Retailing. Critical Concepts* (Vol. III, Part ii) (pp. 47–55). Routledge.
Meijs, M. (2002). The Myth of Manageability of Corporate Identity. *Corporate Reputation Review, 5*(1), 20–34.
Milgrom, P., & Roberts, J. (1986a). Price and Advertising Signals of Product Quality. *Journal of Political Economy, 94*(4), 796–821.
Milgrom, P., & Roberts, J. (1986b). Relying on the Information of Interested Parties. *The RAND Journal of Economics, 17*(1), 18–32.
Mouzas, S., Henneberg, S., & Naudé, P. (2007). Trust and Reliance in Business Relationships. *European Journal of Marketing, 49*(9/10), 1016–1032.
Muniz, A. M., Jr., & O'Guinn, T. C. (2001). Brand Community. *Journal of Consumer Research, 27*(4), 412–432.
Newell, S. J., & Goldsmith, R. E. (2001). The Development of a Scale to Measure Perceived Corporate Credibility. *Journal of Business Research, 52*, 235–247.
Ourusoff, A. (1992). What's in a Name? *Financial World, 161*(September I), 32–46.
Porter, M. E. (1996). What Is Strategy? *Harvard Business Review, 74*(6), 61–78.
Putnam, R. (1995). Bowling Alone: America's Declining Social Capital. *Journal of Democracy, 6*(1), 65–78.
Rotter, J. B. (1971). Generalized Expectancies for Interpersonal Trust. *American Psychologist, 26*(5), 443–452.
Schoenherr, T., Narayanan, S., & Narasimhan, R. (2015). Trust Formation in Outsourcing Relationships: A Social Exchange Theoretic Perspective. *International Journal of Production Economics, 169*, 401–412.
Shields, R. (1996). Foreword to Michel Maffesoli. In *The Time of the Tribes: The Decline of Individualism in Mass Society* (pp. 3–18). Sage.
Shrum, W., & Wuthnow, R. (1988). Reputational Status of Organizations in Technical Systems. *American Journal of Sociology, 93*(4), 882–912.

Smith, A. (1976 [1759]). *The Theory of Moral Sentiments*. Clarendon Press.
Spence, A. M. (1974). *Market Signaling: Informational Transfer in Hiring and Related Screening Processes*. Harvard University Press.
Stigler, G. J. (1950). The Development of Utility Theory. *Journal of Political Economy, 58*(4), 307–327 and 373–396.
Stigler, G. J. (1962). Information in the Labor Market. *Journal of Political Economy, 70*(5), 94–105.
Stuart, H. (2002). Employee Identification with the Corporate Identity: Issues and Implications. *International Studies of Management & Organization, 32*(3), 28–44.
Treviño, L. K., & Nelson, K. A. (2016). *Managing Business Ethics – Straight Talk About How to Do It Right* (5th ed.). John Wiley & Sons.
Tyler, T. R., & Kramer, R. M. (1995). Whither Trust? In R. M. Kramer & T. R. Tyler (Eds.), *Trust in Organizations: Frontiers of Theory and Research*. Sage Publications.
van Riel, C. B. M. (1995). *Principles of Corporate Communication*. Prentice-Hall.
van Riel, C. B. M., & Balmer, J. M. T. (1997). Corporate Identity: The Concept, Its Measurement and Management. *European Journal of Marketing, 31*(5–6), 340–355.
van Riel, C. B. M., & Fombrun, C. J. (2007). *Essentials of Corporate Communication: Implementing Practices for Effective Reputation Management*. Routledge.
Volkswagen. (2020). Volkswagen Supports Its 40,000 Suppliers with Instructions for Protective Measures in Production. https://www.volkswagenag.com/en/news/2020/04/Volkswagen_supports_its_40_000_suppliers.html
Wilson, R. (1985). Reputation in Games and Markets. In A. E. Roth (Ed.), *Game-Theoretic Models of Bargaining* (pp. 65–84). Cambridge University Press.

9

Your Fraud, Our Country: Impacts on National Brands and Reputations

9.1 The "Made In" Brand

Similar to companies, countries also send signals to observers, in such a way that a set of perceptions around them is developed. Beyond affecting the way indigenous people are seen around the world, these perceptions may also have important economic effects. The relationship between products and countries, for example, seems to be a special type of spillover in which the qualities of one are absorbed by the other (Magnusson et al., 2014). As argued by Suh et al. (2016), the country of origin effect relates to the influence that a country's image can have on a buyer considering a product or service from another country. Due to both stereotypes and a nation's real output, the country of origin effect shall be either positive or negative to products and brands, depending on the status of the country in question (Han & Terpstra, 1988; Sauer et al., 1991). National brands such as "Made in China", "Made in Germany", or "Made in Italy" carry the weight of the qualities and defects attributed to the country of origin. As exemplified by Chattalas et al. (2008, p. 55), "despite potentially large differences in price, consumers are likely to prefer French to Austrian champagne; Italian to Finnish fashion; German to Chinese cars;

M. Fracarolli Nunes, C. Lee Park, *Business Ethics and Environmental Fraud*,
https://doi.org/10.1007/978-3-030-73800-6_9

and Japanese to Mexican electronics". Although illustrative of the issue discussed, these comparisons have no absolute value. Among other entailments, this means that they cannot be used in reference to the worth of a specific country or product, nor to compare elements within the same groups. Instead, the country of origin effect refers to specific combinations in which both a product and its geographic provenance are considered, giving rise to a particular and well-delimited sentiment. These contrasts suggest that different "made in" brands carry not only the technical know-how developed by peoples over time, but also part of their culture (Holt, 1998). Apparently, buying a product "made in" a given country would mean buying a piece of it as well.

In face of the eventual pros and cons resulting from such associations, companies may either stress or disguise them, depending on the expected outcomes (Yasin et al., 2007). The Volkswagen group, for example, seems to be in the first category, with the non-German companies it acquired having their national identities preserved, or even highlighted. That would be the strategy adopted in the management of brands like Bentley and Lamborghini, both absorbed by the Volkswagen group in the late 1990s (Volkswagen AG, 2020a, 2020b). The importance of such issues may be inferred by the way the brands are presented. Phrases such as "Bentley Motors remains the definitive British luxury car company" (Bentley, 2020) denote the attempt to preserve the national origins of the company. Lamborghini, in turn, is still presented as "[t]he Italian sports car manufacturer" (Volkswagen AG, 2020b), even after more than two decades have passed since the acquisition of the company by the German group. Other originally foreign brands owned by the group appear to follow a similar path. Ducati is introduced as "[t]he Italian motorcycle brand" (Volkswagen AG, 2020c), while Scania stands as a "long-standing Swedish brand" (Volkswagen AG, 2020d). Likewise, the Czech origins of Škoda are clearly displayed (Volkswagen AG, 2020e), as well as the French ones of Bugatti (Bugatti, 2020). In turn, the originally Spanish brand SEAT is presented in a hybrid form, with phrases like "SEAT combine temperament and precision" (Volkswagen AG, 2020f) merging the typical stereotypes associated with the Spanish and German culture. Despite preserving the national identity of the acquired brands, Volkswagen also profits from the positive reputation associated with German cars.

With nearly 77% of all cars produced in the country being sold abroad (Chazan, 2019), Germany stands as the leading car exporter in the world (Sullivan, 2018). Accordingly, the country answered for nearly 22% of all car exports in 2016 and 2017, as much as all other European countries combined. Accounting for more than €25.4 billion (US $28.2 billion) in sales volume in 2018, the United States is the main foreign market for the German automotive industry, followed by China (€23.9 billion or US $26.5 billion), the United Kingdom (€22.5 billion or US $25 billion), France (€16.2 billion or US $18 billion), and Italy (€11.4 billion or US $12.6 billion) (Statista, 2019). With annual sales of €423 billion (US $470 billion) in 2017, the car industry sustains 820,000 jobs in Germany, representing around 5% of German gross domestic product (Chazan, 2019). The automotive industry could be hardly dissociated from Germany: as discussed in Chaps. 5 and 11, the invention of the automobile is attributed to the German engineer Carl Benz (Dietsche & Kuhlgatz, 2014), just like the main developments of the diesel technology are linked to Rudolf Diesel, who despite being born in Paris had German ancestry.

The success achieved by German brands also comes from less organic factors such as intentionally built coordinated efforts to build positive brand, corporate images, and reputations. That includes the investments in advertising in the most diverse media channels (e.g. television, radio, newspapers, magazines, social media), as well as all the mechanisms employed for this purpose. Sullivan (2018) highlights the fact that car advertising is one of the rare occasions in which the German language is used in international marketing (outside German-speaking countries)—expressions such as *vorsprung durch technik* (advancement through technology), *freude am fahren* (driving pleasure), and simply *das auto* (the car) have been used by Audi, BMW, and Volkswagen for several years in their overseas marketing campaigns to emphasize the "German-ness" of their products.

Among the factors that have helped to consolidate German brands as a synonym for performance is the great success they have achieved in sports competitions over the years. This includes the various successes achieved by Audi in rallies (Robson, 2008), as well as the intense participation of companies like BMW (Lewin, 2016) and Mercedes-Benz (Jenkins et al., 2016) in motorsport championships. In particular, the performance of these teams in important showcases such as Formula One helped to consolidate German brands' positive image on a global level, making room for market gains around the world. Even if in a less direct way, the career of German pilots may also have contributed in this regard. Despite racing mostly for Italian teams (e.g. Benetton and Ferrari), the success of Michael Schumacher, for example, may have greatly contributed to the association between his home country and excellence in terms of automotive performance. With seven world titles, Schumacher dominated the Formula One championships in the 2000s, and remains the most successful driver in the category (Menezes, 2013). Some even consider him the best driver of all times (Gibson, 2016), which causes heated debates with fans of other sports legends such as world champion Ayrton Senna (Smith, 2020), who died in 1994 in an accident at the Imola race track in Italy (L'Équipe, 2020). Michael Schumacher suffered an accident in a ski trip back in 2013, and has since remained in a critical state of health (Doyle, 2020). Despite this, the name of the German pilot remains a benchmark for performance, naming a range of limited editions of both cars (e.g. Fiat Stilo Michael Schumacher, Motor1, 2018) and watch models (e.g. Audemar Piguet Royal Oak Michael Schumacher, Audemars Piguet, 2020); Omega Speed Master Michael Schumacher, (Omega, 2020), which confirms its value and its relevance in the promotion of brand images.

The esteem of the German automotive industry is also due to the remarkable commercial success of some of its models, some of which are linked to the war efforts of Nazi Germany. Following Adolph Hitler's desire to produce a car that was accessible to the average German worker, Ferdinand Porsche developed the model (Price, 2003), which, in the course of the following decades, became the best-selling car of all times (Hiott, 2012). It is estimated that a total of 22.7 million Beetles have been commercialized between 1938 and 2019, comprising the three generations of the model (Tidey, 2019). Accordingly, the first generation—produced between 1938 and 2003—represents nearly 93% of this volume (21 million units), while the second one—produced between 1998 and 2011—accounts for 1.16 million vehicles. The third generation, in turn, produced between 2011 and 2019—had a much more modest performance, having sold only 530 thousand units. To these days, the first generation of the Beetle still composes a non-neglectable part of the car fleet in some Latin American countries Mexico (Associated Press, 2019). In the words of Volkswagen Group for America's Chief Executive Officer (CEO), Mr. Scott Keogh, "[i]t's impossible to imagine where Volkswagen would be without the Beetle" (Wamsley, 2019). Upon the announcement of the discontinuation of Beetle production in 2019, Volkswagen CEO by the time, Mr. Hinrich J. Woebcken, stated that "[t]he loss of the Beetle after three generations, over nearly seven decades, will evoke a host of emotions from the Beetle's many devoted fans" (Tidey, 2019). Another emblematic model produced by Volkswagen is the Combi, which became a symbol of the hippie movement in the United States in the 1960s and 1970s (Agence France Press, 2013).

The prominence that these and other German models have achieved among generations of consumers partially explains both their success and the seriousness of environmental fraud perpetrated by Volkswagen. In a way, they have become part of the affective memory of many people who connect with models and brands in different ways. While some have the pleasant memory of a first car, others keep in their minds the feelings associated with distant moments of their childhood happily spent in their rear seats. The memories of trips with friends and families are also very common, just like remembrances of landmark events in their lives, like the cars that conducted them to their wedding ceremonies, for example. These strong emotional connections with brands and companies are embedded in the concept of extended selves (Belk, 1988) discussed in Chap. 8, and helps to explain the impact of the breach of trust generated when corporate scandals involving environmental fraud are revealed.

Although German brands seem to have a special status among consumers, companies from other countries also benefit from positive perceptions. Italian cars, for instance, have long been associated with sportiveness, just like English cars are often related to the royalty of the country. Indeed, members of the British royal family are said to have a love affair with Land Rover (The Telegraph, 2019). Swedish vehicles, in turn, are linked to perceptions of high-quality engineering, with the automotive industry of the country being particularly famous for the safety of its cars. Volvo, in turn, has long profited from the reputation of producing the safest cars in the world (Volvo, 2020).

In addition to understanding the importance of the country effect, the comprehension of the process through which national identities and images are formed is critical. In this sense, the discussion of the social and historical foundations that build the way in which countries are perceived (both by their own citizens and by those of other countries) is useful, with these and other aspects being approached next.

9.2 National Image, National Identity, and Stereotypes

The usual distance between people and foreign countries contributes to the creation of distorted views, which often lead to prejudices and reductions. Typically, this translates into some characteristics of the inhabitants of a country or their culture being exaggerated, in such a way that they serve to identify them, but also to segment and ridicule. In this way, stereotypes fulfill the function of offering simplified information (Bodenhausen & Wyer, 1985), which, although normally imprecise, works as a reference for the general public. While France, for example, is internationally famous for the high quality of its fashion, cuisine, perfumes, wines, cheeses, architecture, art, philosophy, literature, and culture, French citizens also have a reputation for a pretense negligence with some hygiene habits (Villeminot, 2019). Even if this shall eventually be true for a small portion of the population—which is probably not significantly greater than in other countries—the perception is often erroneously extended to the French in general. Likewise, at the same time Italy shares many of the positive traces attributed to France (e.g. fashion, cuisine, sophistication, culture), it is also associated with mafias and criminal organizations (Calderoni, 2011), while Brazilians are seen as a welcoming and cheerful people (Lourenção et al., 2019) but also corrupt (Fischer et al., 2014).

This contrast between positive and negative images seems to affect basically all countries in the eyes of external observers, being, perhaps, exacerbated when there are current or historical conflicts and rivalries. The relations between former colonies and metropolises, for example, can be marked by great tension, even long after the end of their common history. In other cases, although there is not a particular rivalry, relationships are plagued by what appears to be mutual disgust, at least by a part of the respective populations. The modern relationship between Brazil (former colony) and Portugal (former metropolis) illustrates these dynamics. Even if most Brazilians and Portuguese base their relationships on a high level of respect and even mutual admiration, the citizens of these countries are constantly at the center of jokes and anecdotes in which their intelligence and moral integrity are questioned by each other. The development and reinforcement of this sort of negative stereotypes can be part of a complex process of construction of a national identity.

In the case of former colonies, the separation and even the opposition of what the former metropolis represent would reinforce its allegedly positive characteristics, creating a kind of limit or boundary between good and evil, right and wrong, past and present. It is possible that, somehow, there is a parallel between human psychology and that of a nation. In fact, these tensions between ex-colonies and ex-metropolis may be the national version of some Freudian concepts, especially those that deal with the need for the symbolic death of a father figure for the affirmation of the individual's identity. Evidently, the transposition of this rationale from individual's psychology to a possible collective consciousness around the concept of nation is not trivial. Unlike the individual, who can be more easily delimitated—although this in itself represents a risky simplifying remise—nations are formed not only by a large group of individuals but also by institutions, culture, and values, which are themselves mutants in time and interrelate in a continuous historical process that crosses different generations.

Still on the relations between individual and national psychologies, it seems that processes of scapegoating through stereotypes also work in the construction of national identities, even if in a possibly pernicious way. In fact, it may be argued that these mechanics end up functioning as a sort of denial, in which the citizens of a given nation refuse to acknowledge their flaws. These processes can be extremely damaging to countries in the long run, as the shifts in focus to external agents do not allow problems to be recognized, treated, and, ultimately, solved. The transfer of guilt to others leads to a position that, although comfortable from the point of view of self-images, can severely distort reality. Indeed, if problems are perceived to be rooted somewhere away, one does not take responsibility for solving it. As it seems to be the case in human psychology, perhaps the first step in solving a problem is recognizing that it exists, which the process of scapegoating through stereotypes does not permit.

It is common, for instance, for Brazilians to blame the excessive colonial control exercised by Portugal as one of the sources of corruption in the country. As discussed by Lee Park et al. (2018), the exorbitant regulation would have led the colonists (i.e. Portuguese and their descendants living in the colony) to develop methods to circumscribe the strict rules, which, among other things, aimed to make mineral exploration in the country viable. More specifically, restrictions sought to guarantee the payment of taxes arising from this activity—typically 20% or one-fifth (Renger, 2006). Likewise, the corruption schemes involving contractors and the Brazilian public power are typically pointed out as having their origins in the Portuguese colonizer. As discussed by Brazilian historian Eduardo Bueno (2017), the construction of Salvador—the colony's first capital—by the Portuguese was marked by various corruption schemes, having been partially conducted by contractors who had already been tried and convicted of corruption in Portugal years before. Although it is undeniable that these Portuguese practices may in fact have influenced Brazilian attitudes, the blaming of colonizers would avoid, or, at least, make it more difficult for the Brazilian people to recognize their own responsibility for corruption in the country.

It is also possible that the processes of scapegoating through stereotyping take place due to projections, which, just like a mirror, mean the recognition of one's own flaws in others. When it comes to ex-colonies and ex-metropolises, these mechanisms should be more likely, as, in many cases, the two share many cultural and historical traits. Yet, this may not always be faithful to reality, since, in some cases, the colonization process has been limited to the economic exploitation of regions without the colonizer infiltrating the culture of the indigenous people. In other situations, however, metropolis and colonies formed one same state, which was divided after complex processes of independence. These cases seem to be common in the colonization and independence processes of the American continent, and, in special, in Iberian America (i.e.

colonized by Portugal and Spain). The territory that today forms Brazil became the seat of the Portuguese empire when the court was moved from Lisbon to Rio de Janeiro in the early nineteenth century (Cardeman & Goldfeld Cardeman, 2016). As a measure of protection, the Portuguese crown was escorted by the English navy on this long transatlantic crossing, in order to avoid the dangers that the Napoleonic wars represented. Thus, from 1808 to 1821, Rio de Janeiro was the center of power of a vast Portuguese empire (Jaspar, 1965).

In that way, as discussed by the Brazilian historian Fernando Novais (2016), the utilization of the name Brazil to designate the territory that today forms the country is thus a classic form of anachronism, since, at that time, this same territory was, in a way, a part of Portugal itself. Likewise, the use of the expression "Colonial Brazil", which is commonly applied in the division of the country's historical phases, represents another case of anachronism. In addition to the fact that the territory was part of Portugal at the time, the expression is imprecise because it presupposes that Brazil would be predestined to exist, which, from a historical point of view, is not reasonable. It can be considered then that the notion of Brazil cannot be adopted before the independence of the country, which occurred only in 1822. The separation from Portugal would somehow represent a sort of birth certificate of the country.

Following its independence, however, Brazil remained in the monarchist regime, under the government of the same royal house of Portugal (Bastos, 2008). This monarchic period translated into the government of the Emperors Dom Pedro I and his son Dom Pedro II, and extended until 1889, the year in which the republic was proclaimed (Abreu, 2015). While its neighbor countries went directly from the stage of colony to republic, Brazil became the only country in the American continent to have been governed by a royal house. In addition to the historical curiosities, these complex relationships show the extent to which the path of two nations—now totally independent from a political point of view—can be confused, and how difficult it can be to forge a national identity. As Brazil and Portugal share the same language, much of their culture and history, the use of stereotypes indeed seems to be a way to separate what, somehow, seems to be inseparable.

9.3 National Tribalism

It remains difficult, however, to say whether national feelings are part of the culture or of a collective unconscious linked to the impression of being part of something bigger. In fact, the notion of belonging to a nation could be seen as a broader form of tribalism, in which the citizens of a country are distinguished from other groups, with territorial boundaries functioning, therefore, as the limits of these different groups. Unlike what could be understood as a more classical forms of tribalism, however, the idea of national states overcomes the matters associated with genetics, in such a way that different groups can recognize themselves as belonging to something greater (i.e. the nation) (Prager, 2018). Thus, in addition to geographic issues, the type of tribalism that arises from the concept of nation would be conditioned to historical and cultural aspects such as language, religion, and moral values, among others. At the same time this link to a motherland can exacerbate tensions between countries and eventually lead to wars—what seems to have been the case over the past few centuries, especially among the national states in Western Europe—it allows groups of different ethnic origins to recognize themselves as belonging to something greater and common to them (i.e. the nation). These movements can prevent, or, at least, diminish, the outcomes of the rivalries that result from ordinary forms of tribalism.

People's perception of themselves may also be influenced by internal analysis (i.e. interpretations of the country by a compatriot author). As discussed by Reily (2000), the representation of Brazilians as friendly, happy, cordial, and industrious by Sérgio Buarque de Holanda (1971 [1936])—one of the most influent Brazilian historians—became a common sense categorization among the population of the country. For these cases, more than an image, the notion of identity could be applied. In reality, the development of one single national identity is often difficult, as stereotyping can occur within same country. In these cases, cultural and economic differences between regions are often exacerbated and may become a source of prejudice and discrimination between compatriots that do not recognize themselves as equal. This appears to be the case in countries such as Italy, Germany, France, and Japan. In fact, northern and southern Italians sometimes disagree in the most diverse domains—typically those related to politics—and disdain each other (Bohlen, 1996). These rivalries are even more evident in sports disputes in which teams from these locations are opposed. The Italian case is classic with soccer teams from the South and the North developing a great rivalry. Adds to that the fact that the north of the country is industrially developed, with many world-famous companies keeping the factories and headquarters in the region. Among others, this includes companies of the automotive (e.g. Ferrari) and fashion (e.g. Prada) industries, two of the most famous Italian icons. The south, on the other hand, has its image linked to a more modest economic development, and mainly to criminal organizations (i.e. mafias) (Chubb, 1982). Germany, in turn, still suffers from the marks left by the division of the country during the Cold War with its western portion (capitalist) reaching a significantly greater economic development than that of its eastern part (communist) (Krueger & Pischke, 1995). The 40 years spent under the influence of the Soviet Union also left important traces in the culture of the country which still reflects in the relations between German compatriots (Brosig-Koch et al., 2011). In the case of both Italy and Germany, it is possible that their late unification—in 1870 (US Department of State, 2020) and 1871 (Hamerow, 2015), respectively—stresses these differences, with the union of different counties, duchies, and other administrative units still compromising the perception of citizens that they belong to a common nation. Likewise, the co-existence of different local dialects—particularly in Italy (Maiden & Parry, 2006)—seems to reinforce the citizens' connection to their regional roots, thus hampering the development of a greater sense of belonging to the nation.

Unlike Italy and Germany, France has a history of centralism (Cole, 2008), with the state having formed around the monarchic figure (i.e. the king) (Maral, 2015). This, however, has not prevented rivalries from developing, especially between the inhabitants of the capital Paris and those of the rest of the country, in particular citizens of other large and historically important French cities such as Marseille, Lyon, Bordeaux, and Rouen. The fact that some regions were incorporated by France only relatively recently (e.g. Corse) may also explain the difficulties of resistance of their inhabitants in identifying themselves as French. Likewise, historic regions such as Normandy and Picardy have very marked local cultures, what, in some way can damage the perception of belonging to the nation.

9.4 Final Considerations

As discussed throughout the chapter, the formation of national images and identities can be a complex process, mixing historical, economic, and cultural issues. When these matters are transposed to marketing initiatives, they can assume an even more important dimension, being decisive for the success or failure of products in global markets. German car brands are often advertised in German (even outside Germany), probably as a way to reinforce the association of these brands to the positive perceptions that German engineering and technology rely on. While that is still the case for Audi—*vorsprung durch technik* (advancement through technology) (Volkswagen AG, 2020f), Volkswagen's slogan *das auto* (the car) was set to be gradually retired as part of the company's efforts to reposition itself after the outbreak of the Dieselgate scandal in September 2015 (Cremer, 2015). Accordingly, launched in 2007, the saying had the advantage of simplicity, having, however, come to be criticized by Volkswagen leaders as they were anxious to announce a reformed corporate culture. In this set, the slogan would not be adequate for a company seeking to project its newfound humility that was brought by the disclosure of its public embarrassment. The Volkswagen Dieselgate illustrates the extent to which a company's immoral attitudes can damage the reputation of its home country. Yet, negative perceptions often cannot be associated with a specific event, being the result of intricate processes in which some countries end up being stigmatized. Despite being currently the largest industrial power in the world and advancing in areas of the most refined technologies (e.g. military, biotechnology), China, for example, is still associated with cheap and low-quality products, which can sometimes harm its business transactions.

In what seems to be a quest to circumvent these issues, many Chinese products exhibit on their label the brand Made in P.R.C. (Popular Republic of China), instead of the traditional Made in China one

(Kilpatrick, 2015). This trend seems to have accelerated in the aftermath of the COVID-19 crisis, apparently for two main reasons: first, China was identified by some media outlets and chiefs of state (e.g. U.S. President Donald J. Trump) as being largely responsible for the pandemic (Viala-Gaudefroy & Lindaman, 2020). Thus, the boycott to Chinese products would have a somewhat punitive objective, so that the damage caused in the economies around the world by the lockdown (i.e. a set of restrictive measures allegedly intended to diminish the circulation of the virus) would be returned to the country that would have supposedly been responsible for it (Bickerton, 2020). A second factor refers to the fragility of the industrial sectors in many countries. At the peak of the crisis, entire populations suffered from the lack of basic products, ranging from simple surgical masks to prevent the spread of the virus to respirators for the treatment of those already infected (Ranney et al., 2020). The sudden increase in the demand for these and other products put pressure on prices and led to a worldwide stockout (OECD, 2020). With these products being largely manufactured in China, many government officials found themselves in a difficult situation in terms of national security.

These and other examples discussed throughout the chapter illustrate the relevance of the perceptions that are formed about countries. In addition to influencing international trade and the chances of success for national economies, positive national images can be decisive for the entry of products into foreign markets. Likewise, negative images can present themselves as huge barriers to entry, which, although invisible at first, can prevent access to products and services in certain regions simply because of their geographic origin. In this sense, the management of national brands must be a permanent and joint effort between governments and companies. The damage caused by the Volkswagen Dieselgate, for example, can be extended to the entire German industry, with important impacts on the country's economy. Alongside raising doubts about the honesty of German managers, the fact that the company needed cheating to reach legal emission levels can have an important impact on the image of technological superiority of German products. As discussed in Chap. 8, damages to intangible resources can be long-lasting, and sometimes impossible to reverse. This would explain the company's efforts to change both its logo and the slogan that followed it. Whether these measures will in fact be sufficient to mitigate the negative impacts of the scandal both for Volkswagen itself and for other German companies remains to be seen.

Building on the discussion on the impacts of environmental fraud in firms' intangible resources (Chap. 8), we examine how each of the constructs approached may be affected in the country level. Once more, the Volkswagen Dieselgate serves as the ideal example of the practice, with the idiosyncrasies of the case contributing to its potential to significantly harm German reputation around the world. The close association between Volkswagen and its country of origin, for instance, may make it difficult for consumers to differentiate one from the other. Among other things, the Nazi origin of the Beetle—a personal request of Adolph Hitler, as previously discussed—reinforced this link throughout the decades. Despite not compromising the acceptance of the model (as its massive sales numbers denote), it may be argued that this association was unfavorable to Volkswagen, with the company being connected with a particularly negative passage of Germany's History.

It seems, however, that stakeholders have not fiercely punished German companies for their eventual links with the Nazi regime. Instead, many of these firms evolved to become global players, supporting Germany's remarkable economic recovery after World War II. It is possible that the general high quality of German engineering was capable to offset these negative feelings, turning what could be a burden into an advantage. As discussed, Volkswagen itself reinforced its German origins, with the use of slogans in the German language playing an important role in that direction. Yet, while the strategy may have helped Volkswagen in its search to become a market leader, it shall also have boosted the negative impact of the Volkswagen Dieselgate to other German companies. The fact that Bosch—also a German company—was involved in the scandal reinforces its national aspects. Even if the firm denies being directly associated with the case, its presence in newspapers' headlines around the world may have sedimented the idea that it was related to the unethical conducts in question. Likewise, the image of Volkswagen's leaders admitting to the fraud and apologizing may have worked as an additional element in the construction of negative perceptions around Germans in general. Lately, the scandal took place in the automotive industry and involved the misuse of the diesel technology, both greatly associated with the country. Altogether, these factors make the analysis of intangible resources at a national level relevant, with each of the constructs previously discussed standing as important dependent variables in that regard.

As pointed out throughout the chapter, "Made in" brands have the power to influence consumption behaviors, being eventually decisive to the success (or failure) of products and services commercialized in a global scale. In face of the matters discussed above, it may be argued that the scandal represented a serious threat to the value of the "Made in Germany" brand, having put into question not only the quality of German products, but also the integrity of German managers. In that way, the association of goods and services originated in the country with Volkswagen's fraudulent behavior shall compromise their appeal among foreign consumers, significantly harming the competitiveness of German companies. The scandal may too be particularly damaging in terms of stakeholders' trust. With the fraud being based on a cheating scheme, it may harm the validity of the messages sent by German firms, possibly affecting the quality of their relationships with stakeholders. In case this mistrust indeed comes to spill over other German companies, the damages to the economy of the country in the long-term may be particularly serious in terms of consumers' and employees' beliefs, but also in suppliers', investors', and creditors' willingness to transact with German companies.

Similarly, national credibility may be affected in the two dimensions discussed (i.e. trustworthiness and expertise). Particularly around the latter, the fact that Volkswagen needed to use a cheating technology to meet environmental standards of a foreign country might raise questions around the capacity of German engineers to provide real technological solutions. The development of negative perceptions in that regard can be critical to German companies, as the belief on their superior quality has proven to be an important factor in consumers' decision and, by consequence, a source of sustainable competitive advantage. On what relates to Germany's National image, the Dieselgate may have damaged the positive way in which the industry of the country has traditionally been perceived by foreigners. This effect was accelerated by the considerable media cover that the case received, with Volkswagen's unethical conducts being exposed in detail. Adds to that the fact the company's admission to the fraud, recognizing its inappropriate conducts. That was made clear in numerous occasions, with the words of Volkswagen's US CEO, Mr. Michael Horn, being, perhaps, the most representative of this movement. In referring to the fraud perpetrated by Volkswagen, he publicly stated "[s]o let's be clear about this: our company was dishonest with the EPA and the California Air Resources Board, and with all of you" (Ramey, 2015). Beyond the automatic repercussion of such affirmation, the speech was ridiculed in TV shows (WatchMojo.com, 2015), what probably added to the extent of the damages.

Although the impacts of the case on external observers were significant, the damages to the way Germans perceive themselves must not be neglected. In this sense, it is possible that the revelation of the fraud had a negative effect on the people's morale, as one of its main assets (i.e. the positive perceptions about German companies) was impaired. The impacts of the case in German national identity may then be seen as potential issue on the long run, which may only be offset if the country comes to recover its esteem. Finally, bringing all these issues together and summarizing the effects of the case in the overall perception about the country, German national reputation may have been seriously damaged, what shall negatively impact the economy of the country for decades. Indeed, reputational issues are particularly critical to the country, mainly because of its acts under the Nazi regime. Since the end of World War II, Germans have been portrayed as villains in a series of films, reinforcing the negative image of the country. The revelation of a massive fraud conducted by a German company certainly does not help reverting these perceptions.

References

Abreu, A. A. (2015). *Dicionário Histórico-Biográfico da Primeira República (1889–1930)*. Editora FGV.

Agence France Press. (2013, December 11). VW Combi: californien et hippie for ever! *Le Point*. https://www.lepoint.fr/automobile/le-combi-volkswagen-regne-encore-sur-le-coeur-des-hippies-californiens-11-12-2013-1767534_646.php#

Associated Press. (2019, July 10). Beetlemania: Inside the Tiny Mexico City Hilltop Neighborhood Where Almost EVERYONE Relies on the Original No-Frills VW Beetle. *Mail Online*. https://www.dailymail.co.uk/news/article-7231277/As-Beetle-ends-iconic-original-thrives-Mexico-City-hills.html

Audemars Piguet. (2020). Royal Oak Offshore Chronograph Michael Schumacher. https://www.audemarspiguet.com/en/watch-collection/royal-oak-offshore/26568IM.OO.A004CA.01/

Bastos, M. R. (2008). Retratos do poder imperial no Brasil. *Revista FAAP FACOM, 19*, 42–51.

Belk, R. W. (1988). Possessions and the Extended Self. *Journal of Consumer Research, 15*(2), 139–168.

Bentley. (2020). The Extraordinary Life of W.O. Bentley. https://www.bentleymotors.com/en/world-of-bentley/the-bentley-story/history-and-heritage/historic-people/w-o-bentley.html

Bickerton, J. (2020, June 6). Half of Britons Boycotting Chinese Goods as Anger Over Coronavirus Mounts. *Express*. https://www.express.co.uk/news/uk/1292096/UK-coronavirus-news-China-Chinese-boycott-Covid-19-pandemic

Bodenhausen, G. V., & Wyer, R. S. (1985). Effects of Stereotypes in Decision Making and Information-Processing Strategies. *Journal of Personality and Social Psychology, 48*(2), 267–282.

Bohlen, C. (1996, November 15). North-South Divide in Italy: A Problem for Europe, Too. *The New York Times*. https://www.nytimes.com/1996/11/15/world/north-south-divide-in-italy-a-problem-for-europe-too.html

Brosig-Koch, J., Helbach, C., Ockenfels, A., & Weimann, J. (2011). Still Different After All These Years: Solidarity Behavior in East and West Germany. *Journal of Public Economics, 95*(11–12), 1373–1376.

Buarque de Holanda, Sergio. (1971 [1936]). *Raizes do Brasil* (6th ed.). Jose Olympio.

Bueno, E. (2017). A construção da capital do Brasil. https://www.youtube.com/watch?v=jO53X99cE6Y

Bugatti. (2020). Limited Edition of the Chiron. Celebrating the 110th Anniversary of the Brand. http://bugatti.com/media/news/2019/bugatti-chiron-110-ans-bugatti/

Calderoni, F. (2011). Where Is the Mafia in Italy? Measuring the Presence of the Mafia Across Italian Provinces. *Global Crime, 12*(1), 41–69.

Cardeman, D., & Goldfeld Cardeman, R. (2016). *O Rio de Janeiro nas Alturas*. Mauad Editora Ltda.

Chattalas, M., Kramer, T., & Takada, H. (2008). The Impact of National Stereotypes on the Country of Origin Effect: A Conceptual Framework. *International Marketing Review, 25*(1), 54–74.

Chazan, G. (2019, August 1). Car Industry Woes Weight on Germany's Prospects. *Financial Times*. https://www.ft.com/content/0e477fae-b383-11e9-8cb2-799a3a8cf37b

Chubb, J. (1982). *Patronage, Power and Poverty in Southern Italy: A Tale of Two Cities*. Cambridge University Press.

Cole, A. (2008). *Governing and Governance in France*. Cambridge University Press.

Cremer, A. (2015). 'Das Auto' No More: Volkswagen Plans Image Offensive. *Reuters*. https://www.reuters.com/article/us-volkswagen-emissions-communications-i-idUSKBN0U514L20151222

Dietsche, K. H., & Kuhlgatz, D. (2014). History of the Automobile. In K. Reif (Ed.), *Fundamentals of Automotive and Engine Technology*. Springer Vieweg.

Doyle, L. (2020, November 27). Michael Schumacher Health Update: Where Is Michael Schumacher Now? Can He Walk? *Express*. https://www.express.co.uk/news/world/1171248/Michael-Schumacher-health-update-where-is-Michael-Schumacher-now-walk

Fischer, R., Ferreira, M. C., Milfont, T., & Pilati, R. (2014). Culture of Corruption? The Effects of Priming Corruption Images in a High Corruption Context. *Journal of Cross-Cultural Psychology, 45*(10), 1594–1605.

Gibson, S. (2016, August 25). 25 Reasons Why Michael Schumacher Is the Greatest F1 Driver of All Time. *The Telegraph*. https://www.telegraph.co.uk/formula-1/2016/08/25/25-reasons-why-michael-schumacher-is-the-greatest-f1-driver-of-a/

Hamerow, T. S. (2015). *Social Foundations of German Unification, 1858–1871, Volume I: Ideas and Institutions*. Princeton University Press.

Han, C., & Terpstra, V. (1988). Country of Origin Effects for Uni-National and Bi-National Products. *Journal of International Business Studies, 19*(2), 235–255.

Hiott, A. (2012). *Thinking Small: The Long, Strange Trip of the Volkswagen Beetle*. Ballantine Books.

Holt, D. B. (1998). Does Cultural Capital Structure American Consumption? *Journal of Consumer Research, 25*(1), 1–25.

Jaspar, B. (1965). Rio de Janeiro, Capitale du Portugal (1808–1821). *Revue Des Deux Mondes (1829-1971)*, 521–537

Jenkins, M., Pasternak, K., & West, R. (2016). *Performance at the Limit: Business Lessons from Formula 1® Motor Racing*. Cambridge University Press.

Kilpatrick, R. (2015, January 8). Manufacturers Switch 'Made in China' for 'Made in PRC'; in Bid to Boost Sales Abroad. *That's Mag*. https://www.thatsmags.com/china/post/8250/manufacturers-switch-made-in-china-for-made-in-prc-in-bid-to-boost-sales-abroad

Krueger, A. B., & Pischke, J. S. (1995). A Comparative Analysis of East and West German Labor Markets: Before and After Unification. In *Differences and Changes in Wage Structures* (pp. 405–446). University of Chicago Press.

L'Équipe. (2020, October 31). À Imola, la Formule 1 et ses pilotes rendent hommage à Ayrton Senna. https://www.lequipe.fr/Formule-1/Actualites/A-imola-la-formule-1-et-ses-pilotes-rendent-hommage-a-ayrton-senna/1189530

Lee Park, C., Fracarolli Nunes, M., Muratbekova-Touron, M., & Moatti, V. (2018). The Duality of the Brazilian *Jeitinho*: An Empirical Investigation and Conceptual Framework. *Critical Perspectives on International Business, 14*(4), 404–425.

Lewin, T. (2016). *The BMW Century: The Ultimate Performance Machines*. Motorbooks International.

Lourenção, M. T. D. A., Montanari, M. G., Giraldi, J. D. M. E., & Costa, A. L. (2019). Brazil's Image and Brazilian Personality: A Systematic Review from the Viewpoint of Cordiality. *Revista de Gestão, 26*(3), 274–292. https://doi.org/10.1108/REGE-01-2018-0007

Magnusson, P., Krishnan, V., Westjohn, S. A., & Zdravkovic, S. (2014). The Spillover Effects of Prototype Brand Transgressions on Country Image and Related Brands. *Journal of International Marketing, 22*(1), 21–38.

Maiden, M., & Parry, M. (Eds.). (2006). *The Dialects of Italy*. Routledge.

Maral, A. (2015). *Le Roi-Soleil et Dieu*. Tempus Perrin.

Menezes, J. (2013, December 30). Michael Schumacher: The Seven-Time World Champion's Career in Formula One. *Independent*. https://www.independent.co.uk/sport/motor-racing/michael-schumacher-seven-time-world-champion-s-career-formula-one-9030267.html

Motor1. (2018, January 4). Fiat Stilo Michael Schumacher Limited Edition. https://www.motor1.com/photo/2825006/fiat-stilo-michael-schumacher-limited-edition/

Novais, F. (2016). Fernando Novais: Portugal e Brasil – antigo sistema colonial. https://www.youtube.com/watch?v=JsAXNoumgS8

OECD. (2020, May 4). The Face Mask Global Value Chain in the COVID-19 Outbreak: Evidence and Policy Lessons. http://www.oecd.org/coronavirus/policy-responses/the-face-mask-global-value-chain-in-the-covid-19-outbreak-evidence-and-policy-lessons-a4df866d/

Omega. (2020). Speed Master Racing. https://www.omegawatches.com/planet-omega/60th-anniversary-speedmaster/racing-1996

Prager, D. (2018). Fireside Chat Ep. 57 – What's Good About Nationalism? https://www.youtube.com/watch?v=iOvohNJQGNw

Price, R. L. (2003). *The VW Beetle: A Production History of the World's Most Famous Car, 1936–1967*. Penguin.

Ramey, J. (2015, September 22). Volkswagen US CEO on Diesel Emissions Fiasco: 'We Totally Screwed Up'. *Autoweek*. https://www.autoweek.com/news/a1877321/volkswagen-us-ceo-our-company-was-dishonest/

Ranney, M. L., Griffeth, V., & Jha, A. K. (2020). Critical Supply Shortages – The Need for Ventilators and Personal Protective Equipment During the Covid-19 Pandemic. *New England Journal of Medicine, 382*(18), e41(1–3).

Reily, S. A. (2000). Introduction: Brazilian Musics, Brazilian Identities. *British Journal of Ethnomusicology, 9*(1), 1–10.

Renger, F. (2006). O quinto do ouro no regime tributário nas Minas Gerais. *Revista do Arquivo Público Mineiro, 42*(2), 90–105.

Robson, G. (2008). *Audi Quattro*. Veloce Publishing Ltd.

Sauer, P., Young, M., & Unnava, H. (1991). An Experimental Investigation of the Processes Behind Country-of-Origin Effects. *Journal of International Consumer Marketing, 3*(2), 29–59.

Smith, L. (2020, August 5). Hamilton Better Than Senna and Schumacher, Says Walker. *Motorsport*. https://www.motorsport.com/f1/news/hamilton-senna-schumacher-comparison-walker/4849818/

Statista. (2019, November 6). Leading import countries for motor vehicles from Germany based on export value 2018. *Statista*. http://www.statista.com/statistics/587701/leading-import-countries-german-motor-vehicles-by-export-value/

Suh, Y., Hur, J., & Davies, G. (2016). Cultural Appropriation and the Country of Origin Effect. *Journal of Business Research, 69*(8), 2721–2730.

Sullivan, A. (2018, June 21). Does the World Still Love German Cars? *Deutsche Welle*. https://www.dw.com/en/does-the-world-still-love-german-cars/a-44333631

The Telegraph. (2019). The Royals and Their Love Affair with Land Rover, in Pictures. https://www.telegraph.co.uk/cars/features/land-rover-70th-anniversary-royals-get-4x4-feeling/prince-charles-land-rover-trainin-goriginal-descriptionprince/

Tidey, A. (2019). VW Discontinues the Beetle: Here Are the Key Numbers Behind the Iconic Car. *Euronews*. https://www.euronews.com/2018/09/14/vw-discontinues-the-beetle-here-are-the-key-numbers-behind-the-iconic-car

US Department of State. (2020). Issues Relevant to U.S. Foreign Diplomacy: Unification of Italian States. https://history.state.gov/countries/issues/italian-unification

Viala-Gaudefroy, J., & Lindaman, D. (2020, April 21). Donald Trump's 'Chinese Virus': The Politics of Naming. *The Conversation*. https://theconversation.com/donald-trumps-chinese-virus-the-politics-of-naming-136796

Villeminot, F. (2019, September 19). The French and Hygiene: Why Is the Negative Stereotype So Hard to Wash Off? *France 24*. https://www.france24.com/en/20190919-french-connections-france-hygiene-cleanliness-society-washing-shower-teeth-culture-health

Volkswagen AG. (2020a). Bentley. https://www.volkswagenag.com/en/brands-and-models/bentley.html

Volkswagen AG. (2020b). Lamborghini. https://www.volkswagenag.com/en/brands-and-models/lamborghini.html#

Volkswagen AG. (2020c). Ducati. https://www.volkswagenag.com/en/brands-and-models/ducati.html

Volkswagen AG. (2020d). Scania. https://www.volkswagenag.com/en/brands-and-models/scania.html

Volkswagen AG. (2020e). Škoda. https://www.volkswagenag.com/en/brands-and-models/skoda.html

Volkswagen AG. (2020f). Brands and Models. https://www.volkswagenag.com/en/brands-and-models.html

Volvo. (2020). Focus on Safety from the Start. https://www.volvocars.com/intl/discover-volvo/safety#:~:text=Three%20recent%20Volvo%20models%2C%20the,important%20guide%20for%20European%20consumers

Wamsley, L. (2019). The Last VW Beetle Rolls Off the Assembly Line in Mexico This Week. *NPR*. https://www.npr.org/2019/07/09/739865991/the-last-vw-beetle-rolls-off-the-assembly-line-in-mexico-tomorrow?t=1599554909738

WatchMojo.com. (2015). 10 Volkswagen Scandal Facts. *WMNews*, Ep. 47. https://www.youtube.com/watch?v=E7UaX2HzSGU

Yasin, N. M., Noor, M. N., & Mohamad, O. (2007). Does Image of Country-of-Origin Matter to Brand Equity? *Journal of Product & Brand Management, 16*(1), 38–48.

10

Impacts on Market Value

10.1 Market Value and Value

Market value is a term used to express the financial worth of firms (CFI, 2020), typically those that have their shares publicly traded. Broadly, it results from the multiplication between the total number of shares by the spot price of each (Kramer, 2020). If, on the one hand, the number of shares may occasionally change—for reasons such as stock splits (Brennan & Copeland, 1988), the issuance of new shares (Pontiff & Woodgate, 2008), share repurchases (Grullon & Michaely, 2004), or even delisting (Goetzmann & Garry, 1986)—it is the real variation in the price of stocks that cause market values to fluctuate. Understanding the reasons that shall lead to such variations is, therefore, at the core of the market value debate and provides the bases to the discussion of the potential impacts of environmental fraud in that regard.

Just like any market, stock markets are influenced by the laws of demand and supply (Kalay et al., 2004), with changes in any of these variables causing prices to oscillate. Yet, the determination of stock prices may also be affected by a range of other elements, including managers' decisions (Woolridge & Snow, 1990), the expected state of the global

M. Fracarolli Nunes, C. Lee Park, *Business Ethics and Environmental Fraud*,
https://doi.org/10.1007/978-3-030-73800-6_10

economy (Pearce & Roley, 1984), trade agreements (Daelemans et al., 2018), and political prospects (Gaikwad, 2013), among others. Issues such that of war tensions (Schneider & Troeger, 2006), protectionism (Godsell et al., 2018), the development of new technologies (Pastor & Veronesi, 2009), the nature of legal environments (Durnev & Kim, 2005), and regulatory restrictions (Bailey & Jagtiani, 1994) may also cause investors to revalue their positions. Altogether, these factors may make the determination of the fair price of a share a considerably complex task, often demanding intensive analysis of highly specialized professionals.

Before entering the discussion on how market values are calculated, a debate on the notion of value itself can be useful. This consideration is relevant as determining the value of something—whatever it is—can be quite arduous, inaccurate, and, most of the time, inexact exercise. The reasons for such difficulties come from the fact that the perception of value is somewhat subjective (Oishi et al., 1999), meaning that it can enormously vary among individuals. It is possible that one same object has a great value for one person, but little or none for another. A wheelchair, for example, should be valued by a physically disabled individual who needs it for mobility. A person who does not suffer from any disability, however, may see the wheelchair as just an object that is valuable to others, but not for themselves. Within this view, the perception of value appears to be linked to the idea of necessity. From a more utilitarian perspective, things would be perceived as more valuable as they offer solutions to certain problems. Thus, the perceived value of an object and even of a person would be determined by their respective capacities to provide solutions for those who have problems.

The reasoning may be applied to basically any instance. The value of an employee's salary, for example, would be linked to the extent of their contribution to solving the issues the employer may face. An employee with few qualifications will, in principle, have a low potential to solve problems, which is reflected in their more modest salary. A qualified professional, in turn, has the expectation of providing more elaborate and comprehensive solutions to company's challenges, justifying a better remuneration. Although the value of salaries depends on a number of other factors (e.g. demand and supply of labor, Katz & Murphy, 1992, macroeconomic conditions, Carlin & Soskice, 1990), the idea that its determination is linked to individuals' capacity to offer solutions seems to partially explain the salary gaps between employees at different hierarchical levels, with the notion of value being also linked to the idea of responsibility and, perhaps, meritocracy.

Likewise, the determination of products' prices would be associated with the functional value that consumers perceive in them, that is, their capacity to offer practical solutions. As discussed in Chap. 5, however, the power of a product to influence how a consumer is seen by others (i.e. social value) and how it feels about themselves (i.e. emotional value) would be also critical upon purchasing decisions (Sheth et al., 1991). Luxury products, for example, tend to have great social value (Ajitha & Sivakumar, 2017), since they send signals about the pretense financial situation of those who own them. Similarly, a green product can confer a high social status for its consumers, as they are seen as environmentally responsible (Griskevicius et al., 2010). At the same time, both luxury and green products may lead consumers to feel better about themselves by giving them either a sensation of power (for luxury products) or a sense of moral superiority (for green products). It may be argued, however, that both social and emotional values would be just different manifestations of functional value, since the search for being well evaluated by others, or for feeling good about oneself, would be needs which the products would be filling. Adds to that the epistemic and conditional values which can also greatly influence the recognition of a product's worth (Sheth et al., 1991).

Although the determination of value is subjective, different perceptions must converge so that people may exchange goods and services. For a commercial transaction to occur, for example, both parties must agree on the value of what is being negotiated. While such agreements can be reached quickly for ordinary products in day-to-day situations (e.g. the price of an apple in a supermarket), the convergence of values for more abstract things such as the price of a stock can be much more laborious. Overcoming the eventual divergences in perceptions requires the creation of methodologies that seek to minimize the influence of personal aspects and make the determination of value something close to an objective calculation. With regard to companies, this issue has been addressed with the development of several methods that, although different in nature and applicability, are all based on firms' ability to generate financial results. Even if there is no consensus on how to calculate the value of stocks (and by consequence the market value of companies), some techniques are more accepted and employed. Among them, the method known as discounted cash flows has been particularly popular. In essence, it allows the calculation of a company's value through the sum of the present value of its future cash flows, with the method being divided into basically two fundamental parts: (1) the estimation of future cash flows; and (2) the determination of an appropriate discount rate to bring these cash flows to present value.

As it is common with basically all methods, the ones used to calculate market values are not free from criticism. Likewise, the theories and concepts on which they rely are also often put into question. For Kruschwitz and Löffler (2006, p. 19), for example, Finance theory would be dominated by paradigms that are not supported by reality-grounded theoreticians. That includes the notion of "expected utility, the concept of perfect markets, the postulate that the markets are free of arbitrage and the equilibrium concept". The idea of expected utility would be originated in the work of mathematicians Daniel Bernoulli and Gabriel Cramer (Bernoulli, 1738), who argued that, in face of risky monetary options, the choices of reasonable individuals could not be adequately described by the search to maximize expected profits or wealth. Instead, they should be analyzed by the utility of their returns (Fishburn, 2013), with utility referring to "people's choices and decisions, (…) preferences, and judgments of preferability, worth, value, goodness or any of a number of similar concepts" (Fishburn, 1968, p. 335). In other words, the idea of expected utility moves the analysis from money itself (i.e. profits and wealth), to the individual value perceived on it. In that way, the prediction or explanation of one's rational choices regarding risky monetary options should be redirected to their preferences.

Beyond supporting the idea that these paradigms are not observable in reality, the recognition that "managers and investors do not always behave rationally" has pushed the development of alternative views, including the one known as behavioral finance (Kruschwitz & Löffler, 2006, p. 19). Coherently, Barberis and Thaler (2002) highlight that, as a field, behavior finance argues that some financial phenomena shall be understood when the premise that all agents are rational is relaxed. Accordingly, the reasoning would be based on two main building blocks: limits to arbitrage—as discussed before—and psychology, which focuses on cataloguing the sorts of deviations from full rationality that one might expect. Regardless of criticism to mainstream Finance theory, the dominant views in the field—built over neoclassical economics—are still based on the idea that there is no "free lunch" in the market (Kruschwitz & Löffler, 2006). Among the most relevant is the Efficient Market Hypothesis.

More than a general criticism of the Finance theory, these arguments bring the discussion on value determination back to its subjective aspects. Even if these attacks on the assumptions adopted by Finance scholars are valid, from a practical point of view they do not contribute to the determination of market values. Once more, it must be noted that all methods are flawed and that the development of the Finance theory fulfills the important role of objectively expressing perceptions of value. Ultimately, it is about quantifying feelings and emotions. Given the complexity of such a task, it is necessary to have some tolerance for possible shifts from reality. Evidently, the degree of these shifts must be constantly observed, and eventually criticized, so that we remain with useful theories and methods.

10.2 What Affects Market Value

In addition to the matters discussed above, market values may vary due to issues that are both internal and external to companies. Indeed, prospects for financial performance are sensitive to the most distinct factors. The launch of a new product by a competitor, for example, can mean a significant loss of market share for a company. The drop in revenues and the increase in production costs that may follow it should reduce its ability to generate cash, and therefore decrease its market value. Likewise, upon the approval of a project, prospects must be updated, incorporating the additional value expected to be created. The same mechanics must be applied to all issues that may generate or destroy future cash flows. This includes the expectation of mergers and acquisitions (Rhodes-Kropf &

Viswanathan, 2004), employees going on strikes (Becker & Olson, 1986), supply chain disruptions (Hendricks & Singhal, 2005), among many others.

With regard to discount rates specifically, these shall greatly vary according to the risk associated with a company (Koziol, 2014). For the purposes of the current debate, risk may be simplistically understood as the probability that the company will not generate the results expected from it. The greater the perceived risk, the greater the rate of return required by the financiers of the operation (e.g. shareholders, creditors). These expected rates of return (i.e. cost of equity and cost of debt) have a direct impact on the calculation of market values when the method of discounted cash flows is employed (Lundholm & O'keefe, 2001). Decisions referring to the capital structure of companies (i.e. the relationship between the financing coming from shareholders and creditors) can also have a considerable influence on the levels of returns required (Cummins & Lamm-Tennant, 1994). Often, the greater a company's debt is, the higher the interest rate demanded by lenders to provide new loans will be. These issues comprehend the basic subjects addressed in the literature of Corporate Finance, with the concept of WACC (Weighted Average Cost of Capital) summarizing the most common calculation of the discount rates applied to future cash flows.

10.2.1 The Role of Expectations

In addition to supply and demand relationships and to possible market deviations, stock pricing is dependent on investor's expectations about firms' future (Zweig, 1973). In this sense, companies' internal and external aspects remain under constant scrutiny, with all factors capable of altering forecasts of cash generation being closely monitored (Chung & Jo, 1996). This includes the quality of management decisions and the resources available to firms, with these factors unfolding in a series of others, among which managers' credibility, operational efficiency, firms' capacity to innovate, research and development policies, employees' satisfaction/turnover, the adequacy to market practices, respect for the law, the history of results, and the strategic value of tangible and intangible resources, to name a few.

Likewise, the issues external to companies include everything in their macro-environment, such as the tendencies in consumer markets (Duffee, 2005), the level of economic activity (Pearce, 1983), and legal/political stability in the regions where companies operate (Eleswarapu & Venkataraman, 2006). In this sense, matters such as the choice of governments for non-payment of debts (moratorium) (Smirlock & Kaufold, 1987), fiscal irresponsibility (Stark, 2018), environmental policies, and decisions seen as incorrect from the macroeconomic point of view can cause major fluctuations in the price of shares, none of which is dependent on managers' decisions. Similarly, increased volatility in stock prices are common during periods of election campaigns (Białkowski et al., 2008), especially as public opinion polls reveal the populations' preference for candidates. As aspirants are seen as more hostile to companies' advance in voting intentions and the likelihood of their electoral success increases, investors may choose to redirect their capital to other environments that are more aligned with what they perceive as favorable (Andrade, 1998). The electoral expectations associated with the mobility of speculative money are, therefore, a potential source of variation in stock prices.

In the attempt to navigate these complex issues, it is common for companies to hire services of economic and political analysts, as well as consulting firms which specialize in the identification and study of trends in this regard (Eurasia Group, 2020). In a way, this could be seen as an effort by companies to better manage the uncertainties of the environments in which they operate, adjusting their decisions accordingly. The combination of these external factors with the internal ones previously discussed forms the expectations of stakeholders. Their beliefs may condition the implementation of productive and speculative investments, both of which with great potential to affect the prices of stocks (even if through distinct ways). The price of stocks can therefore be perceived as a mirror of the expectations that managers and investors have for the companies' activities in the future.

Thus, it may be argued that stock pricing is, to some extent, an exercise in futurology, being in essence subjective. In this context, the development and application of financial techniques that normally translate into complex mathematical models would represent an attempt to predict the future with some level of objectivity. Given the complexity of the real world, however, as well as the multitude of events and subtle changes that can occur over time, the *ceteris paribus* premise under which many models rest is repeatedly challenged. It is common, for instance, that after events of greater magnitude—as is the case of the Volkswagen Dieselgate—the models used to price stocks suddenly become outdated and unable to absorb the new reality that is presented. Models are, in fact, simplifications of reality, meaning that it would be unreasonable to expect them to incorporate all possible variations (particularly those that are nearly unimaginable). It should be noted then that, although useful, mathematic and econometric models of stock prices forecast are only tools that aim to assist decision-making by investors. Under conditions of certain normality, they can offer valuable support that, based on the fundamentals of the companies examined and those of the markets where they operate, can serve as a beacon in the dark. Problems occur upon the occurrence of significantly abnormal events that usually leads to severe price bumps. On these occasions, the instability of stock prices is most evident due to investors' difficulty to recalibrate their expectations.

In the case of severe corporate scandals, for example, it is practically impossible to quickly evaluate consequences. As discussed in Chap. 6, a series of legal issues usually follow the discovery of corporate misconducts. Given the intricacy of these matters, it is difficult to assess the cost of such processes which may extend for several years, even decades. Still, as the investigations advance, new facts are usually revealed, what pushes investors to constantly reevaluate the impact of these scandals in companies' expected future cash flows. The inability of mathematic and econometric models to provide accurate predictions is also evident in the stock price differences that can be typically observed upon a company's initial public offer (the process is usually referred to its initials IPO). At launch, the shares are offered at a price usually calculated by large investment banks which generally hold great expertise in the subject (Daily et al., 2005). With some frequency, however, the price of the stocks suffers abrupt increases or falls right after the launch (Chen & Mohan, 2002).

These imprecisions suggest that initial calculations are not in consonance with the market.

Specifying the reasons for such variations is certainly a difficult task. It is possible, for example, that news about the company, about the market, or even about the economic and political conjectures of the country in which the company operates occurred shortly before the initial offer of the shares, causing the updated investors' calculations to diverge from those initially proposed as the target price. Another possibility is that rumors have spread across the market, influencing investors' decisions. It is also possible the models used to calculate the launch price are simply incorrect, or that there was an error in their manipulation or in the interpretation of their results. Whatever the case, these and other inaccuracies denote the difficulty in predicting the behavior of the markets, even when the calculations are performed by specialized personnel with the application of the most advanced methodologies.

10.2.2 Operational Incapacity, Technological Transition, Impact on Intangible Resources, and Legal Costs

As discussed in Chap. 6, the Volkswagen Dieselgate is marked by the disclosure of illegal practices adopted by the company. As these practices came to light, Volkswagen's stock prices suffered a sharp drop (Fracarolli Nunes, 2018), followed by other harsh fluctuations. A discussion on the main reasons supporting them is thus critical. Based on the topics previously addressed, it may be clear that fluctuations in stock prices are, in general, due to changes in investors' expectations, particularly on what relates to the capacity of companies to generate future cash flows. Building on this assumption, and taking the Volkswagen scandal as a prime example of environmental fraud, we propose a debate on the main reasons capable to significantly cause changes in investors' expectations. We focus on four main axes: (1) operational incapacity; (2) impact on intangible resources; (3) technological transition; and (4) legal costs.

Operational Incapacity

The disclosure of the Dieselgate fraud revealed that Volkswagen needed cheating and shortcuts to achieve superior performance. Before that, the company appeared to be successful in producing diesel-powered cars that were able to comply with strict environmental laws. That may have led investors to believe that the company indeed possessed a superior technology and was capable to exploit a promising market. As discussed throughout the chapter, these perceptions fueled the creation of positive expectations which, in general, translated into higher stock prices. Within this view, the practice of environmental fraud appears as a potential reason for the creation of market bubbles which attract more attention and investors as they grow. The one created by Volkswagen's illicit practices, however, could hardly be perceived as such. In this sense, the revelation of the fraud turned into a major disappointment, not only from the technical point of view but also from the moral one. Similarly to other processes in which the price of artificially inflated assets are suddenly brought to reality (e.g. the fall in the stock prices of internet-based companies in the early 2000s) (Griffin et al., 2011), the disclosure of the environmental fraud practiced by Volkswagen stood as the bursting of a bubble.

Impact on Intangible Resources

As discussed in Chap. 8, the disclosure of environmental fraud may have a severe impact on various components of companies' intangible resources, which, in turn, may lead to market value losses. The negative effects on the firms' brands, for example, can end up causing negative effects on the generation of future cash flows, as consumers come to associate the logo, the visual identity, or any other aspect related to the company with immoral/illegal practices. In these cases, much of the brand's emotional and social values shall be destroyed, and, by consequence, its attractiveness and capacity to influence customers' decisions. It may be argued then that part of the abrupt loss in market value that Volkswagen absorbed upon the disclosure of the Dieselgate scandal refers to the possible damages to its brand and to the drop in sales that this could represent.

In this sense, compromising trust can also be quite problematic, with effects extending to the most diverse groups of stakeholders (Pirson & Malhotra, 2011). If distrust is implemented among the company's creditors (e.g. banks), for example, they may no longer rely on the accounting numbers presented, which should impair their propensity to grant loans. Such a situation can prove to be extremely adverse as companies will have to seek other sources while probably having to bear a higher capitation cost (i.e. higher interest rates). The increase in these financial expenses would result in a lower generation of cash available to be distributed to investors, what—according to the discounted cash flow rationale—would justify the fall in the value of shares. The breach of trust could also lead partners to avoid the company, being suppliers, perhaps, the most problematic group in this sense (Yeung et al., 2009). If the company is indeed perceived as dishonest, it is possible that suppliers would prefer simply not to transact with it any longer, directly impacting the company's ability to deliver its final products. The difficulties or even the total interruption of operations would also support a drop in the price of the company's shares. In less extreme situations, suppliers may require more guarantees what may include anything from payments in advance to the signing of more strict contracts to avoid opportunism. This last alternative may be framed in the rationale of the Transactional Cost Economics (Coase, 1937). Accordingly, the need to implement controls for opportunistic behavior represents an important factor in increasing companies' costs. In turn, the demand for advance or cash payments is expected to have a negative impact on company's finances, representing great pressure in terms of working capital.

It should be noted that the payment terms offered by suppliers are an important source of spontaneous financing for companies, in such a way that the obtaining of advantageous conditions in this sense must be analyzed at a strategic level. Emerging ramifications from more established disciplines seek to address these and other issues that appear to pertain to a gray area between fields of knowledge usually treated as distinct. For the topics discussed, the interaction between the quality of buyer-supplier relationship and financial performance is part of what has been called supply chain finance.

Damage to employees' trust can also be quite harmful (Galford & Drapeau, 2003). A workforce that does not believe in the words of its leaders may be more prone to cases of disobedience, indiscipline, and strikes, among other reactions that may be detrimental to the normal conduct of operations. In this set, insecurity can manifest in different ways and target the most distinct objectives. It is possible, for example, that the disclosure of environmental fraud leads employees to wonder whether the company is willing to honor its commitments with them. This may include the diligent payment of their salaries, the maintenance of benefits (e.g. health insurance), the maintenance or training and professional development programs, and the continuation of eventual career plans, among others. These questions can lead employees to seek positions in other companies, eventually in competitors. In any case, these issues may result in companies facing major operational difficulties and lose an important part of their know-how, especially if more experienced employees leave their positions. Given the costs that arise from such a troubled context (e.g. lower productivity, lower quality of products and services) and the eventual loss of revenues, these dynamics justify a repricing of the company's shares (i.e. drop in market value).

In addition to these matters, the hiring of staff can also be negatively impacted. Indeed, a company associated with environmental fraud can scare off workers who would normally seek to integrate it. It is possible, therefore, that the best professionals choose to seek positions in other firms, leading the company to miss opportunities for innovation and process improvements. The interruption of the flow of more qualified intellectual capital can mean a loss of competitiveness. Difficulties in renewing the workforce may also put pressure on the salaries of those who already work for the company, causing additional difficulties in terms of cash generation. Once again, these issues contribute to losses in market value.

Yet, the loss of trust among consumers is, perhaps, the most damaging (Lau & Lee, 1999), as the disclosure of environmental fraud—as well as of any other type of fraud—may call into question the credibility of firms involved in such issues. Following the discovery of unethical conducts, companies may have great difficulty in convincing consumers of their intentions, what, if ever possible, shall require a significant struggle. Among other efforts, a massive investment in corporate communication is likely to be necessary. In the attempt to reorient the perception around their brands, companies should invest in advertisements in the most diverse media channels, as well as intensify the association of their brands with the defense of environmental causes. In addition to the high costs that communication strategies represent, their implementation may increase the perception of corporate hypocrisy in case companies fail to convince their stakeholders that they are really proposing a sincere change in their conducts.

Also, the effectiveness of these initiatives may be compromised by the urgency of their implementation. Unlike a carefully planned repositioning strategy, the rebuilding of a brand after a major negative event—including the disclosure of environmental fraud—occurs on an emergency basis and amid a whirlwind of adverse news, lawsuits, charges from investors, and changes in command, among other sources of instability. It is possible, therefore, that the great pressure that these contexts represent leads companies to adopt hasty measures which may not only be ineffective but also harmful to future efforts. It may also be the case that, seeking to get rid of extremely adverse situations quickly, those responsible for post-crisis communication are dominated by their emotions and take actions that end up aggravating the problem. Within a broad perspective, the chaos generated by a major crisis can lead to errors, so that the high costs and risks associated with these actions support the fall in stock prices.

As discussed in Chap. 8, at the same time intangible resources are fragile and may be easily destroyed, they take a long time to be built. Given the importance of sustainability-related aspects, environmental fraud can cause long-lasting negative effects, especially on the perception of younger consumers. In that way, the breach of trust shall negatively affect companies' ability to generate cash flows, justifying the drop in the value of shares.

Technological Transition

In addition to communication activities, the pressure for quick responses and to alleviate discomfort can lead companies to adopt measures that shall have a long-term impact, decisively affecting their business models.

In some cases, this may mean a total re-branding, with the company seeking to suppress its old ties with the fraud. It is also possible that the firm seeks to communicate a change in attitude through its operational practices. This seems to be the case for Volkswagen, which shortly after the Dieselgate redesigned its corporate strategy toward the production of electric cars. This change seems to aim at the detachment of the company's image to that of the diesel technology, offering the organization a second chance among consumers. These alterations would work as a kind of blank sheet under which the company could rebuild its image. This type of "reset" would be necessary in face of the difficulties and the high costs of repairing the damage to the old image of the company. It is possible also that this change of focus was already part of the company's long-term strategy, since the automotive industry as a whole had already been confronted with this issue (see Chaps. 6 and 11). The discovery of the environmental fraud perpetrated by the company, however, seems to have accelerated this change. While the reasons that led the company to quickly seek a new figure have already been discussed—as well as the means by which this happened—the effects of this sudden change in Volkswagen's potential to generate future cash flows demand a more detailed analysis of its business model.

As pointed out in Chap. 6, Volkswagen had its history linked to internal combustion motors. Diesel engine technology, in particular, seems to have been of great importance in the company's trajectory, having helped it establish as one of the largest automakers in the world. Over the years, the company developed competencies in this sense, with the know-how acquired providing it with a privileged competitive position. At the same time these developments allow the company to improve its productive processes, they also favor the conquest of increasingly larger portions of market segments, often resulting in important gains of scale. With the company producing more units than its competitors, problems such as idle capacity are avoided, allowing all investment in physical assets to be fully applied in the generation of value. This results in the expectation of higher rates of return since the capital invested by shareholders works for longer than the capital invested by competing companies. This expectation of higher returns, in turn, can act as an important attraction for investors, who not only contribute to the appreciation of the company's shares but also to its capacity to access alternative sources to finance their operations and projects.

In this sense, a technological transition would demand a radical reconfiguration of the productive processes, with the total or partial abandonment of diesel technology causing the loss of competitive advantages achieved over decades. This also includes redesigning the supply chain, since electric cars require new types of materials and parts. The relationships built with suppliers over the years would be lost, with the company needing to restart its long-term relationships with new ones. Thus, the transition to electric car technology can represent a significant loss to the company's operational performance, justifying the loss of market value.

Legal Costs

Along with the issues discussed above, the perspective of legal costs represents a major source of volatility in the price of shares (Bhagat & Romano, 2002), as it becomes necessary to consider the breadth that processes linked to environmental causes can have, especially if the damages caused are easily identifiable. At this point, it is crucial to differentiate between cases of environmental disasters and environmental fraud. If, on the one hand, both can receive great media attention (e.g. BP Oil Spill and Volkswagen Dieselgate), they differ enormously in terms of the speed with which their effects are felt. The harmful effects caused by the additional pollution of cars equipped by Volkswagen with cheating software, for example, will extend for years. In addition, the fact that there are several sources of pollution makes it practically impossible to assign due responsibility to the fraudulent company, so that it is unlikely to be linked to the damage caused. Thus, in general, it can be said that, while the damage caused by environmental disasters is easily identifiable, sudden, and blunt, the losses arising from environmental fraud practices are diluted, with this collectivization of the harm contributing to a greater likelihood of impunity. In this context, the investigative work of the authorities becomes even more important.

From the point of view of the costs of legal proceedings, however, this can contribute to greater subjectivity in the analyses and, consequently, to a great elasticity in the calculation of indemnities. Although the calculations associated with environmental disasters are also not simple and not at all objective, the fact that their effects are, in general, more delimited should contribute to more precise verdicts. In addition, the fact that the damages of environmental fraud are diluted and in many cases perceived only in the long-term can cause lawsuits to extend through decades after the discovery of the frauds, what greatly increases the inaccuracy of any projections of legal costs. These uncertainties greatly increase the risk of operations, which should be reflected in the fall in the value of the shares. Several articles have analyzed the stock market response to social and environmental failures. Wood et al. (2018), for instance, examined the economic impacts of negative environmental events for the automotive industry. The investigation of 41 different cases distributed over more than three decades (from 1984 to 2016) revealed that the announcement of environmental fails caused a mean stock market reaction of -1.01%. By way of comparison, Rupp (2001) found that safety recalls in the automotive industry typically account for a stock market reaction of -0.28%. Coherently with our discussion on the potential of environmental fraud to negatively impact companies' intangible resources (Chap. 8), these authors point to the impairment of trust as one of the possible reasons explaining this outcome. Fracarolli Nunes (2019), in turn, shows that the effects of such issues may not be limited to the source company (i.e. the one more directly associated to the problems), disseminating through supply chains. With regard to the Volkswagen Dieselgate specifically, the study shows that suppliers were negatively affected, with market value losses varying from -2.05% to -8.73%. Likewise, Fracarolli Nunes and Lee Park (2016) suggest that the scandal negatively impacted American companies, with the costs associated to market value losses being estimated in US $1.56 billion in the industry level of analysis, and in US $4.88 billion in the supply chain level.

In what refers to the impact of the scandal on Volkswagen itself, Fracarolli Nunes (2018) estimates that the company lost around 30% of its market value when a four-day-event window is considered (i.e. two days prior to the event, and two days after it). Bouzzine and Lueg (2020) extend the analysis on the effects of the Dieselgate, extrapolating the usually short event windows considered. More specifically, the authors did not limit their analysis to the days orbiting the announcement of the fraud but, instead, identified and tested the effects of a total of ten events related to the case. In line with Fracarolli Nunes and Lee Park (2016), the authors show that the effects of the Dieselgate were not restricted to Volkswagen, having also significantly affected the stock returns of its industry peers. As evidenced by the authors, however, Volkswagen's market value was only impaired upon the initial announcement of the fraud, with the negative effects of the other nine subsequent events examined being concentrated on industry peers.

References

Ajitha, S., & Sivakumar, V. J. (2017). Understanding the Effect of Personal and Social Value on Attitude and Usage Behavior of Luxury Cosmetic Brands. *Journal of Retailing and Consumer Services, 39*, 103–113.

Andrade, P. (1998, June 2). Culpa por fuga de capital é de FHC, diz Lula. *Folha de São Paulo*. https://www1.folha.uol.com.br/fsp/brasil/fc02069804.htm

Bailey, W., & Jagtiani, J. (1994). Foreign Ownership Restrictions and Stock Prices in the Thai Capital Market. *Journal of Financial Economics, 36*(1), 57–87.

Barberis, N., & Thaler, R. (2002). A Survey of Behavioral Finance. *Working Paper 9222*. National Bureau of Economic Research.

Becker, B. E., & Olson, C. A. (1986). The Impact of Strikes on Shareholder Equity. *ILR Review, 39*(3), 425–438.

Bernoulli, D. (1738). Specimen Theoriae Novae de Mensura Sortis. *Commentarii academiae scientiarum imperialis Petropolitanae, 5*, 175–192.

Bhagat, S., & Romano, R. (2002). Event Studies and the Law: Part I: Technique and Corporate Litigation. *American Law and Economics Review, 4*(1), 141–168.

Białkowski, J., Gottschalk, K., & Wisniewski, T. P. (2008). Stock Market Volatility around National Elections. *Journal of Banking & Finance, 32*(9), 1941–1953.

Bouzzine, Y. D., & Lueg, R. (2020). The Contagion Effect of Environmental Violations: The Case of Dieselgate in Germany. *Business Strategy and the Environment, 29*, 3187–3202.

Brennan, M. J., & Copeland, T. E. (1988). Stock Splits, Stock Prices, and Transaction Costs. *Journal of Financial Economics, 22*(1), 83–101.

Carlin, W., & Soskice, D. (1990). *Macroeconomics and the Wage Bargain* (Vol. 99). Oxford University Press.

CFI. (2020). Market Value. How Much an Asset or Company is Worth in a Financial Market. https://corporatefinanceinstitute.com/resources/knowledge/valuation/market-value/

Chen, C. R., & Mohan, N. J. (2002). Underwriter Spread, Underwriter Reputation, and IPO Underpricing: A Simultaneous Equation Analysis. *Journal of Business Finance & Accounting, 29*(3–4), 521–540.

Chung, K. H., & Jo, H. (1996). The Impact of Security Analysts' Monitoring and Marketing Functions on the Market Value of Firms. *Journal of Financial and Quantitative Analysis, 31*(4), 493–512.

Coase, R. H. (1937). The Nature of the Firm. *Economica, 4*(16), 386–405.

Cummins, J. D., & Lamm-Tennant, J. (1994). Capital Structure and the Cost of Equity Capital in the Property-Liability Insurance Industry. *Insurance: Mathematics and Economics, 15*(2–3), 187–201.

Daelemans, B., Daniels, J. P., & Nourzad, F. (2018). Free Trade Agreements and Volatility of Stock Returns and Exchange Rates: Evidence from NAFTA. *Open Economies Review, 29*(1), 141–163.

Daily, C. M., Certo, S. T., & Dalton, D. R. (2005). Investment Bankers and IPO Pricing: Does Prospectus Information Matter? *Journal of Business Venturing, 20*(1), 93–111.

Duffee, G. R. (2005). Time Variation in the Covariance between Stock Returns and Consumption Growth. *The Journal of Finance, 60*(4), 1673–1712.

Durnev, A., & Kim, E. H. (2005). To Steal or Not to Steal: Firm Attributes, Legal Environment, and Valuation. *The Journal of Finance, 60*(3), 1461–1493.

Eleswarapu, V. R., & Venkataraman, K. (2006). The Impact of Legal and Political Institutions on Equity Trading Costs: A Cross-country Analysis. *The Review of Financial Studies, 19*(3), 1081–1111.

Eurasia Group. (2020). What We Do. https://www.eurasiagroup.net/services/whatwedo

Fishburn, P. C. (1968). Utility Theory. *Management Science, 14*(5), 335–378.

Fishburn, P. C. (2013). *The Foundations of Expected Utility* (Vol. 31). Springer Science & Business Media.

Fracarolli Nunes, M. (2018). Supply Chain Contamination: An Exploratory Approach on the Collateral Effects of Negative Corporate Events. *European Management Journal, 36*(4), 573–587.

Fracarolli Nunes, M. (2019). The Impact of Negative Social/Environmental Events on the Market Value of Supply Chain Partners. In L. De Boer &

P. H. Andersen (Eds.), *Operations Management and Sustainability* (pp. 151–178). Palgrave Macmillan.

Fracarolli Nunes, M., & Lee Park, C. (2016). Caught Red-Handed: The Cost of the Volkswagen Dieselgate. *Journal of Global Responsibility, 7*(2), 288–302.

Gaikwad, N. (2013). Research Note Presidential Prospects, Political Support, and Stock Market Performance. *Quarterly Journal of Political Science, 8*(4), 451–464.

Galford, R., & Drapeau, A. S. (2003). The Enemies of Trust. *Harvard Business Review, 81*(2), 88–95.

Godsell, D., Lel, U., & Miller, D. (2018). Financial Protectionism, M&A activity, and Shareholder Wealth. *SMU Cox School of Business Research Paper*, pp. 18–23.

Goetzmann, W. N., & Garry, M. (1986). Does Delisting from the S&P 500 Affect Stock Price? *Financial Analysts Journal, 42*(2), 64–69.

Griffin, J. M., Harris, J. H., Shu, T., & Topaloglu, S. (2011). Who Drove and Burst the Tech Bubble? *The Journal of Finance, 66*(4), 1251–1290.

Griskevicius, V., Tybur, J. M., & Van den Bergh, B. (2010). Going Green to be Seen: Status, Reputation, and Conspicuous Conservation. *Journal of Personality and Social Psychology, 98*(3), 392–404.

Grullon, G., & Michaely, R. (2004). The Information Content of Share Repurchase Programs. *The Journal of Finance, 59*(2), 651–680.

Hendricks, K. B., & Singhal, V. R. (2005). An Empirical Analysis of the Effect of Supply Chain Disruptions on Long-run Stock Price Performance and Equity Risk of the Firm. *Production and Operations Management, 14*(1), 35–52.

Kalay, A., Sade, O., & Wohl, A. (2004). Measuring Stock Illiquidity: An Investigation of the Demand and Supply Schedules at the TASE. *Journal of Financial Economics, 74*(3), 461–486.

Katz, L. F., & Murphy, K. M. (1992). Changes in Relative Wages, 1963–1987: Supply and Demand Factors. *The Quarterly Journal of Economics, 107*(1), 35–78.

Koziol, C. (2014). A Simple Correction of the WACC Discount Rate for Default Risk and Bankruptcy Costs. *Review of Quantitative Finance and Accounting, 42*(4), 653–666.

Kramer, L. (2020). How Is a Company's Stock Price and Market Capitalization Determined? *Investopedia*. https://www.investopedia.com/ask/answers/how-companys-stock-price-and-market-cap-determined/

Kruschwitz, L., & Löffler, A. (2006). *Discounted Cash Flow: A Theory of the Valuation of Firms*. John Wiley & Sons.

Lau, G. T., & Lee, S. H. (1999). Consumers' Trust in a Brand and the Link to Brand Loyalty. *Journal of Market-Focused Management, 4*(4), 341–370.

Lundholm, R., & O'keefe, T. (2001). Reconciling Value Estimates from the Discounted Cash Flow Model and the Residual Income Model. *Contemporary Accounting Research, 18*(2), 311–335.

Oishi, S., Diener, E., Suh, E., & Lucas, R. E. (1999). Value as a Moderator in Subjective Well-Being. *Journal of Personality, 67*(1), 157–184.

Pastor, L., & Veronesi, P. (2009). Technological Revolutions and Stock Prices. *American Economic Review, 99*(4), 1451–1483.

Pearce, D. K. (1983). Stock Prices and the Economy. *Federal Reserve Bank of Kansas City Economic Review, 68*(9), 7–22.

Pearce, D. K., & Roley, V. V. (1984). *Stock Prices and Economic News* (No. w1296). National Bureau of Economic Research.

Pirson, M., & Malhotra, D. (2011). Foundations of Organizational Trust: What Matters to Different Stakeholders? *Organization Science, 22*(4), 1087–1104.

Pontiff, J., & Woodgate, A. (2008). Share Issuance and Cross-sectional Returns. *The Journal of Finance, 63*(2), 921–945.

Rhodes-Kropf, M., & Viswanathan, S. (2004). Market Valuation and Merger Waves. *The Journal of Finance, 59*(6), 2685–2718.

Rupp, N. G. (2001). Are Government Initiated Recalls More Damaging for Shareholders? Evidence from Automotive Recalls, 1973–1998. *Economics Letters, 71*(2), 265–270.

Schneider, G., & Troeger, V. E. (2006). War and the World Economy: Stock Market Reactions to International Conflicts. *Journal of Conflict Resolution, 50*(5), 623–645.

Sheth, J. N., Newman, B. I., & Gross, B. L. (1991). Why We Buy What We Buy: A Theory of Consumption Values. *Journal of Business Research, 22*(2), 159–170.

Smirlock, M., & Kaufold, H. (1987). Bank Foreign Lending, Mandatory Disclosure Rules, and the Reaction of Bank Stock Prices to the Mexican Debt Crisis. *Journal of Business, 60*(3), 347–364.

Stark, J. (2018). The Irresponsible EBC. *Project Syndicate*. https://www.economics.utoronto.ca/gindart/2018-02-19%20-%20The%20irresponsible%20ECB.pdf

Wood, L. C., Wang, J. X., Duong, L. N., Reiners, T., & Smith, R. (2018). Stock Market Reactions to Auto Manufacturers' Environmental Failures. *Journal of Macromarketing, 38*(4), 364–382.

Woolridge, J. R., & Snow, C. C. (1990). Stock Market Reaction to Strategic Investment Decisions. *Strategic Management Journal, 11*(5), 353–363.
Yeung, J. H. Y., Selen, W., Zhang, M., & Huo, B. (2009). The Effects of Trust and Coercive Power on Supplier Integration. *International Journal of Production Economics, 120*(1), 66–78.
Zweig, M. E. (1973). An Investor Expectations Stock Price Predictive Model Using Closed-End Fund Premiums. *The Journal of Finance, 28*(1), 67–78.

11

Is Diesel Dead?

11.1 Brief History of Diesel Technology

Rudolf Christian Karl Diesel, the inventor of diesel engines, was born in Paris, 1858, in a family of German immigrants (Thomas Jr., 1978), and since a young age showed interest in mechanics. Following the outbreak of the Franco-Prussian War (1870–1871), the Diesel family was expelled from France, having found refuge in London, UK. Shortly afterward, young Rudolf moved to Germany, where he graduated in 1880 from the Munich Technical University (German: *Technische Universität München*). Among his concerns was the low energy conversion of steam power plants (Klooster, 2009) And, after years of working on more efficient alternatives, he had the patent for his "new, rational heat engine" granted in 1892 (Daimler, 2020a).

Technically, the novel concept had important differences in respect to spark-ignition engines. While the latter fired a compressed mixture of air and fuel, Diesel's invention was designed to condense the intake air, with the fuel being injected just before the ignition. Due to the heat produced by the compression, the mixture went into spontaneous combustion, eliminating the need for sparkles (Daimler, 2020a). From this point, the

M. Fracarolli Nunes, C. Lee Park, *Business Ethics and Environmental Fraud*,
https://doi.org/10.1007/978-3-030-73800-6_11

development of his concept accelerated. In 1893, for example, a description of Diesel's engine was published as the "Theory and Construction of a Rational Heat Motor" (German: *Theorie und Konstruktion eines rationellen Wäremotors)* (Britannica, 2020), and with the joint support from the Krupp firms and the Maschinenfabrik Augsburg—later MAN (Daimler, 2020a)—a series of increasingly successful models were produced. That culminated in the demonstration of a 25-horsepower, four-stroke, single vertical cylinder compression engine in 1897 (Britannica, 2020).

The high efficiency of Diesel's engines made them an immediate commercial success (Britannica, 2020). In fact, the Diesel technology quickly consolidated into the second position among internal combustion motors, even if only in stationary forms at first. Rudolf Diesel, however, never hid his enthusiasm and ambition for a much wider use of his invention. In a letter to publisher Julius Springer in 1892, he claimed that it was "destined to completely revolutionize engine engineering and replace everything that exists" (Mollenhauer & Tschoke, 2010, p. 5). Shortly before his disappearance in 1913, Rudolf also stated to be convinced that the development of a Diesel automobile engine was a sheer matter of time (Daimler, 2020a).

Before that, however, diesel engines debuted in heavier vehicles. In 1922, Benz equipped a tractor prototype with a diesel power plant. One year later, the first diesel truck was introduced by Benz & Cie (Daimler, 2020b), and in February 1936, the Mercedes-Benz 260 D was showcased. Equipped with a 2.6-liter OM 138 four-cylinder engine, it was the first series-production diesel passenger automobile (Daimler, 2020c). Diesel engines continued to gain ground, particularly in Europe. In the decades that followed, however, the continent went through great economic turbulence, particularly due to World War II (1939–1945). Likewise, the oil crises in the 1970s had a direct impact on the consumption of oil derivates, as well as on the development of diesel engines. It was not until the 1990s that diesel became the dominant car fuel in Europe (Lussenhop, 2015). By the time, countries such as the United Kingdom, France, Italy, and Germany offered important incentives, making the acquisition of diesel cars more attractive. Curiously, the stimuli were justified by an allegedly greater environmental efficiency of the fuel, as its combustion would produce 15% less CO_2 than that of gasoline (Vidal, 2015).

Authors such as Cames and Helmers (2013), however, suggest that the European preference for diesel would be linked to the effects that the oil crises of the 1970s had on the energy matrix of the countries in the region. With the offer of crude oil significantly shortened, nations faced serious threats to their energetic security and economy, being pushed to quickly lower their oil consumption. Measures on that regard include France's option for the construction of nuclear plants, as well as Germany's preference for natural gas—instead of oil—as its main heating input. These strategic moves ended up causing an excess of diesel in the market, as European refiners continued to produce it. In this context, governments would have urged automakers to consider diesel-powered vehicles as a viable alternative to their own strategic plans (Plumer, 2015). As a result of these "dieselization" policies (Hivert, 1999), diesel cars became the most popular choice among European consumers, rising from a market share of 22% in 1997 to 53% in 2007 (Hivert, 2013).

Unlike in Europe, the market for petroleum in the United States has historically been dominated by gasoline-powered cars, with the diesel technology being, to some extent, marginalized (Fosten, 2012). In fact, since the 1930s—when Mercedes-Benz started selling small numbers of diesel-powered units in the country—sales were never expressive, with the exception of a short period between the second half of the 1970s and the first half of the 1980s (Kurani & Sperling, 1988). Accordingly, from 1977 to 1981, the market share of diesel cars increased from 0.4% to 6.1% nationwide (9% in California), with the 1970s oil crises also playing a major role in the rise. Among the initiatives adopted to diminish the North American dependence on foreign oil was the approval by the American Congress of the Energy Policy and Conservation Act of 1975. Through the Corporate Average Fuel Economy (CAFE) program, it required automakers to increase the fuel efficiency of new passenger cars and light-duty trucks sold in the American market (National Research Council, 2002). Considered more energetically efficient, diesel emerged as a potentially viable alternative to gasoline, as automakers struggled to meet the new fuel consumption demands (Kurani & Sperling, 1988).

Likewise, diesel benefited from consumers' expectation of cost savings, with the fuel being initially perceived as economically superior to gasoline.

The popularity of diesel cars in the United States, however, did not last long, with sales dropping rapidly in the coming years. By 1985, diesel-powered cars had returned to their modest position in the American market, accounting for only 0.8% of the new vehicles commercialized (Kurani & Sperling, 1988). As discussed by the authors, this sharp fall would reflect consumers' misunderstanding of the economic benefits of diesel, as comparisons with gasoline were often made in terms of cost per gallon (instead of more accurate measures such as cost per mile, or fully allocated total costs). With gasoline's absolute price being typically lower, the misconception that it allowed for a better economic performance crystallized among consumers. In fact, the difference in prices per gallon can still be observed in the United States. As of June 2020, retail prices for regular gasoline and diesel corresponded to US $2.08/gallon and US $2.41/gallon, respectively (U.S. Energy Information Administration, 2020a). Accordingly, the disparity in final prices reflects the differences in the cost of distribution and market (21% for gasoline and 31% for diesel), refining (17% for gasoline and 13% for diesel), and crude oil in each gallon (39% for gasoline and 33% for diesel), while both fuels are subject to the same tax burden (23%).

Adds to that, the negative perception on the quality of diesel engines in the United States, which, to a large extent, is due to the poor performance of a specific General Motors' (GM) model. As pointed out by Kurani and Sperling (1988), the GM 5.7-liter diesel engine presented numerous technical problems, consolidating the idea that diesel engines had high maintenance cost and low reliability. Among consumers' complaints was its frequent need for oil changes, issues with fuel pumps, an inadequate system to isolate water from the fuel, an unsteady engine block, skimpy main bearings, and a transmission that was unsatisfactorily matched with the power characteristics of diesel engines. Altogether, these faults would have caused the drop in diesel car sales in the period, as well as a lasting damage to its reputation. That translates in steady low participation of diesel-powered cars in the American market. In 2010, for example, only 2.68% of the new vehicles commercialized in the United States relied on diesel (Fosten, 2012). These figures remained practically unchanged until the disclosure of the Volkswagen Dieselgate, with diesel cars accounting for 3% of the American automotive market in 2015 (Lussenhop, 2015).

In addition to the negative effects of the Volkswagen Dieselgate—as discussed in Chaps. 6 and 10—diesel technology has been the target of fierce attacks, usually linking its use to environmental and public health issues. On that regard, the World Health Organization (WHO) calls pollution “the new tobacco” (Ghebreyesus, 2018), and relates the consumption of diesel to lung, urinary bladder, and pancreas cancer, among others (WHO, 2014). Studies on the association between the exposition to engine exhausts and childhood cancer are also commonly referred to by the organ. Likewise, expressions such as “air pollution is choking our cities and causing a global health crises” (Greenpeace, 2020) have commonly been associated with the consumption of diesel.

As a result, diesel’s market share suffered a sharp drop in European countries. In Germany, for example, the percentage of new diesel passenger cars went from 48% in 2014 to 32% in 2018. France, in turn, displayed a share decrease from 63% to 39% in the same period, with countries such as the UK (from 50% to 32%), Sweden (from 59% to 38%), Greece (from 64% to 36%), and Spain (from 66% to 36%) showing similar paths (Statista, 2019). Likewise, the number of German consumers that desired their next vehicle to be equipped with a diesel engine dropped 35% from 2014 to 2018 (Deloitte, 2018). These numbers suggest that diesel is indeed in decline and that it may even disappear from the automotive sector over the next decades. Among the problems that may prevent, or, at least, make this trend less likely, are the high costs of transition to new technologies, as well as the serious social and environmental issues that are typical of the alternatives available.

11.2 Sustainable Alternatives?

Among the most popular options for diesel’s so-called sustainable alternatives is its replacement by fuels that come from renewable sources, with biofuels becoming increasingly popular after the 1970s oil crises. Brazil, for example, opted to substitute a large portion of its petroleum-based fuel consumption with ethanol. Taking advantage of its wide territorial extension, climatic conditions, and centuries-old expertise in the cultivation and processing of sugar cane, the country implemented what is perhaps the largest fossil fuel substitution program ever (Nitsch, 1991). The Proálcool (i.e. *Programa Nacional do Álcool*, or National Alcohol Program) program lasted from 1975 to 1994, and was responsible for a significant change in the Brazilian energetic matrix, as well as for a technological development from which the country benefits until today. Around 73% of Brazilian car fleet is equipped with ethanol-powered engines, or is capable to use both ethanol and gasoline (Rapid Transition, 2018). That includes both engines that use only ethanol as fuel and flex vehicles (i.e. cars that can be fueled with either gasoline or ethanol in any proportion). It is estimated that the use of ethanol in the Brazilian fleet is responsible for a reduction in greenhouse gas (GHG) emissions that exceed 40 million CO_2 equivalent (CO_2eq) every year (Farina et al., 2013). This represents more than the total 2012 annual emissions of countries such as Croatia (30 million CO_2eq), Dominican Republic (33 million CO_2eq), Estonia (23 million CO_2eq), Gabon (35 million CO_2eq), Jamaica (15 million CO_2eq), Lithuania (29 million CO_2eq), and Uruguay (34 million CO_2eq), for instance (The World Bank, 2020).

With other countries encouraging the use of ethanol, its global production increased from 29 billion liters (7.7 billion gallons) in 2000 to more than 117 billion (30.9 billion gallons) in 2017. The share of ethanol production used as *carburant* also increased from 59% to more than 84% in the same period (Statista, 2020). This sharp growth can be attributed, to a great extent, due to Federal policies destined to accelerate U.S. biofuels industries (Schnepf & Yacobucci, 2013). Among the initiatives in that direction is the creation of the Renewable Fuel Standard (RFS)—“a federal program that requires transportation fuel sold in the United States to contain a minimum volume of renewable fuels” (U.S. Department of Energy, 2020a). Originally established by the American Congress with the enactment of the Energy Policy Act of 2005 (EPAct Public Law 109–58), the initial RFS (called RFS1) stipulated that a minimum of 4 billion gallons (around 15.1 billion liters) of renewable fuels were to be used in 2006, with figures rising to 7.5 billion gallons (around 28.4 billion liters) until 2012 (Schnepf & Yacobucci, 2013).

Also, the EPAct established a series of incentives to the acquisition of new alternative fuel vehicles (AFVs), including the provision of a tax credit for 50% of the incremental vehicle cost, in addition to a 30% tax credit of the increased cost for those vehicles that either meet or exceed the most demanding emission standards under the Clean Air Act. Likewise, vehicles that either meet or exceed California's Super Ultra Low Emission Vehicle Standards are objected to the same incentives. The credit would be available for the acquisition of qualified light-, medium-, and heavy-duty dedicated AFVs which operate on natural gas, propane, hydrogen, or fuel blends composed of at least 85% methanol, with mixed fuel vehicles also qualifying for reduced credit amounts (U.S. Department of Energy, 2020b).

The Energy Independence and Security Act of 2007 (EISA Public Law 110–140) considerably augmented the biofuel mandate volumes of the EPAct and the period of its application until 2022. The expended RFS (called RFS2) demanded the annual use of biofuels to increase from 9 billion gallons (34 billion liters) by 2008, to 36 billion gallons (136.2 billion liters) by 2022, from which at least 16 billion gallons (60.5 billion liters) should come from cellulosic biofuels, and 15 billion gallons (56.7 billion liters) from corn-starch ethanol (Schnepf & Yacobucci, 2013). Accordingly, beyond this increase in volumes and extension of mandates, the RFS 2 encompassed three important differences in relation to RFS 1: (1) the division of total renewable fuel requirements in four distinct but related categories (total renewable fuels, advanced biofuels, biomass-based fuels, and cellulosic biofuels); (2) the determination that biofuels pertaining to each category must achieve a minimum reduction of GHG emissions; and (3) the resolution that all renewable fuels must be originated from feedstocks that comply with amended definitions of renewable biomass, what include certain restrictions regarding the use of land. These policies led the United States—the largest ethanol producer of the world—to increase its production from 6.5 billion gallons (24.7 billion liters) in 2007 to 15.7 billion (59.7 billion liters) in 2019. Similarly, Brazil—the second-largest producer—saw its annual production grow from 5 billion gallons (19 billion liters) to more than 8.5 billion gallons (32.1 billion liters) in the same period (U.S. Department of Energy, 2020c).

In face of this remarkable evolution, the debate on the social impacts of ethanol production has gained momentum in the last years. The fact that the fuel is derived from feedstock (e.g. sugarcane, corn, potatoes), for example, has put into question the consequences of large-scale production on the amounts of food available for consumption. In that way, the use of food for purposes other than nutritional ones reduces the quantities available for this end and poses a threat to food security, defined as existing "when all people, at all times, have physical, social and economic access to sufficient, safe and nutritious food which meets their dietary needs and food preferences for an active and healthy life" (FAO, 2020). Within a trade-off perspective, as the production of biofuels advances, people may simply not have access to the minimum amounts of food necessary to meet their basic nutritional needs. In addition, the reduction of food available is expected to pressure prices, limiting the access of the poor to nourishment.

Indirectly, the production of biofuels ends up influencing the price of agricultural land, which, in one way or another, pushes food prices. In fact, the production of biofuels can generate impacts that go beyond the most easily identifiable ones. Increased land prices shall lead, for example, to the process of land concentration by large groups, with small and medium producers tending to sell their properties. Likewise, expensive land prices can act as an important barrier to entry (Porter, 1980, 2008), preventing the access of new small and medium producers, and reinforcing the concentrations cycle. Along with the direct social impacts associated with these movements (e.g. displacement of rural populations to urban areas), the concentration of food production in a few producers shall have deleterious consequences such as the formation of cartels.

From an environmental perspective, the production and consumption of biofuels have also been the target of major criticism. As pointed out by a working group of the Intergovernmental Panel on Climate Change (IPCC, 2014, p. 616),

> Biofuels have direct, fuel-cycle GHG emissions that are typically 30–90% lower per kilometre travelled than those for gasoline or diesel fuels. However, since for some biofuels, indirect emissions—including from land

use change—can lead to greater total emissions than when using petroleum products, policy support needs to be considered on a case by case basis.

In fact, the production and distribution of biofuels are noticeably dependent on machines, equipment, and vehicles that are powered by diesel engines (e.g. tractors, harvesters, trucks, ships). Given the considerable social and environmental impacts associated with the production of biofuels, their positioning as sustainable alternatives becomes less robust, or even impossible. Certainly, this is complex and demands caution. The debate proposed here is not intended to determine a verdict or claim that all forms of biofuels are bad for people or for the planet. Instead, we seek to raise awareness of the potential collateral effects that might result from the adoption of arguably environmentally friendly alternatives.

11.2.1 Natural Gas

As discussed by Mokhatab et al. (2012), the emergence of natural gas as a fuel of choice would be due to its lower environmental impacts when compared to more traditional alternatives. For Economides (2012, p. 19), the process of de-carbonization of fuels—which would have "little to do with often strident environmental ideologues"—will make natural gas the next most important fuel of the world economy. Pushed by the United States' decision to use natural gas as a substitute for coal and oil, consumption forecasts indicate an acceleration in demand. In that way, the emerging or speculated consumption by China and India, the great energy needs of the United States, and the maturing of its domestic production also support the optimism around the uses of natural gas. From a geopolitical point of view, the fact that there are many suppliers in the world represents yet another advantage of natural gas over oil. In operational terms, natural gas would be also easier to handle, process, transport, and store. However, despite the alleged environmental benefits of natural gas over coal, the replacement of the latter for the former would be not taking place as expected because of political and economic pressures (Greiner et al., 2018).

The commercial production of natural gas in the United States started in 1821, with interest in the commodity significantly growing in the 1970s (Curtis, 2002). According to the U.S. Energy Information Administration (2020b), most of the production increase since 2005 is due to horizontal drilling and hydraulic fracturing techniques applied in tight geological formations (e.g. shale, sandstone, and carbonate). Popularly known as "shale gas", these resources have allowed the United States to significantly diminish its dependence on imported oil (Maverick, 2020). In fact, the United States generates nearly all of the natural gas that it consumes, with annual production reaching 30.6 trillion cubic feet (866.4 million cubic meters) in 2018 (U.S. Energy Information Administration, 2020b).

Despite the apparent benefits to the economy and geopolitics of the countries that exploit these resources, the production of shale gas has been aimed at numerous criticisms from the environmental point of view. Howarth et al. (2011), for example, argue that between 3.6% and 7.9% of the methane from shale gas production escapes to the atmosphere in the lifetime of a well. As highlighted by the authors, these methane emissions would be at least 30% greater than those from conventional gas. Jenner and Lamadrib (2012), in turn, stress the risks that shale gas production poses to water safety, as the extraction may contaminate drinking water aquifers (Vengosh et al., 2013).

A renewable alternative to natural gas has been gaining ground in recent years. Produced from anaerobic digestion (i.e. the disintegration of organic material in the absence of oxygen), biogas—a mixture of methane (CH_4) and carbon dioxide (CO_2)—can be produced from organic waste, food crop residues, intermediate crops, and livestock farming. The purification of biogas, in turn, results in biomethane, which holds the same properties as natural gas (Engie, 2020). Accordingly, the product finds use as fuel for heating, transportation, and the generation of electricity, among other ends. In addition, the digestate produced may be also returned to the soil. Broadly, these characteristics allow biogas to be classified as a renewable and sustainable source of energy, which supports the belief that its exploitation shall grow considerably in the coming years.

11.2.2 Electric Cars

Along with the advances in biofuels, natural gas, and biogas, the transition to electric vehicles seems to be a major trend in the automotive industry. In the United States, for example, 26% of consumers claim to prefer their next car to be either all battery-powered or hybrid (Deloitte, 2019). Likewise, 32% of German, 27% of Indian, 33% of South Korean, 56% of Japanese, and 56% of Chinese consumers express their preference for fully or partially electrically powered vehicles (Deloitte, 2019). These figures reflect the idea that electric cars are viable and sustainable alternatives to fossil fuels. With all-electric cars producing zero direct emissions (i.e. emissions through the tailpipe, evaporation from the fuel system, or during fueling processes) (U.S. Office of Energy Efficiency and Renewable Energy, 2020), they have become popular among celebrities and authorities, as public figures seek to associate their images with "doing good". That may explain, at least partially, their wide acceptance by consumers and the general public.

Yet, electric cars may not be as sustainable as they seem to be at a first glance. Along with the numerous social and environmental issues associated with the use of batteries, the generation of the electricity they consume may be itself very problematic, even if drawn from arguably sustainable sources. Among the main causes of rejection of renewable energy is the fact that it is intermittent and, therefore, unreliable. Unlike oil, energies such as solar or wind are directly dependent on climate conditions, which makes the generation planning and forecasting processes extremely complex. Adds to that the difficulties to efficiently store electric energy, what, in many cases, has also contributed to the maintenance of fossil fuels as the preferred source of energy. While the issues related to the influence of climate conditions are still present, the storage of electric energy has profited from a remarkable development in the last years, with batteries standing as the main tools in this regard. Out of the most popular solutions is the use of rechargeable lithium-ion batteries, which, along with transforming portable electronics, is the technology of choice for electric vehicles (Xie & Lu, 2020).

As discussed by Lu et al. (2013), a range of positive characteristics is associated with lithium-ion batteries, especially when they are compared to other commonly used alternatives. One of them is the perception that lithium batteries have high energy and power densities, and a long service life. While these ideas pushed their wide application in consumer electronics, when it comes to cars, lithium-ion batteries have shown problems in terms of safety, durability, uniformity, and cost, what has limited its use. Still accordingly, these issues would be due to the need for lithium-ion batteries to operate within a safe and reliable area, delimited by temperature and voltage windows. According to the instructions provided by most battery manufacturers, reliable operating temperatures would range from -20° to 55 °Celsius (from -4° to 131 °Fahrenheit) for discharging and 0° to 45 °Celsius (32° and 113 °Fahrenheit) for charging. The typical operating voltage of lithium-ion batteries, in turn, would be between 1.5 Volts and 4.2 Volts. The non-observation of such limits leads to the rapid attenuation of battery performance, as well as to safety issues.

In 2017, Tesla CEO Elon Musk took an important step in the popularization of lithium-ion batteries (Australian Associated Press, 2017). After challenging himself to upgrade South Australia's energy grid, Tesla built a 100 megawatt lithium-ion battery, the largest in the world (Ellsmoor, 2019). Owned by French renewable energy company Neoen, the battery had a capital cost of €56 million (approximately US $66 million) (Wahlquist, 2018). Two years after its installation, it has responded to three major system outages, contributing to restore stability to the network, while lowering the operational costs of the grid (Thornhill, 2020). Accordingly, this and other grid-scale batteries offer an operational alternative to the instability of wind and solar power, with South Australia functioning as a testbed for the transition from fossil fuels, as more than half of the power used in the state is originated from renewable sources. As pointed out by Ellsmoor (2019), the battery helped improve the viability of renewables sources of energy in South Australia, as this was its prime power source. In addition to their widespread industrial applications, the importance of lithium-ion batteries is also recognized by the academic community, with the 2019 Nobel Prize in Chemistry being awarded to John Bannister Goodenough (The University of Texas at Austin, USA), Michael Stanley Whittingham (Binghamton

University, State University of New York, USA), and Akira Yoshino (Asahi Kasei Corporation, Tokyo, Japan/Meijo University, Nagoya, Japan) "for the development of lithium-ion batteries" (The Nobel Prize, 2019).

If, on the one hand, the technological improvements allow for greater dissemination of renewable sources of energy (Xie & Lu, 2020), the production of some of the inputs used in the fabrication of batteries has important social and environmental impacts. The extraction of lithium, for example, depends on complex mining processes which are often associated with severe degradation of natural spaces (Drapper, 2019). Ellsmoor (2019) adds that the production of lithium-ion batteries demands the mining and manufacturing of a range of rare metals, causing significant emissions. Beyond lithium, major components such as nickel and cobalt are finite resources, with the amount available of each being unlikely to meet future demand for batteries. In that way, the increasing use of lithium batteries would expose one of the most problematic facets of the transition to a low carbon economy, as the successful dissemination of lithium as the base product for a battery-based economy (Sanderson, 2020) led the metal to be known as "white petroleum" (Ellsmoor, 2019). The seek for new sources of lithium is fed by expectations of scarcity, with important discrepancies between production and consumption being forecast until 2045 in the European Union, for example (Sterba et al., 2019). Currently, identified lithium reserves are estimated to total about 80 million tons, being mainly found in Bolivia (21 million tons), Argentina (17 million tons), Chile (9 million tons), the United States (6.8 million tons), Australia (6.3 million tons), and China (4.5 million tons) (U.S. Department of the Interior, 2020). From the sustainability point of view, the exploitation of lithium is also controversial, being seen either as an important economic opportunity for the poor in one extreme or as the cause of environmental degradation in the other. While the words of Bolivian Vice President Álvaro García Linera seem to fit the first group—with the politician predicting lithium mining to be the engine of the Bolivian economy (Drapper, 2019)—it has also been pointed out as a threat to natural sights such as the "salar the Uyuni", which happens to be largest salt desert in the world (National Geographic,

2019). Possible substitutes for lithium are calcium, magnesium, mercury, zinc, and aluminum (U.S. Department of the Interior, 2020).

Altogether, these negative social and environmental impacts raise doubts about the real sustainability of electric cars, as well as that of all the electronic devices equipped with lithium-ion batteries. Among the possible solutions to the environmental problems caused by the use of lithium-ion batteries is the expectation that the battery recycling market will be strengthened as more batteries are produced. The increase in recycling is expected then to diminish the need for new raw material and, by consequence, the necessity of mining (Ellsmoor, 2019). Still after the author, however, by 2025, lithium demand is expected to increase to nearly 1.3 million metric tons of lithium carbonate equivalent (LCE), what represents over five times the 2019 demand. As previously discussed, The Volkswagen Group has set to launch more than 70 different electric car models until 2029, with similar paths being observed in the strategies of other automakers. Along with pressuring the prices of the metal, the mining of known reserves, and stimulate the discovery of new ones, these figures put the continuity of many industrial operations at risk, especially those that compose the value chains of both the automotive and electronics industries. This idea is reinforced by the U.S. Department of the Interior (2020) statement, as "lithium supply security has become a top priority for technology companies in the United States and Asia".

11.2.3 Sources of Energy

The environmental impacts of electric cars are also associated with the way the electricity they consume is generated. On that regard, Vliet et al. (2011) argue that electric cars may significantly increase GHG emissions, particularly if the type of fuel used to generate the electricity comes from an old coal-based plant. Compared to a whole renewable source, the additional pollution in these cases would be estimated to be around 155 g of CO_2 equivalent per kilometer. Likewise, the use of electricity generated from renewable sources may not be as sustainable as one may initially think, as these processes may cover impacts that are often neglected or ignored. The use of solar panels, for example, figures among these cases. As discussed by Hu et al. (2016), although the conversion of solar energy in electricity induces regional cooling, the conversion of such energy to heat—particularly in urban areas—increases both regional and global temperatures, compensating the initial cooling effect. Yet, as pointed out by the authors, this process disturbs global atmospheric circulation, what results in changes in regional precipitation. Beloin-Saint-Pierre et al. (2009), in turn, stresses issues related to the irradiation received by photovoltaic installations, as well as to the high consumption of electricity in the production of photovoltaic systems in solar energy systems.

Typically regarded as one the most sustainable sources of energy, the production of electricity through wind has been subject to several state incentives, including tax cuts (International Energy Agency, 2016) and subsidized credit (BNDES, 2011). Nevertheless, although energy generation itself is indeed associated with low GHG emissions (Raadal et al., 2014), a series of environmental issues are indirectly linked to it. Among these problems is the mortality and injuries of birds (Smallwood & Thelander, 2008) and bats (Arnett et al., 2016). As discussed by Barrios and Rodriguez (2004), wind turbines are often aligned along coasts or mountain ridges, profiting from air currents that can be used by soaring birds, what increases the risk of collision. Accordingly, although some authors claim that wind farms would be less dangerous to birds than other human-made structures (e.g. power lines) (Nelson & Curry, 1995; Osborn et al., 1998), the belief would not correspond to more recent evidence. Beyond the casualties of wild animals themselves, from a broader perspective, the installation of wind turbines is associated with more profound impacts. Still after Barrios and Rodriguez (2004), the equipment is associated with the disturbance of the foraging and breeding of waterfowls (Winkelman, 1989; Pedersen & Poulsen, 1991), what would result in habitat losses (Osborn et al., 1998; Larsen & Madsen, 2000; Guillemette & Larsen, 2002).

From a social viewpoint, the presence of wind turbines is associated with adverse effects on the health of the population living or working around them. Jeffery et al. (2013) highlight that the proximity to industrial wind turbines has caused a series of complaints from rural patients regarding a decrease in their quality of life. That includes reports of sleep disturbances, cognitive dysfunction, anxiety, depression, and stress, among other related issues. Negative sentiments such as anger, grief, and a sense of injustice would also be common. Accordingly, the suggested causes of these unintended and pernicious effects would be the noise caused by wind turbines, infrasound shadow flicker, ground current, and dirty electricity. Also, despite usually appreciated, the design of wind turbines is also often criticized, with the equipment being argued not to fit landscapes' esthetical harmony (Firestone et al., 2015). On top of that is the increased demand for lithium-ion batteries that comes with the dissemination of wind power generation (Bixiao et al., 2017). This means that, like other forms of intermittent generation, the production of wind-sourced energy is indirectly responsible for the negative social and environmental damages associated with the production of lithium-ion batteries, as previously addressed.

Defined as "the electricity generated by hydropower; the production of electrical power through the use of the gravitational force of falling or flowing water" (Bagher et al., 2015, p.17), hydroelectricity is among the types of energy said to be environmentally friendly, being considered one of the most important alternatives of renewable energy for decades. In fact, this force has been used for more than 2000 years, with people in Ancient Greece profiting from flowing water to operate mills that grounded wheat into flour (National Geographic, 2020). As pointed out by Itaipu Binacional (2020), following the World Summit on Sustainable Development held in Johannesburg, South Africa, in 2002 and the 3rd Water Forum in Kyoto, Japan, in 2003, a consensus was reached by representatives of more than 170 countries, according to which all hydroelectric generation must be considered renewable and deserve international support.

Coherently, such conclusion was supported by the fact that, beyond being a renewable source of energy itself, the production of hydroelectricity enables the utilization of other renewable sources. That would be due to the flexibility and storage capacity of hydroelectric plants, what, among other things, allow the use of intermittent sources of renewable energy such as solar and wind generation. Furthermore, the production of hydroelectricity would be associated with national energetic security issues and price stability. Once river water is a domestic resource, it is not subject to market fluctuations, which is not the case for non-renewable alternatives such as fuels and natural gas. Likewise, the economic efficiency of hydroelectric plants helps enabling the use of thermal power plants. Other advantages such as the storage of drinking water in the reservoirs, the contribution of hydroelectricity to a higher stability and reliability of electric system, and the low GHG emission levels associated to its production would altogether contribute to the positive image with which the generation of hydroelectricity has been counting on.

Despite these argued advantages, hydroelectricity has also triggered considerable criticism, mainly because of its asserted social and environmental damages. The Union of Concerned Scientists, for example, seems to be among the most prominent opponents of the construction of hydroelectric power plants. Founded by scientists and students of the Massachusetts Institute of Technology, it currently gathers around 250 scientists, analysts, and policy and communication experts who engage in issues related to climate change, sustainable development, racial and economic equity, among others (The Union of Concerned Scientists, 2020). Accordingly, the problems with the generation of hydroelectricity could be divided into three main areas: land use, wildlife impacts, and life-cycle global warming emissions (The Union of Concerned Scientists, 2013). With respect to the first, the problems would be associated with the areas flooded by plants' reservoirs, with their extent considerably varying, mainly in function of the slope of the terrain. While a 10 MW run-of-the-river plant located in a hilly location may need only 2.5 acres (0.008 square kilometers) for its reservoirs (National Renewable Energy Laboratory, 2012), the Balbina hydroelectric power plant in Brazil—a 250 MW facility installed in a flat area—demanded 2360 square kilometers to be flooded, an area that is the same as that of the U.S. state of Delaware (Fearnside, 1989). Along with the destruction of forests and wildlife habitat, the flooding of these areas would also compromise agricultural and scenic land, with entire communities often having to be removed to make room for the water (Yardley, 2007).

Regarding more specific wildlife impacts, it is argued that hydroelectric facilities can produce major impacts on aquatic ecosystems, with fish as well as other organisms being injured and eventually killed by turbine blades. Also, as reservoirs are more stagnant than river waters, they tend to concentrate higher amounts of nutrients and sediments, what shall lead to the proliferation of algae and other aquatic weeds. These weeds may then push other river animals and plant life, demanding control through either manual harvesting or by the introduction of fish that shall consume these plants (National Renewable Energy Laboratory, 2012). In addition, evaporation rates in reservoirs are considerably higher than in flowing rivers, and, in case too much water is stored, parts of the river downstream from the reservoir can simply dry out, with hydroelectric operators being required to release minimum amounts of the retained water in certain periods. If not properly held, animal and plant life shall be harmed. Moreover, when compared to normal river water, reservoir water is normally colder and has lower rates of dissolved oxygen. That means that, once released, it may impact the conditions of the river, and by consequence, fauna and flora living in these ecosystems. These problems can be mitigated by the installation of aerating turbines to increase the dissolution of oxygen in the water, as well as multi-level water intakes that may help ensure that the water released is originated from all levels of the reservoir and not only from the bottom, which, beyond being the coldest, has the lowest level of dissolved oxygen.

When it comes to life-cycle global warming emissions, the Union of Concerned Scientists (2013) point out that, along with the emissions produced during the installation and dismantling of hydroelectric power plants, recent research suggests that emissions during their operation shall also be significant. Indeed, it seems that the level of emissions varies according to the climate conditions of the area where reservoirs are installed, as well as to the size of the facility. In that way, this suggests that, while small and large plants installed in semi arid regions have relatively modest levels of emissions, the operation of plants located in tropical areas or temperate peatlands results in significantly higher rates of life-cycle global warming emissions, as, once an area is flooded, vegetation and soil decomposes, releasing both carbon dioxide and methane. Still after the group, while numbers shall vary in face of site-specific characteristics, current estimates indicate that these emissions can be over 0.5 pounds of carbon dioxide equivalent per kilowatt-hour (National Academy of Sciences, 2010; IPCC, 2014). By way of comparison, emissions for natural gas-generated electricity are estimated to be between 0.6 and 2 pounds of carbon dioxide equivalent per kilowatt-hour. The numbers for coal-generated electricity, in turn, are predicted to be between 1.4 and 3.6 pounds of carbon dioxide equivalent per kilowatt-hour (IPCC, 2014).

11.3 Diesel Is Not Dead

Despite the trend and developments in that direction, a complete shift of the automotive industry to electric cars seems to be unlikely, as such change requires considerable investments (Chazan, 2019). In fact, it seems that companies' propensity to replace diesel with other sources of energy has been slowing down. If, on the one hand, such discourse was practically homogeneous in the aftermath of the Volkswagen Dieselgate, companies now show that they continue to believe in diesel as the main fuel for cars. In discussing diesel's prospect, Daimler (2020d) is explicit on its views, as the company claims to be "convinced that diesel will continue to be a fixed element of the drive-system mix in the future". Accordingly, in face of its energy efficiency, "it makes more sense to improve diesel than to ban it" and thus they also state that diesel "will remain the backbone of our mobility for many years to come".

Companies historically associated with the diesel technology have been campaigning for its use. Volvo (2020), for instance, claims that its diesel engines "deliver exceptional fuel economy, performance and handling in all driving conditions". In discussing the image of the fuel in Australia, the company argues that, despite being "immensely popular in Europe", it has only in recent years "overcome dated views about being a dirty and smelly fuel". For BMW (2020), "aside from the enormous economic importance, clean diesel's contribution towards climate goals is often underestimated". On that regard, the company stresses diesel engines' lower CO_2 emissions when compared to petrol equivalents. Similarly, Daimler (2020d) (Mercedes-Benz' parent company) points out to a reduction in NOx emissions from diesel, and to the operability of software updates in that direction. Likewise, Volkswagen has just presented a new generation of four-cylinder Diesel engines, as the EA288 evo models "not only comply with the current limits of the EU6d-temp exhaust emission standard, but are also already prepared for the future EU6d standard (which applies to new models from September 2019)" Volkswagen (2020). Among other innovations introduced is the "twin dosing", which would lead to an 80% reduction in NOx emissions from diesel engines (Volkswagen, 2019).

In face of these initiatives and all the difficulties in replacing diesel with other sources, it seems that diesel technology will continue to equip cars for a long time. Regardless of all the criticism it triggers, diesel still stands as economically competitive. As a result of the continuous investment in the development of diesel engines, the environmental effects of its use are expected to be mitigated in the coming years, what may contribute to its re-acceptance as a dominant fuel in the automotive industry. Evidently, given the complexity of the issue, predictions in this regard are, to a great measure, unreliable, as they are also dependent on the technological development of all other alternatives, as well as on the dynamics of societies' perception on the issue. It remains to be seen, however, whether diesel will be able to get rid of its negative image, which, as discussed, has been solidly built over decades. In any case, the resilience of the diesel technology has already been proven, meaning that one may be not surprised to see its rise again.

References

Arnett, E. B., Baerwald, E. F., Mathews, F., Rodrigues, L., Rodríguez-Durán, A., Rydell, J., Villegas-Patraca, R., & Voigt, C. C. (2016). Impacts of Wind Energy Development on Bats: A Global Perspective. In C. C. Voigt & T. Kingston (Eds.), *Bats in the Anthropocene: Conservation of Bats in a Changing World*. Springer.

Australian Associated Press. (2017, December 1). South Australia Turns on Tesla's 100 MW Battery: 'History in the Making'. *The Guardian*. https://www.theguardian.com/australia-news/2017/dec/01/south-australia-turns-on-teslas-100mw-battery-history-in-the-making

Bagher, A. M., Vahid, M., Mohsen, M., & Parvin, D. (2015). Hydroelectric Energy Advantages and Disadvantages. *American Journal of Energy Science, 2*(2), 17–20.

Barrios, L., & Rodriguez, A. (2004). Behavioural and Environmental Correlates of Soaring-Bird Mortality at On-Shore Wind Turbines. *Journal of Applied Ecology, 41*(1), 72–81.

Beloin-Saint-Pierre, D., Blanc, I., Payet, J., Jacquin, P., Adra, N., & Mayer, D. (2009, September). *Environmental Impact of PV Systems: Effects of Energy Sources Used in Production of Solar Panels.* 24th European Photovoltaic Solar Energy Conference, Hamburg, pp. 4517–4520—ISBN 3-936338-25-6. https://doi.org/10.4229/24thEUPVSEC2009-6DV.3.7ff.ffhal-00487349

Bixiao, G., Jian, W., Ju, Q., & Qingjun, H. (2017). The Lithium-ion Battery Standby Power of Wind Turbine Pitch System. *Energy Procedia, 105*, 3539–3544.

BMW. (2020). *The Diesel Engine.* https://www.bmwgroup-werke.com/steyr/en/highlight/diesel-engine.html

BNDES. (2011). *Energia Eólica.* https://www.bndes.gov.br/SiteBNDES/bndes/bndes_pt/Hotsites/Relatorio_Anual_2011/Capitulos/o_bndes_em_numeros/destaques/energia_eolica.html

Britannica. (2020). *Rudolf Diesel.* https://www.britannica.com/biography/Rudolf-Diesel

Cames, M., & Helmers, E. (2013). Critical Evaluation of the European Diesel Car Boom-Global Comparison, Environmental Effects and Various National Strategies. *Environmental Sciences Europe, 25*(1), 15.

Chazan, G. (2019, August 1). Car Industry Woes Weight on Germany's Prospects. *Financial Times.* https://www.ft.com/content/0e477fae-b383-11e9-8cb2-799a3a8cf37b

Curtis, J. B. (2002). Fractured Shale-Gas Systems. *AAPG bulletin, 86*(11), 1921–1938.

Daimler. (2020a). *Rudolf Diesel and His Invention.* https://media.daimler.com/marsMediaSite/en/instance/ko/Rudolf-Diesel-and-his-invention.xhtml?oid=9361302

Daimler. (2020b). *Debut of Diesel Engines in Tractors and Trucks.* https://media.daimler.com/marsMediaSite/en/instance/ko/Debut-of-diesel-engines-in-tractors-and-trucks.xhtml?oid=9361501

Daimler. (2020c). *February 1936: The Diesel Engine Celebrates Its Premiere in the Passenger Car.* https://media.daimler.com/marsMediaSite/en/instance/ko/February-1936-the-diesel-engine-celebrates-its-premiere-in-the-passenger-car.xhtml?oid=9915149#:~:text=February%201936%3A%20the%20diesel%20engine%20celebrates%20its%20premiere%20in%20the,17.&text=Stuttgart%20%E2%80%93%20The%20Mercedes%2DBenz%20260,series%2Dproduction%20diesel%20passenger%20car

Daimler. (2020d). *Diesel*. https://www.daimler.com/innovation/diesel/en/

Deloitte. (2018). *2018 Deloitte Global Automotive Consumer Study*. https://www2.deloitte.com/content/dam/Deloitte/de/Documents/consumer-industrial-products/2018_GACS_Data%20Deck_Germany.pdf

Deloitte. (2019). *2019 Deloitte Global Automotive Consumer Study*. https://www2.deloitte.com/content/dam/Deloitte/us/Documents/manufacturing/us-global-automotive-consumer-study-2019.pdf

Drapper, R. (2019). This Metal Is Powering Today's Technology—At What Price? *National Geographic*. https://www.nationalgeographic.com/magazine/2019/02/lithium-is-fueling-technology-today-at-what-cost/

Economides, M. J. (2012). Foreword. In S. Mokhatab, W. A. Poe, & J. G. Speight (Eds.), *Handbook of Natural Gas Transmission And Processing*. Elsevier.

Ellsmoor, J. (2019, June 10). Electric Vehicles Are Driving Demand for Lithium—With Environmental Consequences. *Forbes*. https://www.forbes.com/sites/jamesellsmoor/2019/06/10/electric-vehicles-are-driving-demand-for-lithium-with-environmental-consequences/#1915401b62e2

Engie. (2020). *Biogas/Biomethane*. https://www.engie.com/en/activities/renewable-energies/biogas-biomethane

FAO. (2020). *Food Security Statistics*. http://www.fao.org/economic/ess/ess-fs/en/

Farina, E., Rodrigues, L., & de Sousa, E. L. (2013). A política de petróleo e a indústria de etanol no Brasil. *Interesse Nacional*, Julho-Setembro, pp. 64–75.

Fearnside, P. M. (1989). Brazil's Balbina Dam: Environment Versus the Legacy of the Pharaohs in Amazonia. *Environmental Management, 3*(4), 401–423.

Firestone, J., Bates, A., & Knapp, L. A. (2015). See Me, Feel Me, Touch Me, Heal Me: Wind Turbines, Culture, Landscapes, and Sound Impressions. *Land Use Policy, 46*, 241–249.

Fosten, J. (2012). Rising Household Diesel Consumption in the United States: A Cause for Concern? Evidence on Asymmetric Pricing. *Energy Economics, 34*(5), 1514–1522.

Ghebreyesus, T. A. (2018, October 27). Air Pollution Is the New Tobacco. Time to Tackle This Epidemic. *The Guardian*. https://www.theguardian.com/commentisfree/2018/oct/27/air-pollution-is-the-new-tobacco-time-to-tackle-this-epidemic

Greenpeace. (2020). *Air Pollution*. https://www.greenpeace.org.uk/challenges/air-pollution/

Greiner, P. T., York, R., & McGee, J. A. (2018). Snakes in the Greenhouse: Does Increased Natural Gas Use Reduce Carbon Dioxide Emissions from Coal Consumption? *Energy Research & Social Science, 38*, 53–57.

Guillemette, M., & Larsen, J. K. (2002). Postdevelopment Experiments to Detect Anthropogenic Disturbances: The Case of Sea Ducks and Wind Parks. *Ecological Applications, 12*, 868–877.

Hivert, L. (1999, September 30–October 1). *Dieselization and the New Dieselists Behavior: Recent Developments in the French Car Fleet.* Proceedings of the 1999 European Energy Conference Technological Progress and the Energy Challenges, Session 13, Transport and CO_2 Policies, Paris.

Hivert, L. (2013). Short-Term Break in the French Love for Diesel? *Energy Policy, 54*, 11–22.

Howarth, R. W., Santoro, R., & Ingraffea, A. (2011). Methane and the Greenhouse-Gas Footprint of Natural Gas from Shale Formations. *Climatic change, 106*(4), 679–690.

Hu, A., Levis, S., Meehl, G. A., Han, W., Washington, W. M., Oleson, K. W., van Ruijven, B. J., He, M., & Strand, W. G. (2016). Impact of Solar Panels on Global Climate. *Nature Climate Change, 6*(3), 290–294.

International Energy Agency. (2016). *Tax Incentives for Renewable Energy.* https://www.iea.org/policies/6008-tax-incentives-for-renewable-energy?page=5&sector=Generation

IPCC. (2014). *Climate Change 2014—Mitigation of Climate Change.* Working Group III Contribution to the Fifth Assessment Report of the Intergovernmental Panel on Climate Change. https://www.ipcc.ch/site/assets/uploads/2018/02/ipcc_wg3_ar5_full.pdf

Itaipu Binacional. (2020). *10 Motivos Para Promover a Hidreletricidade.* https://www.itaipu.gov.br/energia/10-motivos-para-promover-hidreletricidade

Jeffery, R. D., Krogh, C., & Horner, B. (2013). Adverse Health Effects of Industrial Wind Turbines. *Canadian Family Physician, 59*(5), 473–475.

Jenner, S., & Lamadrib, A. J. (2012). *Shale Gas vs. Coal.* https://papers.ssrn.com/sol3/papers.cfm?abstract_id=2025627

Klooster, J. W. (2009). *Icons of Invention: The Makers of the Modern World from Gutenberg to Gates.* Greenwood Press.

Kurani, K. S., & Sperling, D. (1988). Rise and Fall of Diesel Cars: A Consumer Choice Analysis. *Transportation Research Record, 1175*, 23–32.

Larsen, J. K., & Madsen, J. (2000). Effects of Wind Turbines and Other Physical Elements on Field Utilization by Pink-Footed Geese (Anser brachyrhynchus): A Landscape Perspective. *Landscape Ecology, 15*, 755–764.

Lu, L., Han, X., Li, J., Hua, J., & Ouyang, M. (2013). A Review on the Key Issues for Lithium-Ion Battery Management in Electric Vehicles. *Journal of Power Sources, 226*, 272–288.

Lussenhop, J. (2015, September 23). Why Do American Car Buyers Shy Away from Diesel? *BBC*. https://www.bbc.com/news/world-us-canada-34329596#:~:text=When%20the%20vehicles%20are%20actually,the%20market%20%2D%20about%203%25

Maverick, J. B. (2020). How Has Fracking Decreased U.S. Dependence on Foreign Oil? *Investopedia*. https://www.investopedia.com/ask/answers/012915/how-has-fracking-helped-us-decrease-dependence-foreign-oil.asp

Mokhatab, S., Poe, W. A., & Speight, J. G. (2012). *Handbook of Natural Gas Transmission and Processing*. Elsevier.

Mollenhauer, K., & Tschoke, H. (Eds.). (2010). *Handbook of Diesel Engines* (Vol. 1). Springer.

National Academy of Sciences. (2010). *Electricity from Renewable Resources: Status, Prospects, and Impediments*. The National Academies Press. http://www.nap.edu/openbook.php?record_id=12619

National Geographic. (2019). *Bolivie: l'extraction du lithium menace le plus grand désert de sel du monde*. https://www.nationalgeographic.fr/environnement/comment-produire-de-lhuile-de-palme-sans-detruire-les-forets

National Geographic. (2020). *Hydroelectric Energy*. https://www.nationalgeographic.org/encyclopedia/hydroelectric-energy/

National Renewable Energy Laboratory (NREL). (2012). In M. M. Hand, S. Baldwin, E. DeMeo, J. M. Reilly, T. Mai, D. Arent, G. Porro, M. Meshekand, & D. Sandor (Eds.), *Renewable electricity futures study* (Vol. 4). NREL/TP-6A20-52409. Golden, CO.

National Research Council. (2002). *Effectiveness and Impact of Corporate Average Fuel Economy (CAFE) Standards*. National Academy Press.

Nelson, H. K., & Curry, R. C. (1995). Assessing Avian Interactions with Windplant Development and Operation. *Transactions of the North American Wildlife and Natural Resources Conference, 60*, 266–287.

Nitsch, M. (1991). O programa de biocombustíveis Proálcool no contexto da estratégia energética brasileira. *Brazilian Journal of Political Economy, 11*(2), 123–138.

Osborn, R. G., Dieter, C. D., Higgins, K. F., & Usgaard, R. E. (1998). Bird Flight Characteristics Near Wind Turbines in Minnesota. *American Midland Naturalist, 139*, 20–38.

Pedersen, M. B., & Poulsen, E. (1991). *Avian Response to the Implementation of the Tjaereborg Wind Turbine at the Danish Wadden Sea*. Studies on Danish fauna report 47. Denmark Institute of Ecological Studies.

Plumer, B. (2015, October 16). Europe's Love Affair with Diesel Cars has Been a Disaster. *Vox*. https://www.vox.com/2015/10/15/9541789/volkswagen-europe-diesel-pollution

Porter, M. E. (1980). *Competitive Strategy: Techniques for Analyzing Industries and Competitors*. Free Press.

Porter, M. E. (2008). The Five Competitive Forces That Shape Strategy. *Harvard Business Review, 86*(1), 25–40.

Raadal, H. L., Vold, B. I., Myhr, A., & Nygaard, T. A. (2014). GHG Emissions and Energy Performance of Offshore Wind Power. *Renewable Energy, 66*, 314–324.

Rapid Transition. (2018). *The Rise of Brazil's Sugarcane Cars*. https://www.rapidtransition.org/stories/the-rise-of-brazils-sugarcane-cars/

Sanderson, H. (2020, September 6). The Electric Vehicle Revolution: Cornwall Tries to Revive Its Lithium Mines. *Financial Times*. https://www.ft.com/content/80cbf087-0f3c-432f-9576-122b52bda051

Schnepf, R., & Yacobucci, B. D. (2013). *Renewable Fuel Standard (RFS): Overview and Issues. Congressional Research Service*. https://fas.org/sgp/crs/misc/R40155.pdf

Smallwood, K. S., & Thelander, C. (2008). Bird Mortality in the Altamont Pass Wind Resource Area, California. *The Journal of Wildlife Management, 72*(1), 215–223.

Statista. (2019). *Percentage Share of New Passenger Cars in Europe with Diesel Engines in 2014 and 2018, by Country*. https://www.statista.com/statistics/425113/eu-car-sales-share-of-diesel-engines-by-country/

Statista. (2020). *Production d'éthanol au niveau mondial de 2000 à 2017*. https://fr.statista.com/statistiques/571264/ethanol-production-monde/

Sterba, J., Krzemień, A., Fernández, P. R., García-Miranda, C. E., & Valverde, G. F. (2019). Lithium Mining: Accelerating the Transition to Sustainable Energy. *Resources Policy, 62*, 416–426.

The Nobel Prize. (2019). *Press Release: The Nobel Prize in Chemistry*. https://www.nobelprize.org/prizes/chemistry/2019/press-release/

The Union of Concerned Scientists. (2013). *Environmental Impacts of Hydroelectric Power*. https://www.ucsusa.org/resources/environmental-impacts-hydroelectric-power

The Union of Concerned Scientists. (2020). *About*. https://www.ucsusa.org/about

The World Bank. (2020). *Total Greenhouse Gas Emissions (kt of CO_2 Equivalent)*. https://data.worldbank.org/indicator/EN.ATM.GHGT.KT.CE

Thomas, D. E., Jr. (1978). Diesel, Father and Son: Social Philosophies of Technology. *Technology and Culture, 19*(3), 376–393.
Thornhill, J. (2020, February, 28). Two Year on, Elon Musk's Big Battery Bet Is Paying Off in Australia. *Bloomberg Green*. https://www.bloomberg.com/news/articles/2020-02-28/two-years-on-musk-s-big-battery-bet-is-paying-off-in-australia
U.S. Department of Energy. (2020a). *Alternative Fuels Data Center*. https://afdc.energy.gov/laws/RFS.html
U.S. Department of Energy. (2020b). *Energy Policy Act of 2005*. https://afdc.energy.gov/laws/epact_2005.html
U.S. Department of Energy. (2020c). *Global Ethanol Production*. https://afdc.energy.gov/data/10331
U.S. Department of the Interior. (2020). *Lithium Data Sheet—Mineral Commodity Summaries 2020*. https://pubs.usgs.gov/periodicals/mcs2020/mcs2020-lithium.pdf
U.S. Office of Energy Efficiency & Renewable Energy. (2020). *Reducing Pollution with Electric Vehicles*. https://www.energy.gov/eere/electricvehicles/reducing-pollution-electric-vehicles
Vengosh, A., Warner, N., Jackson, R., & Darrah, T. (2013). The Effects of Shale Gas Exploration and Hydraulic Fracturing on the Quality of Water Resources in the United States. *Procedia Earth and Planetary Science, 7*, 863–866.
Vidal, J. (2015, September 22). The Rise of Diesel in Europe: The Impact on Health and Pollution. *The Guardian*. https://www.theguardian.com/environment/2015/sep/22/the-rise-diesel-in-europe-impact-on-health-pollution#:~:text=Diesel%20was%20a%20niche%20market,the%20lungs%2C%20brain%20and%20heart
Vliet, O., Brouwer, A. S., Kuramochi, T., van Den Broek, M., & Faaij, A. (2011). Energy Use, Cost and CO_2 Emissions of Electric Cars. *Journal of Power Sources, 196*(4), 2298–2310.
Volkswagen. (2019). *Innovative Twin Dosing Reduces NO_x Emissions by Approx. 80 Percent*. https://www.volkswagen-newsroom.com/en/press-releases/innovative-twin-dosing-reduces-nox-emissions-by-approx-80-percent-5281
Volkswagen. (2020). *Diesel Direct Injection Engine (TDI)*. https://www.volkswagen-newsroom.com/en/diesel-direct-injection-engine-tdi-3650
Volvo. (2020). *Your Guide to Diesel Engines*. https://www.volvocars.com/au/cars/diesel

Wahlquist, C. (2018, September 27). South Australia's Tesla Battery on Track to Make Back a Third of Cost in a Year. *The Guardian*. https://www.theguardian.com/technology/2018/sep/27/south-australias-tesla-battery-on-track-to-make-back-a-third-of-cost-in-a-year

WHO. (2014). *Diesel and Gasoline Engines Exhausts and Some Nitroarenes* (Vol. 105). https://www.who.int/ipcs/assessment/public_health/IARC_mono105.pdf?ua=1

Winkelman, J. E. (1989). *Birds and the Wind Park Near Urk: Collision Victims and Disturbance of Ducks, Geese and Swans*. RIN Report 89/15. Rijksinstituut voor Natuurbeheer, Arnhem.

Xie, J., & Lu, Y. (2020). A Retrospective on Lithium-ion Batteries. *Nature Communications, 11*(2499), pp. 1–4. https://doi.org/10.1038/s41467-020-16259-9. https://www.nature.com/articles/s41467-020-16259-9

Yardley, J. (2007, November 19). Chinese Dam Projects Criticized for Their Human Costs. *The New York Times*.

12

Lessons Learned, Future Research and Tendencies on Environmental Fraud

12.1 Lessons Learned and Future Research

In face of the relative complexity and novelty of its subject, the book sought to address the relationship between business ethics, environmental fraud, improper competitive advantage, and the age of green in a holistic way. This quest translated into the discussion of assorted topics, particularly those related to the nature, causes, and consequences of ethical deviations involving environmental issues. If, on the one hand, the variety of matters approached offers valuable opportunities for discussion, it may also favor an exaggerated attention to details. Although not particularly negative, the focus on specific aspects shall end up impairing a more general understanding of the themes approached. In the search to strengthen the connection between chapters, a brief review of their individual contributions shall be helpful. The highlight of their limitations, as well as the opportunities for future research they open, can facilitate the accommodation of these contributions both in the literature already established and in the one that is yet to be produced.

Chapter 1 exposes the conceptual discussions of the book, dealing with the most diverse aspects of Business Ethics. Issues such as the

M. Fracarolli Nunes, C. Lee Park, *Business Ethics and Environmental Fraud*,
https://doi.org/10.1007/978-3-030-73800-6_12

historical development of the concept, the influence of business dynamics, and the role played by human nature in the conduction of unethical behavior were approached. Based on a more skeptical view of human nature, the chapter proposes that the mere awareness of environmental issues may not be sufficient for managers to remain within ethical limits. On the contrary, the tightening of societies' surveillance is defended as the most effective way—if not the only one—to ensure that companies fit into a scheme of operations that is truly sustainable. This debate is inserted in the identification of a conflict of interests between economic, social, and environmental objectives. Among the main contributions of the chapter is the development of the tripartite business model.

Considerations about the status of Business Ethics as an independent field of thought were also made, with the main controversies and criticisms directed at it being examined. In dealing with ancient examples and with discussions held by classic authors, the debate contributes to demystifying the idea that today's managers are particularly unethical, or more unethical, than managers of the past. Despite receiving greater attention nowadays, ethical issues have always orbited economic activity, with businesspeople—as any people—often transgressing the limits between right and wrong. This historical perspective dialogues with the arguments presented in the first paragraph of the book, according to which business and ethics have always been in conflict (and will always be), because people and ethics have always been in conflict (and will always be). In that way, the chapter proposes that the development of Business Ethics as a field that represents a pragmatic effort to make business possible. If, on the one hand, the vision may be argued to demote the field of its invisible pedestal (i.e. sometimes considered to be the vector of good in a world of evil men and women), it may allow for the advance of good in practice, not so much due to more elevated moral standards of those who push it, but as it seems to be the only way our "business-centered civilization" shall survive.

Along with this more general debate, the reasons why businesspeople behave the way they do were also considered, with the role of emotions being treated as a possible driver of unethical conducts. Adds to that the severe power and political struggles that take place within organizations, where intrigues, lies, betrayals, and other sorts of unethical conducts contribute to the setting of pernicious corporate habitats. In particular, disputes and conflicts were positioned as potential triggers of hierarchical instabilities, what, along with other factors, may favor the development of negative emotional responses from those holding the power. Yet, at the same time the discussion on the reasons of unethical behavior is intricate, the examination of the factors leading to ethical one must be also complex. It may be argued, for example, that, despite observable to some extent, the rationalization of ethical decisions based on the contrast of risks and returns seems more like a premise to be adopted in decision-making models than a realistic way to explain or predict people's conducts in that regard. It is possible, for instance, that people do not decide rationally because they lack the means to do so. That may include the necessary information, the knowledge of methods, or even the conscience that it is possible. In such cases, ethics would benefit from ignorance.

In any case, future research should focus on the empirical validation of the hypotheses raised, as well as on the challenges presented by emerging business contexts. On that regard, Moor (2006) makes the case for the development of machine ethics as a consequence of the expansion of computers' decision-making roles in practical matters (e.g. computers driving cars). As discussed by the author, technologies are usually evaluated according to how well they accomplish their purposes, with the selection and application of standards being necessary. In that way, not all values would be necessarily ethical. From another angle, it is possible to assume an eventual moral superiority of machines, precisely because they are not subject to the same ego-defense strategies that are common to humans. As discussed by Fracarolli Nunes and Lee Park (2020), this translates into greater learning potential, what may also be true of moral and ethical issues. In addition to the points discussed above, these aspects also lack empirical evidence, which may represent an opportunity for researchers interested in the new frontiers of applied ethics.

Chapter 2, in turn, deals with the conceptual definition of *environmental fraud*, addressing both its similarities and differences with other types of criminal conducts. Building on a discussion on both general and corporate criminology, a debate on the incentives that shall lead managers to engage in unethical conducts is proposed, complementing the views presented in Chap. 1. Environmental fraud is discussed as a particularly harmful conduct, which may have its effects disseminated across societies. The proposition of a definition of the concept complements its previous use (e.g. Liberti, 2006; Everett, 2014), while the main contribution of the chapter resides in the proposition of the fraud severity and range matrix.

Regarding opportunities for future research, the validation of the environmental fraud construct stands as an important step to the development of the stream. The creation and testing of specific scales, for example, is particularly welcome. In addition, the construct may serve as a basis for the conduction of several case studies, among which works referring to the situations discussed throughout the book (e.g. Volkswagen Dieselgate, conventional crops falsely labeled as organic). From a practical point of view, it is possible that the debate happens to assist the creation and implementation of a legal framework more adapted to treat cases of environmental fraud. Likewise, the exposition of the problem can be useful for the development of an increased awareness on the part of stakeholders, who, together with legal authorities, can augment the pressure for companies to conduct their business in a truly sustainable manner.

In the third chapter, the interfaces between environmental fraud and strategy are approached in a more direct manner. In addition to a review of the Strategic Management literature and a critical discussion of its main strands (e.g. Industry Structure and RBV), the chapter offers a debate on environmental fraud's potential to function as a vector of abnormal performance. In addressing this issue, the concept of *improper competitive advantage* is developed to deal with illicit and immoral means with which companies may compete. These discussions contribute to the emergence of a literature specifically focused on ethical shortcuts that can be adopted by firms. In addition to subsidizing a greater understanding of the mechanisms by which competitive advantage can be achieved, the chapter sheds light on themes that are generally ignored by the literature. The main contribution of the chapter resides then in the fact that it treats unethical practices as rational choice, which, despite reprehensible, are often adopted by managers.

In addressing the potential of environmental fraud to lead companies to differentiation, Chap. 3 proposes then a formalization of the debate on illicit practices, in such a way that the methods and techniques typically employed in the investigation of legal and moral initiatives may be used. The discussion does not argue that environmental fraud or any other type of moral deviation shall be accepted. Instead, it defends that these issues must be tackled, which is precisely at the origin of their qualification as improper. However, the recognition that these practices exist and that they have the strategic potential to benefit the companies that apply them contributes to bringing the competitive advantage discussions closer to the reality of the corporate world. Once again, the discussions on the history of Business Ethics (Chap. 1) add to the understanding that illicit practices appear to be inseparable from production, trade, investment, or any other economic activity. It is reasonable to assume, therefore, that ethical deviations will continue to be part of these economic initiatives. Thus, the incorporation of these themes into the more traditional aspects of Strategic Management literature is an attempt to reinforce scholars' comprehension of these practices, as something that, although undesirable, seems to be natural to business practices.

Opportunities for future research are abundant. First, the empirical verification that environmental fraud can lead to differentiated performance would be of great value. Researchers who focus their efforts on this direction may profit from a range of well-developed frameworks which are already applied in the study of "proper competitive advantage". If, on the one hand, this literature still counts with no consensus among scholars—as previously discussed—the divergences have led to the experimentation and the eventual acceptance of a large number of methods that correct and complement each other's results. It is hence expected that this methodological heterogeneity will significantly add to the debate, with its application also being extended to the study of other illegal and immoral initiatives aimed at generating competitive advantage.

Closing the first part of the book, Chap. 4 concentrates on what is here called the *age of green*. As discussed, issues related to sustainability cannot be dealt with in isolation, being possibly more adequately treated as part of a complex intersection between genuine, economic, and political interests. Within this view, the identification of the real intentions of those who carry the banner of environmentalism—and sustainability in general—becomes challenging. It may be argued that the *age of green* is the result of a philosophical and historical process, which over the last centuries helped shape the values of today's society. Future research on the eventual misuses of the sustainability cause may be relevant, with the themes of environmental fraud and corporate hypocrisy being of special interest. Additionally, the many reasons that lead consumers to limit their interest in environmental preservation to their public personas (i.e. the creation of "green façades" not necessarily coherent with their real consumption habits) can be included in these investigations.

Inaugurating the second part of the book, Chap. 5 addresses the automotive industry's background. In addition to the main milestones of its development over more than a century, the chapter also presents brief biographical descriptions of its main creators. Likewise, the development of companies that have made the production of cars one of the main gears of the world economy is discussed. The association between these movements with historical and social events seeks, therefore, to offer readers elements that shall lead to a more structured comprehension of the diverse contexts in which these activities developed. Resuming the discussions of previous chapters, the automotive industry is discussed as a favorable context for the occurrence of environmental fraud. On that regard, Michael Porter's (1996) views on Strategy become critical to the understanding of the ways through which competition between carmakers unfolds. In particular, the fact that these companies have a low potential for differentiation is proposed as an important incentive for managers to seek to increase their profits by illicit means. As discussed in Chap. 3, cost-based competition demands the constant search for reduction of operational charges. This often translates into a constant reduction in the quality of products, greater pressure on suppliers, lower wages, and other initiatives that make the automotive sector an arguably hostile and even unhealthy competitive environment. Likewise, the constant search for operational efficiency makes gains of scale a sort of inescapable objective for these companies. High-volume production appears to be a *condition sine qua non* of competitiveness in the automotive industry. Along with the search for market share gains, the need to reduce costs favors long-term strategic moves, such as mergers and acquisitions.

The debate proposed in the chapter is relevant since societies seem to have developed a symbiotic relationship with automobiles in such a way that everyday life can hardly be imagined without them. Even if people's dependence on automobiles has been decreasing as more alternatives emerge, they continue to represent an ideal of consumption. The fact that the automobile continues to occupy this privileged position even after the intense attacks it has been suffering (e.g. liability for environmental damage) demands a more detailed reflection. Future research may focus on these issues, as well as extend the discussions proposed in the chapter to other industries. Researchers linked to the topic can also delve into the debates of the auto industry itself, revealing new factors that may have contributed to the practices discussed.

In Chap. 6, cases from the automotive industry are addressed from the perspective of environmental fraud. In addition to the Volkswagen Dieselgate, similar situations involving PSA, Renault, and FCA were discussed. Beyond the comparison between the cases and the aggregation of several documentary sources, the main contribution of the chapter rests in the discussion of environmental fraud as an apparently disseminated practice in the automotive industry. In this sense, the ideas developed in Chaps. 3 and 5 are taken up, with the characteristics of the automotive industry being reaffirmed as possible conditioners of environmental fraud. The ingenuity of mechanisms applied in the cheating schemes (i.e. illegal software) is also discussed, as well as the different consequences they have had for each of the companies. While Volkswagen found itself in the midst of a media nightmare and had to face much tougher legal punishments, the discovery of the use of similar software by other companies (FCA, Peugeot, and Renault) reveals much milder impacts, both from the point of view of the exposure of their brands and to the sentences in the courts. As discussed in the chapter, this might be due to the different laws and interpretations that were in force at the time in the United States and Europe. While Volkswagen was directly accused of violating American law, some of these companies appear to have been able to argue that their actions were at the limit of legality in Europe, even though they were very similar to Volkswagen's practices in the United States. These differences seem to have created a gray area that contributes to the difficulty of defining and understanding these new types of deviations.

It is possible that the different treatments given to companies in the United States and Europe are related to the commercial interests of each country. It must be noted that Volkswagen is a German company that disputes the market in the United States. In addition to a strong automotive culture, the country is home to some of the largest automakers in the world (e.g. General Motors, Ford). If, on the one hand, one must not credit the Dieselgate to commercial disputes between Volkswagen and American companies, it is possible that these tensions have contributed to the creation of an atmosphere favorable not only to the investigation, but also to the punishment of the German company. As discussed, despite attempts over the years, Volkswagen has never been able to establish itself as a relevant player in the American market. Its expertise in the use of diesel technology appeared, therefore, as one of its main resources, especially since the company presented itself as the only one able to balance the pros and cons of diesel consumption (i.e. lower operating cost and environmental damage). On the other hand, the other companies are European and, having to explain themselves to similarly European authorities, they had a milder treatment. Again, it is not possible to state that there has been a favoring of these companies by the judicial authorities. As the practices attributed to them were often within a gray area, this could accommodate different interpretations. In any case, attention is drawn to the fact that similar practices have led to such different results in the United States. Researchers interested in the topic shall further investigate the reasons for these differences. This issue may be of great value to economists who are dedicated to matters related to protectionism. In the same way, studies on the complexity of the relations between private companies and the government may find in these cases abundant material.

In Chap. 7, the discussions on environmental fraud are extended beyond the automotive industry. The market of organic products is approached, with their potential for greater margins being discussed as an important incentive for the practice. More specifically, the commercialization of conventional cotton and soy (i.e. produced using fertilizers and pesticides) as being organic is treated as one of the possible forms of environmental fraud. Just like the use of subterfuges in the automobile industry is apparently encouraged by the perverse competitive dynamics that are typical of the sector, rural producers may see in such fraud a possibility of differentiation that allows them to escape the rigors of extremely competitive dynamics. The use of iceberg strategies by logistics service providers is also addressed as a specific type of environmental fraud. As discussed, companies in this sector usually reserve their environmentally responsible operations for the so-called last-mile delivery, that is, for the last part of their operations. Since the final destination of orders is usually found in large cities, the vehicles used in this phase are typically powered by alternative fuels such as biomethane. The use of electric vehicles and even bicycles is also common, which contributes to creating a positive image for these companies.

Logistics service providers are not usually well evaluated in terms of their environmental impact. The fact that their operations are largely supported by the use of fossil fuels contributes to them being identified as environmentally irresponsible companies. With the consolidation of an environmental awareness, the improvement of this image becomes critical. Unfortunately, this does not seem to be happening in a real way. Instead, the concentration of green operations in urban centers can be understood as a form to deceive consumers, making them believe that the entire operation is done in a similar fashion. With most products sold in Europe, the United States and basically all major consumer markets being produced in China—or in other countries that offer relatively cheaper labor (e.g. India, Vietnam, Bangladesh)—they travel large geographic distances, which mostly happens with the use of fossil fuels. The main contribution of the chapter refers to the demonstration that environmental fraud is not exclusive to the automotive industry, reinforcing the discussions about incentives to illicit practices. Future research should seek to identify cases of environmental fraud in other contexts, as well as test whether the incentives discussed here apply in dissimilar contexts.

The impacts of environmental fraud on intangible resources were approached in Chap. 8. In addition to a discussion on the nature and strategic relevance of these resources, the chapter brings a reflection on the different ways in which they can be affected. Broadly, this includes the debate on the potential of unethical conducts to undermine the way companies involved in such issues are perceived among their different audiences. Thus, the chapter contributes to the development of a more holistic view of the perils resulting from the practice of environmental fraud, addressing matters that, in general, are ignored, or treated in isolation. The discussions proposed are, however, eminently conceptual. Despite considering the literature dedicated to each of the resources approached, and being based on the logical articulation between the different concepts addressed, the views discussed shall greatly profit from empirical evidence. Future research should therefore dedicate to identify and measure the real impacts of environmental fraud to intangible resources. In favor of this task is the fact all the constructs analyzed are relatively mature from a conceptual point of view, meaning that they have not only been validated in previous studies, but serve as a reference for current literature. Likewise, researchers have different methods at their disposal, among which are surveys and experiments.

Chapter 9 deals with the potential negative effects that environmental fraud can have on the way countries are perceived. Based on a debate about the creation of national images and stereotypes, the association between brands and countries is discussed as a potential element of differentiation and, consequently, as a source of competitive advantage. Furthermore, the chapter addresses the main difficulties that these associations can cause to companies if their country of origin is not particularly respected or admired in a specific field. Several examples are used pointing out how building a positive image in the past benefits producers in the present. The Dieselgate scandal represents an emblematic case in this sense. With Volkswagen's path being closely linked to Germany's recent history, the damage absorbed by the company appears to have spread to other companies based in the country. In this kind of spillover, firms that share the same origin end up partially absorbing the losses caused by other organizations. The chapter therefore contributes to the understanding of the side effects of environmental fraud on a national scale.

In addition to anecdotal evidence, the chapter is based on a review of the literature, as well as on logical constructions. Future research may empirically address the topic. In this sense, the conjectures presented may serve as a basis for the construction of several hypotheses, with quantitative methods such as surveys or experiments being possibly employed. Once again, given the abundance of scales already validated and accepted in the literature, the use of the constructs discussed here as intangible resources (i.e. brand, trust, corporate image, corporate identity, corporate credibility, and corporate reputation) can be of great practical use.

Likewise, the examples used can serve as a starting point for researchers that seek a more detailed understanding of the phenomenon.

Chapter 10 dealt with environmental fraud's potential to destroy the market value of both the companies directly responsible and those that orbit them (e.g. suppliers, customers, competitors). In addition to a conceptual discussion on the nature of the market value concept, a debate was also proposed on the concept of value, as well as on the main methodologies used in the calculation of share prices. Based on these discussions, the empirical studies that analyzed the impact of the Volkswagen Dieselgate are addressed. In general, they show that the scandal led by the German company had a profound impact in terms of the destruction of market value, both for the source company (i.e. Volkswagen) and for other companies that somehow relate to it. Although comprehensive from a conceptual point of view, the chapter is restricted to analyzing the empirical results of the Volkswagen Dieselgate. If, on the one hand, this is justified by the relevance of the case, the analysis of the impacts of other cases can be quite useful. Future research will therefore be able to investigate the extended effects of the other cases discussed in the book (e.g. FCA, Renault), as well as new cases that may arise. The fact that event studies use secondary and public data (i.e. stock price) works as a great facilitator for projects in this direction. The chapter's greatest contribution lies in the discussion of the mechanisms by which market value is affected. In this sense, the analysis of the impact of environmental fraud on intangible resources was particularly useful.

Chapter 11 provides a brief history of the diesel technology. In addition to the main facts related to the biography of the creator of diesel engines, Rudolf Diesel, the fundamental questions that led the fuel to take on the relevance it has today are discussed. Among other factors, technical and political issues were addressed as important elements in its evolution. Likewise, the growing environmental awareness and the consolidation of the *age of green* are exposed as factors that contribute to the loss of its popularity. Based on these criticisms, the chapter discusses possible alternatives to diesel, highlighting both their positive and negative aspects. In this context, the transition from internal combustion engines to electric ones is critically approached, with the environmental damage associated with this technology being stressed. In particular, the generation of energy from different sources is discussed. Likewise, the problems associated with the use of electric batteries—from the extraction of raw materials necessary for their manufacture to the environmental risks linked to fails in recycling processes—were addressed. When brought together, these discussions provide the basis for further reflection on the environmental viability of electric cars, highlighting the fact that they may not be exactly superior to diesel cars. The environmental problems arising from the production of fuels from renewable sources (i.e. biofuels) were also discussed, making the real environmental impact of these alternatives more evident.

The main contribution of the chapter rests then in the demystification of alternatives to diesel, with the exposure of their negative effects offering new elements for the debate around the use of energies considered as clean. Thus, the debate contributes to a more comprehensive view, preventing complex issues such as the replacement of energy matrices from being treated in a simplistic manner. Researchers on the subject are invited to extend this approach, investigating not only negative effects eventually ignored in the present debate, but also focusing on other energy alternatives that have not been discussed here.

12.2 The Future of Environmental Fraud: Green Finance Under Suspicion

As discussed throughout the book, sustainability has become a dominant issue in the public debate, having moved from a relatively obscure subject to a mainstream concern. In that process, the discussion escaped academic circles, attracting not only environmental activists, but also politicians, journalists, artists, and a legion of people looking for a noble cause to defend. The popularization of the theme and its establishment among a growing public explain, in part, what is here called the *age of green*. In addition to raising awareness on the need to preserve nature, the growth of this environmental awareness has been accelerated.

The dissemination of this message found a strong echo in international organizations (e.g. the United Nations), as well as in traditional media outlets (e.g. newspapers, magazines, radio, and television networks). All this turmoil around the matter did not take long to translate into a charge for industrial activity to drastically reduce its environmental impact. In response, a range of technologies and new products were developed by companies, creating a whole new industry dedicated to green consumption. In this sense, sustainability has served as a sort of amalgamation that connects different interests, creating what seems to be its own dynamics, while its mechanics can affect the development of the most distinct economic activities. Issues related to the environmental impact of companies have traditionally been associated with their operations, having CO_2 and NO_x emissions produced by industrial processes being of particular importance in this regard. Likewise, high and large environmental impacts (e.g. oil spills) are also linked to operational failures. It is also common to associate pollution with consumption and use of products, so that different parts of the production process end up being highlighted as the focus of environmental problems (e.g. design, logistics, recycling). Discussions related to the theme of sustainability (including its social aspects) have traditionally been attacked by the operations management departments of universities and business schools.

However, as discussed throughout the book, it is common for environmental issues to fall outside the scope of operations, being conducted by marketing departments. In many cases, the objective of creating positive corporate images seems to overcome the desire to minimize firms' environmental impacts, what may lead to exaggerations and even falsifications in the messages sent by companies to their different audiences. Recently, another field has taken ownership of environmental issues, placing them at the center of its debates. Traditionally associated with a vision of a rationalist world and the search for profit maximization, the Finance discipline seems to be incorporating themes related to respect for human rights and environmental preservation quite aggressively. These factors have been increasingly used as criteria for making loans and making investment decisions. "Green bonds", for example, have represented an important source of financing for environmentally responsible projects (Adachi, 2020). As discussed by the author, a more comprehensive version of these mechanisms has spread among companies, with interest rates on financing being directly linked to their environmental performance. This is the basic mechanism of the "sustainability-linked-bonds" launched by Suzano—one of the largest pulp companies in the world. According to Marcelo Bacci (Suzano's CFO), if the CO_2 reduction targets set are not met, the cost of financing will be higher, with the company committing to bear higher interest rates. For the executive, the nature of the operation can be defined as "skin in the game".

While sustainability-linked bonds seem to be an important step in the development of companies' commitment to environmental issues, some caveats are important so that these mechanisms are not misused as instruments of environmental fraud (not in Suzano's specific case, but in general). First, it is necessary to emphasize that the environmental performance goals are defined by the companies themselves, which can lead to a prioritization of objectives according to their levels of difficulty. Within this perspective, more complex and eventually more relevant objectives for society can be neglected. Likewise, it is possible that companies will overestimate the achievement of relatively simple goals, which, instead of contributing to real sustainable development, could generate just one more way of manipulating corporate images. It is also possible for companies to define objectives that will naturally be achieved, without these representing any concrete effort or challenge. This would be the case for asset renewals (e.g. trucks, machines, new factories). While the reasons for such renovations may simply be the search for greater productivity, replacing old technologies with new ones would lead to a natural reduction in environmental impacts. If these reductions are used as environmental performance objectives to raise funds, the contribution of such initiatives may be debatable.

In addition, it is necessary to consider the possibility that these instruments do not actually represent any or little concern with environmental issues, serving only as "green packaging" for financial purposes. In this case, this and other Green Finance instruments would not be very different from other forms of greenwashing. Given the sedimentation of *age of green*, however, it is likely that similar mechanisms will be adopted by more companies. Once again, while these initiatives can act as an important incentive for the adoption of environmentally responsible practices, the additional financial pressure these bonds exert on managers can act as an incentive to environmental fraud, with environmental performance being manipulated, exaggerated, and eventually falsified in order to avoid paying for the increase in interest rates predicted by the failure to achieve objectives. In this sense, it is also necessary to pay attention to the verification of these results, with the development of more transparent audit methods being necessary.

References

Adachi, V. (2020). Suzano vai captar ao menos US$ 500 milhões em bônus atrelado a emissão de CO_2. *Capital Reset*, September 20. https://www.capitalreset.com/suzano-vai-captar-ao-menos-us-500-milhoes-em-bonus-atrelado-a-emissao-de-co2/

Everett, L. (2014). *Environmental Fraud: How Palm Oil Turned the Tables on the Green Groups and Their Shadowy Funders!* Aurora Mega Publishing.

Fracarolli Nunes, M., & Lee Park, C. (2020). Machine Learning, the Internet of Things, and the Seeds of Un-behavioral Operations: Conceptual Bases for the Industry of the Future. In P. Bartolo, F. M. da Silva, S. Jaradat, & H. Bartolo (Eds.), *Industry 4.0—Shaping the Future of the Digital World*. CRC Press.

Liberti, F. (2006). Environmental Fraud. *Fraud Magazine*, November/December. https://www.fraud-magazine.com/article.aspx?id=4294967698

Moor, J. H. (2006). The Nature, Importance, and Difficulty of Machine Ethics. *IEEE Intelligent Systems, 21*(4), 18–21.

Porter, M. E. (1996). What Is Strategy? *Harvard Business Review, 74*(6), 61–78.

Index

A

Age of green, 87–101, 131, 172, 279, 283, 289, 290, 292
Alternative fuel vehicles (AFVs), 113, 257
Amazon, 3, 171, 174–175
Apple, 3, 35, 68, 80, 174, 176, 177, 188
Automotive industry, 52, 68, 105–127, 133, 150, 159–178, 196, 209–211, 220, 242, 244, 261, 269, 270, 284–287

B

Barney, Jay, 73, 74, 79, 80
Benz, Bertha, 106
Benz, Carl, 105–107, 209
Bergen Declaration on Sustainable Development, 96
Biofuels, 255–259, 261, 290
Blueprint for Survival, 91
BMW, 209, 269
Bosch, 135, 147, 150, 220
Brand, 4, 17, 63, 64, 135, 142, 149, 161, 168, 178, 185–202, 207–222, 238, 241, 285, 288
Broken window theory, 23
Brundtland, Gro Harlem, 95
Burke, Edmund, 22, 59
Business Ethics, 1–38, 279, 280, 283
Buyers, 75, 116, 123, 124, 166, 188, 190, 200, 207

C

California Air Resource Board (CARB), 134, 137
C&A, 164, 165
Car culture, 115–120
Cash flow, 232–234, 236–238, 241, 242

M. Fracarolli Nunes, C. Lee Park, *Business Ethics and Environmental Fraud*,
https://doi.org/10.1007/978-3-030-73800-6

Child labor, 19, 36–38, 164
Ciulla, Joanne, 25, 26, 29, 31–33
Clean Air Act (CAA), 61, 113, 136–138, 144, 145, 257
Competitive advantage, 17, 52, 67–82, 131, 140, 152, 171, 188, 191, 198, 221, 243, 279, 282, 283, 288
Competitive environments, 5, 16–17, 68, 73, 74, 81, 111, 122, 284
Corporate Average Fuel Economy (CAFE), 113, 253
Corporate credibility, 17, 63, 64, 185–202, 288
Corporate crimes, 5, 13, 47–57, 185
Corporate culture, 6, 12–13, 172, 195, 218
Corporate identity, 64, 185–202, 288
Corporate image, 64, 185–202, 209, 288, 291, 292
Corporate reputation, 17, 64, 185–202, 288
Cost-based competition, 70, 81, 111, 121, 284
Criminology, 47–57, 131, 281
Customers, 2, 10, 11, 22, 35, 69, 70, 75, 99, 123, 124, 132, 138, 141, 167, 171, 173–175, 185, 188, 191, 193, 195, 199, 238, 289

D

Diesel, Rudolf, 209, 251–270, 289
Dieselgate, 17, 58, 60, 112, 131–152, 165, 191, 200, 218–221, 236–238, 242–245, 255, 269, 282, 285, 286, 288, 289
Diesel technology, 133, 143, 149, 152, 209, 220, 242, 243, 251–255, 269, 270, 286, 289
Differentiation Association Theory, 51, 52
Discounted cash flows, 232, 234, 239
Drucker, Peter, 25, 26

E

EA 189, 132, 139, 140, 142
Efficient Market Hypothesis, 233
Electric cars, 37, 122–123, 242, 243, 261–264, 269, 290
Environmental fraud, 17, 33, 47–64, 67–71, 112, 119, 131, 140, 143, 149, 151, 152, 159–178, 185–202, 211, 220, 229, 237, 238, 240–244, 279–293
Environmental Protection Agency (EPA), 55, 60, 61, 132, 134, 136–138, 144–147, 222
Ethanol, 120, 256–258
The European Commission, 141, 166, 169
European Investment Bank (EIB), 139, 140, 150
Expectations, 12, 16, 23, 70, 87, 116, 149, 171, 172, 185, 186, 194, 230, 233–238, 242, 254, 263, 264

F

Fast fashion, 68, 160–165
Federal Express (FedEX), 170, 175

Federal Trade Commission (FTC), 137, 138
Fiat Chrysler Automobiles (FCA), 80, 131–152, 285, 289
Five forces
  bargaining power of customers, 75, 124
  bargaining power of suppliers, 75, 123–124
  internal rivalry, 122
  threat of new entrants, 75, 122–123
  threat of substitutes, 75, 123
Food and beverage industry, 166–169
Fraud, 8, 13, 15, 17, 23, 33, 47–64, 67–71, 112, 119, 131, 132, 135, 137, 138, 142, 143, 147–152, 159–178, 185–202, 207–222, 229, 237, 238, 240–245, 279–293
The fraud severity and range matrix
  day-to-day fraud, 49
  diluted fraud, 49
  punctual fraud, 49
  widespread fraud, 48–50, 58

G

General Motors (GM), 112, 119, 134, 149, 254, 286
Glueck, Eleanor, 52, 53
Glueck, Sheldon, 52, 53
Greed, 1, 6–7, 53, 57
Green Finance, 290–293
Greenwashing, 59–60, 159, 292
Gross, Edward, 7, 55–57

H

H&M, 160, 161, 164, 165
Henry Ford, 109
Hydroelectricity, 266, 267

I

Improper Competitive Advantage, 17, 67–82, 131, 140, 152, 191, 279, 282
Industry structure, 74–79, 282
Intangible resources, 17, 63, 173, 186, 187, 198, 201, 202, 219–221, 235, 237–245, 287–289

L

Legal costs, 237–245
Lithium-ion batteries, 261–264, 266
Logistics, 160, 170–176, 291
Logistics service providers(LSP), 170–172, 175, 287

M

Made in, 207–212, 221
Market value, 63, 64, 133, 174, 229–245, 289
Mercedes-Benz, 107, 209, 252, 253, 269
Military ethics, 27, 30, 31
Modern slavery, 3, 19, 23, 33–36, 164
Musk, Elon, 262

N

National brands, 207–222
National identity, 208, 212–216, 222

National image, 212–215, 218, 219, 221, 288
National reputation, 222
National tribalism, 216–218
Natural gas, 173, 176, 253, 257, 259–261, 267, 269

O

Office Européen de Lutte Antifraud (OLAF), 139, 140
Operational efficiency, 81, 108, 112, 122, 234, 284
Operational incapacity, 237–245
Opportunism, 1, 6, 13–14, 239
OPSON VIII, 169
Organic cotton, 164–165, 167

P

Porter, Michael, 4, 16, 70, 74, 75, 79, 112, 122, 145, 171, 196, 201, 258, 284
PSA, 107, 131–152, 285

R

Renault, 107, 131–152, 285, 289
Renewable Fuel Standards (RFS), 256, 257
Resource-based view (RBV), 74, 79–82, 282
Rousseau, Jean-Jacques, 53, 89, 90

S

Samsung, 68, 176, 177
Scapegoat, 125–127
Scientific Management, 109, 110
Smith, Adam, 88, 194
Solar energy systems, 265
Solar panels, 265
Stakeholders, 17, 22, 33, 58, 60, 61, 63, 131, 142, 149, 159, 185, 186, 189, 194, 196–201, 220, 221, 235, 239, 241, 282
Stereotypes, 116, 207, 208, 212–215, 288
Stockholm Conference, 91–94
Strategy, 11, 14, 57, 70, 71, 73, 75, 80, 95, 112, 113, 122, 127, 132, 140, 143, 149, 152, 161, 173, 178, 191, 195, 196, 201, 208, 220, 241, 242, 264, 281, 282, 284, 287
Suppliers, 10, 11, 22, 72, 75, 111, 115, 121, 123–124, 185, 186, 190, 191, 198, 200, 221, 239, 243, 244, 259, 284, 289
Supply chains, 19, 72, 82, 120, 160, 164, 167–169, 171, 175, 177, 192, 194, 234, 239, 243, 244
Sustainability-linked bonds, 292
Sustainable consumption, 98–100
Sutherland, Edwin, 51–54, 56
SWOT analysis, 73–74

T

Taylor, Frederick, 109, 110
Technological transition, 237–245
The tripartite business ethics model, 26, 30, 31
Trust, 14, 63, 137, 138, 142, 185–202, 211, 221, 239–241, 244, 288

U
United Nations (UN), 88, 90, 92, 93, 95–97, 100, 290
The United Nations Conference on Environment and Development, 96–97
United Parcel Service (UPS), 174–176
The United States Department of Justice, 145, 167

V
Value, 2, 5–7, 11, 12, 16, 17, 19–21, 24, 36, 49–51, 56, 58, 62–64, 68, 75, 79–82, 87, 97, 99, 100, 109, 112, 115–117, 122, 123, 126, 131, 133, 138, 142–144, 147, 166, 169, 174, 187–189, 191–193, 195, 199, 208, 210, 213, 216, 221, 229–245, 264, 281, 283, 284, 286, 289
Volkswagen, 17, 48, 52, 57, 58, 60, 61, 63, 112–114, 119, 131–144, 147–152, 165, 191, 200, 208, 209, 211, 218–222, 236–238, 242–245, 255, 269, 270, 282, 285, 286, 288, 289
Volvo, 196, 211, 269

W
Weber, Max, 12, 23
Wind turbines, 265, 266
World Commission on Environment and Development (WCED), 90, 95

Z
Zara, 72, 160–162, 188
Zero Emission Vehicle (ZEV), 137, 138

The manufacturer's authorised representative in the EU is Springer Nature Customer Service Centre GmbH, Europaplatz 3, 69115 Heidelberg, Germany. If you have any concerns regarding our products, please contact ProductSafety@springernature.com

Printed and bound by CPI Group (UK) Ltd, Croydon, CR0 4YY
30/09/2026
02225326-0011